LEADERS OF PHILOSOPHY

DESCARTES

DESCARTES

by
S. V. KEELING
M.A., D.-ÈS-L., OFFICIER D'ACADÉMIE

*Senior Lecturer in Philosophy
at University College, University of London*

GREENWOOD PRESS, PUBLISHERS
WESTPORT, CONNECTICUT

Originally published in 1934
by Ernest Benn Ltd., London

First Greenwood Reprinting 1970

Library of Congress Catalogue Card Number 78-109759

SBN 8371-4249-0

Printed in the United States of America

TO
M. R.

CONTENTS

	PAGE
FOREWORD	ix

PART I

CHAPTER		
I.	"*Talis erat . . . Naturæ filius*"	3
II.	THE INTELLECTUAL CLIMATE OF THE AGE	29

PART II

III.	THE ART OF RESEARCH IN SCIENCE AND PHILOSOPHY	57
IV.	RECONSTRUCTION IN METAPHYSICS	83
V.	THE NATURAL WORLD AND OUR KNOWLEDGE OF NATURE	119
VI.	BODY AND MIND	141
VII.	KNOWING, KNOWLEDGE AND THE SELF	154
VIII.	THE SELF AND ITS FREEDOM—"*Omnis peccans est ignorans*"	173

PART III

IX.	THE CARTESIAN SCHOOL	201
X.	SOME MERITS AND DEFECTS OF CARTESIANISM, (I)	229
XI.	SOME MERITS AND DEFECTS OF CARTESIANISM, (II)	252
BIBLIOGRAPHY		273
INDEX		277

FOREWORD

A GREAT philosophy must first and chiefly be sought in the philosopher's writings, not in those of another. So of all things I hope least that this book may prove a safe substitute for a first-hand study of Descartes's own works. What seemed to me my proper business was not merely to assemble into one connected story doctrines that Descartes elaborated piecemeal in various contexts, but rather to interpret those doctrines through conceptions and in language more readily understood to-day, and to notice the position certain of his special problems assume in contemporary thought. To present Cartesianism as a philosophy in parts defensible and constructively important as well as in parts indefensible but important in its very errors naturally impelled me to emphasise its internal connexions, and to pay more attention to the dependencies, actual or assumed, between its parts. No attempt has been made to elucidate the antecedent forms of its central and characteristic conceptions or to reinstate Cartesianism in the philosophical *milieu* in which it developed. This has been the special and magnificent contribution of that prince among Cartesian scholars, Professor Etienne Gilson of the Sorbonne. How often I have depended on the results of his fine scholarship will be evident from the frequency of my references to his writings; how great is the debt I owe to them no one can realise more fully than myself.

My aim in the opening chapter is to create an impression of the cast of mind it was that produced one of the most influential philosophies of modern Europe, and only in a secondary way to chronicle the incidents of Descartes's private life. In Part II attention is confined to positive exegesis, and (except in Ch. VI) I refrain from critical commentary in the belief that what is essential in Cartesianism will stand out more forcibly if the continuity of my presentation is kept unbroken. In Part III my principal object is to suggest the character of Descartes's immediate influence by connecting the theories of the chief Cartesians as directly as possible with the theme of substance and causality in Cartesianism. Had more space been available I should have gladly entered fully into the contributions of these unduly neglected thinkers. And in the last two chapters, while attempting a general estimate, I felt free to correct certain unfounded objections often preferred against Descartes, to advance certain criticisms that I consider justified, and to indicate broadly what I take to be the chief claims Cartesianism makes on the interest of philosophical students for all time. An elaborate discussion of the points raised in these last chapters and a full defence of my criticisms there would have been out of place. These I intend to present in a volume of Cartesian studies now in preparation.

The passages quoted from Descartes in the text and footnotes of this book are my own translations from the monumental edition of his *Œuvres complètes* prepared by MM. Charles Adam and Paul Tannery under the auspices of the Ministère de l'Instruction Publique. For the convenience of readers who have not access to this edition I have added, wherever possible, references to corresponding places in the most recent of English versions—*The Philosophical Works of Descartes*, by E. S. Haldane and G. R. T. Ross, published in two volumes by the Cambridge University Press. On crucial points, and particularly on any such arising in the *Regulæ*, the *Discourse* and the *Meditations*, the reader will do well to compare the English rendering with the French or Latin of Descartes himself. The works to which I have had most frequent occasion to refer are indicated by the uniform use of the following abbreviations : 'AT,' *for* the edition of Adam and Tannery ; 'HR,' *for* the translation of Haldane and Ross ; 'Gilson, Études,' *for* E. Gilson, *Études sur le rôle de la pensée médiévale dans la formation du système cartésien* (Paris ; Vrin, 1930).

In conclusion I wish to record my gratitude to all who have helped me : to my first teacher in philosophy, Professor G. Dawes Hicks, who awakened my interest in Descartes; to Dr. C. D. Broad, who stimulated it anew and led me to make a study of Descartes's texts for myself. Perhaps even greater is my indebtedness to Cartesian scholars in France, whose lectures I had not the good fortune to hear, but whose writings have long been for me models of philosophical interpretation. Among them I would name in particular Professor E. Gilson, and the

FOREWORD

late Professors L. Liard, O. Hamelin and G. Milhaud. And especially to Professor J. L. Stocks of the University of Manchester I tender my sincere thanks. But for his extremely kind help in suggesting improvements and criticisms this book would have been much more imperfect than it is.

S. V. KEELING.

MOUSTIERS SAINTE-MARIE,
BASSES-ALPES, FRANCE.
Easter, 1933.

PART I

I

"TALIS ERAT ... NATURÆ FILIUS"

" From birth my mind was, I confess, of such a turn that my greatest satisfaction in study always came not from attending to the proofs of others but from discovering them by my own efforts."—DESCARTES.

" THERE are two qualities which we may fairly demand from the work of any man whom we are to recognise as a really great philosopher with a permanent importance in the history of human thought. In the first place the work must be original, and in the second it must be critical. When I say that the work must be original, I do not mean that it need be startling or revolutionary, but that it must be the achievement of genuine personal intellectual effort. The great philosopher must be one who has thought for himself and has thought hard. . . . And by saying that the work must be critical, I do not mean that it must necessarily be largely devoted to criticism of other men's thoughts, I mean that it must be something more than the construction of a brilliant but undisciplined speculative imagination. The great philosopher cannot, indeed, have too daring an imagination provided only that its exercise is controlled by a profound sobriety of judgment, a massive commonsense." These are the requirements Professor A. E. Taylor proposes, in his Aquinas Sexcentenary Lecture, as a minimum to be satisfied by any philosophy which is fairly to be considered great. That the work of Descartes fulfils those requirements is beyond question, though how eminently it does so those alone may appreciate whose judgment is prepared by a first-hand and detailed acquaintance with his writings. And even though, as Professor Taylor says, a great philosophy need not be " startling or revolutionary," there can be no doubt that Descartes's was both. Now we shall need, in order to set ourselves aright for understanding what is original and meritorious in this new philosophy, not only to dissect the doctrine and interrogate critically its grounds, but also to reinstate it in the contextual circumstances in which it arose and developed.

"Philosophy," says Dr. A. N. Whitehead, "never reverts to its old position after the shock of a great philosopher." Evidently, then, to appreciate the importance of a particular "shock," it is quite as necessary to review the "old position" to which the new current never reverts, as to elicit precisely what it is that is novel in the new position. If one thing is clear and certain about the work of Descartes, it is surely that the upheaval and the consequent new position cannot be regarded as simply no more than resultants of the cultural circumstances in which they originated. The "shock" and its consequences are the results rather of the interplay of three most complex factors, which we may conveniently call "formative," "restrictive" and "determinative." The last seems to consist in circumstances, some personal, others impersonal, in origin. What is original and creative must, of course, issue from the man himself; he alone in re-forming his material, remakes it creatively and critically, and is thus responsible for its final and definitive form. It is, then, the object of the present chapter to convey some impression of the manner of man Descartes was, so that later we may observe how far his temperament and proclivities throw light on the character of his finished work. The determinate form Descartes's conclusions assume, however, is also due in large measure to something quite impersonal—independent of the man himself; namely, to the logic implicit in his philosophical method. The manner in which this impersonal element determines his final results it will be our concern to examine, *inter alia*, throughout the whole second part of the book. The two other factors, "formative" and "restrictive," and how they contributed to the advent of the new position, we may conveniently review together in the next chapter.

Let us then begin by asking whether anything known about the man himself—his inclinations, activities or experiences—accounts in any measure for what is distinctive in his work. Why, indeed, was Descartes led to study philosophy at all? Had he any other dominant intellectual interests? Was his work profoundly influenced by other men, predecessors or contemporaries, or did they act only as the initial 'irritants' of his thought? Does he tend to react constructively, by selective assimilation like Leibniz later, or to react adversely, by wholesale rejection, to the thought of others and to the accepted beliefs of his time ? Were his intellectual endeavours hampered, directly by repression, or indirectly through fear of it ? What attitude did he adopt towards the opinions, sentiments and settled convictions prevailing in the educated circles of his period ? Does he permit his emotional experiences not only to ' set ' but also to ' settle ' important problems for him, without the criticism or support due from reason ? These are all, surely, pertinent questions to raise, and such as can be answered only by first considering the life and character of the individual himself and the social conditions of his epoch. *Nascitur non fit* is doubtless true of the genius in philosophy as in any other department, and though it may be, as Descartes believed, that any man may make discoveries and reach important knowledge will he but follow the right method, it is certainly not " any " man who can find out what that method is.

I

Like Hegel, Descartes gave no sign of remarkable ability in philosophy during his schooling, and when attracted to it later, unlike Spinoza and many of the greatest philosophers, it was not from any profound conviction of a moral value that its study would impart to his life. Unlike Hegel, Descartes's early experience was not one of acute spiritual distress, nor, like Plato, was he inspired in unusual degree by the significance of moral, æsthetic or religious experience, though he was well alive to certain quite practical and humanitarian benefits that should accrue from improving our knowledge of nature. Descartes wrote no autobiography and he had no Boswell. But some five hundred letters from his own hand and the hundred from eminent correspondents, which together form five volumes of the authoritative edition of his works, illuminate for us in greater detail and with more intimacy and directness than a biography by the hand of another could do the intellectual activity of the last twenty and richest years of his life. Among great men Descartes least could have profited from the proddings of even a most tactful, self-effacing Boswell. He evaded anything like a constant contact, preferring occasional chance meetings with a Beeckman, or, more rarely, a visit to his closest friend Mersenne, that delightful and obliging figure in whom, according to Hobbes, there was more than in all the universities together. Mersenne it was who brought Descartes into touch with his most learned and stimulating correspondents in science and philosophy, and who facilitated exchanges of ideas and works in a day before academies [1] and learned societies were founded, and when published transactions, scientific journals and publishers' catalogues were unimagined. Apparently Descartes depended extremely little upon personal discussion for intellectual stimulus. The custom of discussing by correspondence we shall see, however, had frequently the happy effect of leading him to state more fully what, in his own mind, had already been worked out.

The semi-autobiographical places in the *Discourse on Method*, unless they project criticisms of a maturer age into an earlier period,[2] show that philosophy appealed little to Descartes in early manhood. He saw in it mainly " a means of speaking plausibly about all things, and of making ourselves admired by others less learned." It was an unsatisfying and unprogressive study, for, " since many centuries it had been cultivated by the finest minds that ever lived, and yet there is not to be found in it a single thing that is not matter of dispute and that is not, in consequence, dubious." So, " considering how many conflicting opinions there may be about one and the same matter," he adds, " I had not such presumption as to hope to succeed better than others had done." And since physics had not yet been separated off from philosophy, it too falls under the same condemnation; it is nothing but a body of unproved possibilities. Descartes also speaks in terms of dissatisfaction with the other subjects he studied at La Flèche, though not with the manner in which they were taught, for the Jesuit college there was " one of the most celebrated in Europe." He is very

[1] Not until 1637, the year the *Discourse* appeared, and when Descartes was in his forty-first year, was the Académie française founded by Louis XIII.
[2] Cf. G. Cantecor: " A writer who relates his past can quite well be of good faith and none the less deceive himself, forget important facts, set others he recalls in a factitious order, assign to the past preoccupations of more recent date. Every autobiography is liable to such errors, there is no reason why Descartes's account alone should be exempt. In fact, this account contains so many and such serious inaccuracies that the first duty of those who would know the real history of Descartes's thought is to disallow tentatively what he tells us about it, and try to reconstitute it for themselves."—" La Vocation de Descartes," *Revue philosophique*, 1923, p. 373.

far from feeling for it the contempt which Hobbes felt for Oxford, and, writing in 1638, " there is no place in the world where philosophy is better taught than at La Flèche," recommended his correspondent to send his son there rather than to the University of Leyden. Descartes at La Flèche was no more satisfied than Hobbes was at Oxford with his allowance at scholastic physics and logic, but he had not, like his English contemporary, to wait until he was forty before he could " fall in love with geometry." Indeed, the mathematical side at La Flèche was strong, and the subject delighted him more than any other " because of the certainty of its proofs and the evidence of its reasonings." Compared with mathematics, " the works of the ancient pagans that treat of morals are superb, magnificent palaces built on sand and mud." But it was the formal character of mathematics that delighted. The " true use of the science " did not occur to him during these school years, for he then supposed it to consist simply in " being of service to the mechanical arts." Yet he was reaching towards a juster estimate, for he admits to being particularly surprised, since the foundations of mathematics were " so firm and strong," that nothing " loftier " had been erected on them. The physics to which Descartes was introduced at La Flèche were very much those regularly studied in the French universities a century earlier. Not that this should suggest that his teachers were ' behind the times ' or ill-disposed towards the newer knowledge in natural science. On the contrary, it is clear from the School's historian[1] that its professors frequently attempted to convey to their students some idea of the brand-new discoveries being made in optics and astronomy, and of the use of the optical instruments recently invented. Further, we hear [2] that on the third day of the College Commemoration Feast in 1611 a sonnet was read celebrating the discovery, made by Galileo in that year, of some " nouvelles planettes ou estoiles errantes autour de Jupiter."

[1] Cf. de Rochemonteix, *Un Collège de Jésuites aux XVIIe et XVIIIe siècles* : *Le Collège Henri IV de La Flèche*, 1880, Vol. I, pp. 147 ff. The College was founded in 1604, two years before Descartes's entrance, by a privilege of Henri IV, who intended establishing a Catholic university there.

[2] C. Adam, *Vie et Œuvres de Descartes*, p. 29. Paris, 1910. This, the most scholarly and authoritative biography extant, forms the twelfth volume of the Adam and Tannery edition of the *Œuvres*. Unfortunately it is not to be procured separately.

It was part of the common knowledge vouchsafed by Aristotle that the certainty of mathematics derives from its purely formal character, and that this certainty is unattainable by sciences having material objects and natural events for their subject-matter. Scholasticism had summed up the distinction in its 'axiom': *modus scientiæ debet respondere materiæ*. Yet, in spite of the dead-weight of this contrary authoritative opinion, Descartes had satisfied himself, before the end of his college studies, that physics, and for that matter all other sciences too, could be brought to yield results as certain as those found in mathematics. And that they had not already done so was precisely the reason of his dissatisfaction with them. His favourite observation on the education at La Flèche is that it was predominantly a literary one. On the whole there was too much of letters and too little exercise in reasoning to satisfy him. He acquired some taste for poetry, though small skill in writing it, and Greek appears to have been almost neglected by pupils and tutors alike. He had mastered "all that the others there had learned," and, dissatisfied with what he had gained from following the science classes, ran through all the books "treating of those sciences accounted the most curious and extraordinary" that fell his way. His tutors, he tells us, did not rate him at all inferior to his fellows, "even though some of these were destined to fill the places of their masters." And it was probably this taste for intellectual things and his delicate health that led to an unusual measure of leniency being accorded to him in college. We have it from Lipstorp that "it was his regular habit to awaken early in the morning, and while still abed, to occupy himself with meditation until midday . . . and in this way he composed his Algebra." This became his invariable practice through life until his unfortunate visit to Sweden.

In 1614 Descartes left the college he had entered eight years before at the age of ten and turned from La Flèche, where, rather more than a century after, Hume was to compose the major part of his *Treatise*. What had these first eighteen years accomplished for the young Descartes? They had fostered an enthusiasm for mathematics, and especially for solving problems. They had accustomed his mind to methodical thinking as a result of regularly performing formal exercises. They had given him a mastery of Latin—then indispensable as the international language of speech and correspondence among savants—in which, indeed, he wrote as gracefully and easily as in his native language. And, to some extent, they had formed his critical judgment, enabling him to decide what studies he would lay aside, and why he would do so. Weary of text-books, he enters on a period of uncertainty concerning what ultimately he should make of his life and what immediately he should pursue in study or diversion. Uncertainty is at length allayed by a decision to travel, to " read in the great book of the world " awhile—a project most conveniently furthered in those days by soldiering. So at two and twenty he joins the army of Prince Maurice of Nassau. The travels begin, but the uncertainty and lull in intellectual keenness are not thrown off till he reaches Holland and there makes a new acquaintance.

There are three dates of capital importance in Descartes's mental history, and, curiously, it is the same day (10th November) in the three succeeding years, 1618, 1619 and 1620. On the first of these he meets with Isaac Beeckman, a Dutch doctor in medicine, who graduated in France, and is keenly interested in natural science. Beeckman fills the office of *agent excitateur* to his new acquaintance, eight years his junior. During the next nine years a period of " free enquiry " ensues, and Descartes's previous knowledge of physics is subjected to destructive criticism and preparation made for its reconstruction on surer foundations. He proposes to Beeckman a new way of solving certain problems in physics. Enthusiasm is shared and admiration is reciprocal. Both, trained in a natural philosophy based on " substantial forms," decide to set aside these unclear, otiose conceptions, and together create the beginnings of a new science—that now known as mathematical physics. The elation on both sides is evident. Beeckman notes in his diary : " This Poitevin has been in contact with many Jesuits and other men of learning and science. He says, however, that he has never met with anyone but myself (which it delights me to hear) who pursues this kind of study, and connects physics and mathematics with such skill. Nor have I, on my part, ever discussed this kind of study with any other being."[1] Descartes, on his part, admits to Beeckman :

[1] Cf. AT, X, 52 ; also G. Milhaud, *Descartes Savant*, ch. i. Paris, 1921.

"I slumbered and you awakened me;" and, on taking leave of him later, declares: "Wherever I tarry, I promise to begin at once the composition of my Mechanics or Geometry, and to extol you as the inspiration and spiritual father of my studies. . . . You alone, in truth, have shaken my idleness from me; you have brought back to my mind a science that had almost faded from memory, and called back to finer and worthier occupations one who had strayed from them. If therefore something not entirely negligible should issue from me, you have the right to claim it . . . either for your own benefit or in order to correct it." So a new interest, and a creative one, brings to an end the short spell of intellectual lassitude. Neither physics in the accustomed sense, nor pure mathematics, is henceforth to be Descartes's professed and favourite study. This, the awakening of his creative originality, indicates to Descartes that his immediate work is to establish the basis of a new science by applying mathematics to the solution of particular problems in physics, and rendering physics susceptible to mathematical treatment. So, he believes, the break with the natural science of "substantial forms" is well-nigh complete.

He takes leave of Beeckman, and the travels recommence. Passing through Poland, Hungary, Austria and Bohemia, in early winter he finds himself detained on the outskirts of a small German town—probably Ulm. Without society to divert him, or cares to disturb, he remains a whole day shut up in his "poêle," with complete leisure to review his situation. Friendship with Beeckman had given purpose and direction to the reawakened enthusiasm. The "vision" in a dream that occurs on this night, exactly a year after his first meeting with Beeckman, is to clarify that purpose and determine for the future the direction of his intellectual endeavour. In the *Olympica* he makes the entry: "10, November, 1619; I discovered the foundations of a marvellous science," and a year later adds: "10, November, 1620; I begin to understand the foundation of a wonderful discovery."

What is this "marvellous science," and what the "wonderful discovery"? Authorities are not completely agreed. The "marvellous science," however, would seem to be[1] the one

---

[1] This interpretation seems confirmed by the epitaph composed by Chanut, to whom Descartes frequently related his early experiences. It runs: "In

eventually developed from the discovery that all quantities between which numerical relations hold are expressible by lines.[1] Here, then, in this intuition, the way is partly prepared for reducing the primitive concepts of physics to those of geometry, so that " the physics that had till then been connected with medicine and philosophy were now shown reducible to number." " All the sciences are interconnected as by a chain ; no one of them can be completely grasped without the others following of themselves and so without taking in the whole encyclopædia at one and the same time " (*Opuscules de 1619-21*, iv ; AT, X, 255). So the new ideas and tentative hypotheses that had been quickened in Descartes's mind since his meetings with Beeckman issue in this present discovery, namely, that all the sciences, developed along the right lines, would exhibit a certain unity and uniformity of structure. In a perfected knowledge there would be no incomprehensible ' gaps.' The connexions between its objects, however numerous, complicated, difficult to disentangle and order rightly, are ultimately " necessary " connexions, which, with their terms, would exhibit the world as a unified and comprehensible system.

Relating his experience on 10th November, a year later, Descartes speaks, not of a " marvellous science," but of a " marvellous discovery." What has he discovered ? It would appear to be the means necessary and available for realising this single, unified science, whose possibility he had first clearly seen the year before. Hence it is not too much to say that the " discovery " of those means is simply a first glimpse into the nature and possibilities of a *Method*—that " Method of rightly conducting the reason and seeking for truth in the sciences," the details of which are elaborated in the *Rules for the Direction of the Mind*, posthumously published.

otiis hibernis Naturæ mysteria componens cum legibus Matheseos, utriusque arcana eadem clave reserari posse ausus est sperare." The experience evidently left on Descartes an impression profound and permanent. Cf. also, Gilson, *Études*, p. 200.

[1] The fuller import of the discovery, as determined later, may be fairly stated thus : all qualitative differences, intensive no less than extensive, may be correlated with variations in shape and dimension, and these correlations expressed in numerical symbolism. Further, all relations between the properties of numbers, shapes and dimensions are expressible in equations. For fuller explanation see Chapter IV. Tannery makes the great merit of Descartes in this matter to consist in having applied, not algebra to geometry, but geometry to algebra.

The next nine years Descartes devotes to working out his method and applying it to algebra. In 1622 he returns to France, visiting his family and selling his estates in Poitou. The proceeds added to present capital suffice, he tells us, to enable him to live where he may choose, " free from the obligation of making a living from my science." His family, however, had hopes of his marrying and settling there, but in this proposal he sees only a curtailment of his freedom. He replies, *peu galant*, to a young woman of charm and good birth, that he finds " no beauty comparable to the beauty of truth " ; and later, among Parisian society, declares that " a beautiful woman, a good book and a perfect preacher are, of all things in the world, the most difficult to find." No ties of society or marriage, nothing shall compromise the fulfilment of his vow made on the memorable night at Ulm—to devote the rest of his life to the cultivation of reason and the advancement of knowledge by means of his method. This was his dominant reason for not marrying, though it may not have been his only one, for when elsewhere publicly presenting his views on marriage he contrived to lend them a touch of *malice*. " When a husband," he says, " weeps over his dead wife, whom, it sometimes happens, he would be disappointed to see restored to life, it may well be that his heart is oppressed with sadness, that the funeral trappings and the absence of her to whose conversation he is so accustomed stirs his feelings ; some trace of affection or compassion may chance to revive in imagination and draw tears from his eyes in all sincerity. But in spite of this, in his innermost soul he feels a secret joy."

Repudiating marriage, he sets forth on further travels, this time through Switzerland (where he carries out some meteorological observations, studies glaciers, and computes the heights of mountains) and thence to Italy. His regret at being unable to pass the rest of his life here is more understandable in his day, for then there was no country where science was so esteemed and where so many men of science were gathered. Ever prudent, however, Descartes fears the intense heat by day, the treacherous, unhealthy cool of the evening and the fevers that follow. The towns, too, were so inadequately policed that he who would above all avoid brawls with thieves and live care-free dared not settle in them. Believing the keener air

"TALIS ERAT ... NATURÆ FILIUS" 13

of the north more conducive to mental vigour and alertness, he returns to France, making for the capital. Here he spends two years in contact with such men of science as Mydorge the mathematician, Villebressieu the alchemist and engineer, Silhon who was Pascal's Beeckman, the devoted Mersenne, and Morin the astronomer, who, writing to Descartes ten years later, says: " From the hour I had the honour of seeing and knowing you in Paris, I perceived that yours was a mind capable of leaving something rare and excellent to posterity."

In the meanwhile, during the nine years following his second " illumination," Descartes works out his " new discovery " with greater clearness, and by 1629 is completely possessed of his method in all its detail. About this time too[1] he commits it to writing under the title of *Regulæ ad directionem ingenii*. The method is there to be expounded in three parts, each to consist of twelve rules and their explanations. Only half the work was completed, however, and even that was not published until fifty years after his death. But it seems probable that the incomplete manuscript was well known and that copies of it circulated in Holland, for Locke's *Essay* shows many direct traces of its influence, and the first edition of the *Essay* appeared twenty years before the *Regulæ* was published in Amsterdam.

II

We now enter on the third period of Descartes's history, the most fruitful one in philosophical construction. The twenty years from 1628 to his departure for Sweden are spent wholly in Holland except for three brief visits to France. What decided him to settle in Holland ? It is plausible to suppose a desire to revisit Beeckman, though this would hardly account for his decision to settle there permanently. Holland was then a refuge for Catholics no less than for Protestants, and doubtless the country best fitted to offer hospitality to two of the three greatest philosophers of the century, Descartes and Spinoza, as well as to the lesser Bayle, and to two renowned French philologists, Scaliger and Saumaise. Popular imagination, however,

---

[1] The inference was originally Baillet's, but M. Charles Adam and Professor Gustave Cohen both support it.

Professor Cohen suggests,[1] is not always accurate in its conception of Dutch tolerance in this century. Holland was essentially a land of intellectual anarchy : " every sect, even the most senseless, had its followers among the solitary inhabitants, absorbed in their lonely, lofty meditations, from which they emerged only to group themselves into little churches. These churches would tolerate each other, but this does not mean that they would come to each other's support. Authority would shut its eyes and allow the sects to exist together, rather from political and economic necessity than from any deep convictions on the part of those exercising power." If such a measure of toleration suited the purposes of those in authority, certainly Descartes found it no less accommodating. Where better could he find the tranquillity necessary for exacting intellectual work, freedom from importunate visits and social engagements, without complete isolation? For he loved to ramble among the crowd, contemplating, as Valéry puts it, " la multiplication des seuls."

" In this great town where I now am," Descartes writes to de Balzac, " there being not a soul but myself not engaged in commerce, all are so engrossed in their affairs that I could pass my whole life unnoticed by anyone. I stroll every day amid the Babel of a great thoroughfare with as much freedom and repose as you could find in the walks of your garden, and look on the people I pass just as I should on the trees in your forests or the animals in your pastures ; the noise of their bustle does not disturb my reflections more than the babbling of a stream. . . . What other place could you choose in all the world where you could enjoy such complete liberty or sleep with more security, where armies are always afoot for your protection, and where poisoning, treachery and calumnies are less known ? " Nor does this love of living half in contact, half aloof from his fellows argue a churlish disposition or an affectation, but simply a pronounced predilection, at which he hints in a general way in another letter to de Balzac : " I have become so philosophical as to despise most things usually esteemed, and to value others not customarily supposed of much account." This quest for solitude without isolation is the main reason Descartes

[1] Gustave Cohen, *Écrivains français en Hollande dans la première moitié du XVIIe siècle*, p. 389. Paris, 1920.

"TALIS ERAT ... NATURÆ FILIUS"

alleges for settling in Amsterdam in the spring of 1629 and making it his headquarters during the ensuing seven years. Franco-Dutch relations were then friendly. " Holland admired France, and France marvelled at Holland as a physical miracle triumphant by its industry over the encroaching ocean, and as a political miracle, triumphant through its passion for freedom over the might of Spain." To enjoy this freedom was an added attraction, for here Descartes would be exposed to no risk in propounding such revolutionary views as, " there is nothing entirely in our power but our thoughts," or, " never should we allow ourselves to be persuaded except by the evidence of reason," or, " never should we accept as true anything not clearly seen to be so." But, M. Cohen declares, " such proud maxims of a reason independent of the Faith could not yet flourish on French soil."

The first five years of his residence in Holland find him occupied with a variety of pursuits, suggested by his mathematical and physical researches in Paris, and with one important problem of a quite different character which his method raises but does not solve. The Method, we shall see, culminates, broadly speaking, in the principle that whatever is clear and distinct in its conception is true. This Descartes had found a sufficiently useful criterion in practice. But though pragmatically satisfactory, the principle has not been and cannot be demonstrated in the *Regulæ*. Yet it requires demonstration, for it is not self-evident. So far, then, all he can claim for it is the status of a postulate that he has found to be easy of application and to work well on particular occasions. But now he seems to see that the value of his whole method stands or falls with this principle. Were it overturned, the method would be nothing but a collection of judicious guesses and hints, and its interest merely historical and not scientific. He cannot therefore afford to let this proposition remain a simple postulate, liable to be supplanted at any moment by another that works better, or even to be rejected as misleading ; he must try to find some rational ground establishing that the principle is itself a piece of certain knowledge. And the more is he impressed with the necessity of doing so when he recalls that the Pyrrhonists had denied the possibility of any certain knowledge —a view that had recently been revived by Montaigne and

Charron and was now much in the air. The proposition then must be proved. But it cannot be proved directly from the principles of the Method alone, hence the need of an excursion into metaphysics. For the moment, however, Descartes is not prepared to commit his findings in metaphysics to definite statement.

His Paris visit of 1626 had also set him on the track of several scientific problems, and he was constantly having to consider fresh suggestions sent by or through Mersenne. Descartes writes to him: " If you think it strange that I have not completed my treatises begun in Paris . . . it is because, while working on them, I gained more knowledge than I had at the outset, and, wishing to take it into account, was compelled to enlarge my original project." These questions and the greater knowledge gained appear to relate primarily to chemistry and anatomy. The *Monde* was now well towards completion, but Descartes was meanwhile keeping an eye alert for the right sort of material, necessarily observational, to be collected before he could make a preliminary draft of the *De Homine et de Fœtu*. Consequently we hear of daily visits to the slaughter-houses of Amsterdam to examine the anatomy of animals and to carry out dissections on eyes and brains, lungs and hearts, in search for the laws of embryology, or, to use the term he himself coined—" embryogeny." With increase of interest in anatomy, his circle of local friends came to include certain medical men at the University—a further instance of a characteristic tendency to form friendships likely to prove of service to him in his work. It is not before 1633 that he finishes the *Traité du Monde*, that systematic *a priori* physics which results from applying the mathematical method of the *Regulæ* to empirical materials. " I have now become so bold," he writes, " as to venture to discover the reason for the location of every fixed star. They all appear to be irregularly scattered throughout the heavens, yet I doubt not that there is among them some natural order both regular and determinate. Knowledge of this order is the key and foundation of the highest knowledge one can attain about material things, for by its means one may know *a priori* all the various forms and essences of terrestrial bodies, whilst without it one must be content with merely guessing at them *a posteriori*."

"TALIS ERAT ... NATURÆ FILIUS"

Now in the *Monde* (which comprised two parts, the *Traité de la Lumière* and the *Traité de l'Homme*) Descartes reaffirms the Copernican hypothesis of the earth's movement around the sun. On the eve of going to press, however, he is amazed to hear through Mersenne that Galileo, who had advanced the same hypothesis in his *Two Systems of the World*, had been severely censured by the Inquisition and the book publicly burned. Descartes immediately requests Mersenne to stop publication of his book, for he will on no account bring himself into conflict with the Church.[1] He declares that if the offending conclusion is false, so must be all the foundations of his philosophy. For it is " so connected with every other part of my Treatise," he writes, " that I could not disconnect it without making the remainder faulty " (AT, I, 271). He borrows Galileo's book from Beeckman, though only over a week-end. This is long enough, however, for Descartes to find that several other of his own cherished conclusions had already been reached independently by Galileo.

It will pay us to dwell for a moment on the condemnation of Galileo. The *pièces constitutives* of the situation are two : (i) the censure by the Holy Office in 1616[2] of the two theses that the sun is the centre of the world and is completely immobile, and that the earth is not its centre and is not immobile ; and (ii) the *coup de théâtre* of Galileo's condemnation. Descartes's reaction to this situation is instructive, for it indicates both the measure of intellectual freedom existent in his day and the length to which he personally is prepared to persist in expounding conclusions of whose truth he is convinced, in the face of organised opposition. However effective the Inquisition might be in stopping his mouth, it was quite incapable of changing his private belief, and there is little doubt that Descartes gives unconditional though unuttered assent to Galileo's " *Eppur' si muove.*" What appears most to irritate Descartes is to find that his wish to construct a natural philosophy that should be logically independent of matters of faith

---

[1] Descartes's excuse seems rather hypocritically to make a virtue of what for him is all but a necessity : " You will only have a better opinion of me when you learn that I have absolutely decided to suppress the *Treatise* and so lose the results of four years' labour in order to submit with complete obedience to the Church."

[2] For Galileo had first propounded this thesis in an earlier work, *Spots on the Sun*, 1613.

and revelation (the practicability of which proposal he seems to have taken for granted) was not possible of fulfilment, unless, at least, it were accompanied by a course of dangerous and revolutionary action to which he was by no means prepared to commit himself. He had overlooked the viewpoint of the other party to the compromise. Conflict with the Church would be inevitable, for however satisfactory the separation in thought that Descartes proposed might be to reason, the plausibility of its adoption in practice was a pure illusion. This seemed the immediate lesson to be drawn from Galileo's experience. Yet the "opinion de physique," so offensive to the Church, was very much in the air at the time; we learn, for instance, from Gassendi that "everybody in the Low Countries is for the movement of the earth." The Inquisition's punishment of Galileo by heavy fines, imprisonment and subsequent confinement till death, though severe, was not the worst fate that could befall philosophers and men of science. And Descartes knew full well that parallels as bad, and worse, were not far to seek. When he was already four years old had not Bruno been burned at Rome as an atheist for having incorporated in his pantheism Copernicus's discovery of the earth's motion and for having suggested that the biblical account of the Creation was properly mythical? And though there had been greater tolerance in France through Henri IV's reign, within twenty years of Bruno's death another Italian, Vanini, who propounded a form of Naturalism, was burned at Toulouse as an atheist. In the next year Fontanier of Montpellier, who admitted guilt of no greater crime than "teaching an inestimable treasure,"[1] was burned in Paris for atheism. In England, too, Elizabeth and James I had been no less zealous than Rome in persecution and execution. And imprisonment, though not execution, of those who declared their disbelief in the inspiration of the Scriptures or in the divinity of Christ was enforced by the Puritans even so late as two years before Descartes's death.

They were very real risks, then, that the natural philosopher had to face were he intent on publishing his conclusions before a powerful Church whose own holy book was itself a rival cosmogony and a doctrine of God and Man in one. Descartes's *Monde* would be as fair game as any rival cosmogony, so it is

[1] Cf. F. Strowski, *Pascal et son temps*, I, 140-1.

hardly surprising he withheld it from publication. To his
Catholic friends the reason he gave is " obedience to the
Church " as " a dutiful son and subject." But the real explanation would appear to be different. The single aim he imposed
on his will was to keep his days unfettered so they might be
devoted wholly to study. With this desire dominant, prudence
in practical affairs is a natural and reasonable corollary. That
he should have to confess to Mersenne : " I have a thousand
different things to consider together so as to find an expedient
by which to speak the truth without startling anyone's imagination or shocking opinions commonly received " (AT, I, 194)
may be regrettable, but it is scarcely surprising. And his
admission to Pollot later, " it is not my temperament to set
sail against the wind " (AT, IV, 73), is as characteristic as is his
haste to noise abroad that, whatever be the issue, he holds
theology in esteem. Through all his conduct, prudence dictates
both its direction and his justification. His view is suitably
prepared for the public in the *Passions of the Soul* (ccxi) : " It
is imprudent to lose one's life when one can save oneself without
dishonour ; if the odds are heavy against one, 'tis better to
beat an honourable retreat or ask quarter than to expose oneself
unreasoningly to certain death." Whether or not he would have
held that, as Anatole France puts it, " there is something of
impertinence in getting oneself burned for an opinion," and
that " martyrs are wanting in irony," which is " an unpardon-
able fault," he would probably have regarded it a piece of noble
folly to imperil his freedom, and Descartes was not capable of
follies. He would have held, with Parny, that

> Une indifférence paisible
> Est la plus sage des vertus.

But it was not a prudence which slips imperceptibly into that
form of selfishness or self-absorption which makes long and
intimate friendships impossible. There is evident warmth in
his attachment to Beeckman. In frankness and generosity he
compares very favourably with the Dutchman, who finds it no
breach of loyalty to pass off as his own composition the *Compendium Musicæ*—Descartes's first book, which he had dedi-
cated and presented in manuscript to his friend. The cordiality
and good feeling that marked Descartes's relations with Mer-

senne, Mesland, Clerselier and Picot among many, show he is sincere when he writes to Chanut : " The greatest good in life is friendship," and to Voët : " Friendship is a thing too sacred to be abused, for there is no greater good." The constancy here avowed is well borne out in his Protestant connexions. Descartes's intimacy with Regius and Reneri, two enthusiastic disciples who belonged to the Reformed Church, was in no degree modified by the scandal this relationship created among Parisian Catholics who accused him of going *au prêche*, nor by the distrust of Dutch Protestants who would abuse him with such epithets as " Papist " and " Jesuit." Friendship with those of different religion is no crime, he urges in his famous letter to the University of Utrecht. His relations, and very cordial ones, extend even to " that scandalous prior," Claude Picot, free-thinker and bon-vivant, and to the " illustré débauché " and atheist, De Barraux. It is not unnatural that so many intimate connexions of this kind were taken in such an epoch as arguing greater tolerance than piety. In a letter to Huygens, consoling him on the death of his wife, Descartes avoids the customary allusions to the comforts of religion and speaks with a sincerity that is more eloquent because it is so reasonable. There can be no question then of Descartes's sincerity and loyalty in friendship. In brief, M. Leroy seems to sum up the matter justly : " If Descartes is prudent, he is not at all cowardly. He is frank, therefore he detests all Machiavellianism. But he does not thunder forth his detestation. He observes distinctions and his terms are measured."[1]

On the other hand, the sincerity of his public declarations that relate to religion and the Church are quite fairly open to question.[2] In private correspondence he certainly said much that he would never have allowed to appear in print. He admits to Chanut finding it impossible to accept the Bible in its literal sense, and to Mdlle. Schurmann, that he neither believes in the literal inspiration of the Scriptures nor acquiesces in the Mosaic story of the world's Creation, except from regard to the Church. What really is Descartes's attitude to such matters has been very variously interpreted by different scholars. M. Adam,

[1] Maxime Leroy, *Descartes, le Philosophe au masque*, Vol. II, p. 86. Paris, 1929.
[2] On the diversity of recent interpretations see my article ' Cartesiana,' *Journ. of Phil. Studies*, V, 19.

Descartes's most authoritative biographer, warns us not to be misled by the declaration " I defend the cause of God," frequently on Descartes's lips. M. Espinas, however, will not allow there is any *arrière pensée* in Descartes's public utterances in these connexions, and represents him as consumed with zeal for the Church's defence and as desirous of inaugurating a counter-reform—an hypothesis that seems much less plausible. Again, M. Leroy reproaches Descartes's biographers with not allowing sufficient weight to his relations to heretics, atheists, and Rosicrucians ; for, he maintains, some of these friendships, by their intimacy and long standing, reveal a moral affinity and congruence of ideas and aims. As the *Correspondence* shows, Descartes certainly knew how to disguise his thought and choose his language. " The truth must be veiled," he writes ; and again, " Now that I am to be not only a spectator of the world, but am to appear an actor on its stage, I wear a mask." And did he not refuse to place his signature to the *Monde*, so that he " may be ever free to disavow it " ? The " God " he believes established by his metaphysics is, too, a ' philosophical God '—an ultimate ground to explain the existence and order of the physical world, the existence of man and the possibility of knowledge—and this is very far from being the God of the Christian religion as understood by the Roman Church of the seventeenth century.

III

Three years after his scare at Galileo's condemnation, Descartes decided to publish the results of applying his method to problems in mathematics and natural science, after introducing certain modifications into his cosmology, and in 1637 John le Maire of Leyden completed the printing of an epoch-making quarto : *Discourse on the Method of properly guiding the Reason in the Search for Truth in the Sciences. Also the Dioptric, the Meteors, and the Geometry, which are Essays in this Method.* The last clause of this long title gives us the key to what Descartes is most anxious to emphasise. His principal intention in publishing the *Essays* was to present to the public four fully worked-out examples of applications of his Method. For, as he frequently emphasises, its character and importance are to be properly grasped, not by contemplating the rules themselves in their formal statement, but by examining them as they are exhibited in a concrete setting of some kind. He accordingly presents four specimens : three are separate applications of the method to different materials—one (in the *Dioptric*) furnishing his mathematical physics, another (in the *Meteors*) providing solutions to particular and disconnected problems in concrete physics, and the third (inserted in the *Discourse*), a contribution to the physiology of blood-circulation—all illustrating the fecundity and utility of his Method. The fourth application also exhibits these merits, and shows besides that it is possible by means of the Method to reach results that are certain, for in the *Geometry* it is applied to notions that are relatively simple, capable of exact definition, and therefore of being clearly and completely understood. Descartes regards this last application as constituting a complete vindication of his Method, besides being the most important of the four illustrations. In treating many of the problems he contents himself with indicating the means of their solution, and does not fill in every step of each demonstration, which seems to be indirect evidence to show that he is interested more in the method and its applicability than in the material results themselves.

It must be admitted that the results Descartes reached (considered in themselves for the information they give about physical and physiological phenomena, and not for the relief into which they throw the character and merits of the method) are now of little more than historical interest. The *Treatise on Light* was eclipsed by Newton's work in optics, and the problems treated in the *Meteors* were dealt with more successfully later on by experimental methods. But though the detail of Descartes's procedure here can no longer be supported, we must never forget that the more general and original conception which inspired it (namely, that natural data can and should be investigated according to the method and presuppositions of his mathematical physics) has been amply vindicated in having made possible the solid advances from his day down to our own. The *Geometry* remains his great and original contribution to pure mathematics. What was then revolutionary, and is still important in it,[1] has been absorbed into standard treatises on

---

[1] Thanks to recent developments in the philosophy of mathematics, we to-day can state more clearly than Descartes could the point of his contention.

"TALIS ERAT . . . NATURÆ FILIUS"   23

co-ordinate geometry through subsequent generations, and now finds a place in every text-book.

But though much of the contents of these *Essays* is now of importance only to the historian of the sciences, the six-part preface that Descartes composed for them (the famous *Discourse on Method*) remains a philosophical classic to this day. At the time of publication it was a highly revolutionary manifesto, a distinct innovation in respect of both its matter and its literary form. No previous thinker had published a philosophical or scientific treatise in French except Oresme and Ramus.[1] Latin was the language of Bacon's *Novum Organum*, of Clavius's *Geometry*, and of Gassendi's works. It was in Latin, too, that the bulk of the lectures were given, and all theses for degrees were *soutenues* in the universities throughout France and Holland. Descartes, by writing in French, showed, what in fact he declared, that it was not the ear of the learned he hoped to catch, but of all who had wit enough to understand plain meanings : " Those who avail themselves of their natural reason alone may be better judges of my opinions than those who give heed only to the writings of the ancients." He intends his book to be accessible to every one, adding, as did Pascal of his *Provinciales*, " and understandable even to women." Descartes's indifference to the " opinions of the learned," some-

It seems to be this : that what is essential in mathematical demonstration is purely formal. It is a consequence of the properties of the relations studied (*e.g.* such relations as, ' equal,' ' proportional to,' etc.), and not a consequence of the character of the terms those relations relate. So, for mathematics, it is a matter of indifference whether the related terms be lines, figures, numbers or measurable quantities, for the same general theorems may be proved of all alike. Thus the proof is independent of the peculiar differentiating characteristics of the relata, and results established about one type of relata can be translated into statements of relationship between relata of different type. Thus the invention of analytical geometry consists in this : having first established a correlation between points and numbers, and having next expressed these in relation to convenient co-ordinates, we may proceed to demonstrate that certain relations holding between those numbers represent certain relations between the points for which the numbers stand. Conversely, algebraical and arithmetical relationships may be represented by geometrical constructions, and the statistical graph happily illustrates how this is applicable to concrete data.

[1] Nicholas Oresme (died 1382) was the first of French savants to compose philosophical treatises in his native tongue. Besides translating Aristotle's *Politics* and *Ethics*, he wrote in French treatises on physics and the standard work of the fourteenth century on political economy.—Peter Ramus (1515–72), massacred on the Eve of St. Bartholomew, represented the culmination of anti-Aristotelian tendencies. His principal work, *La Dialectique*, was composed in French in 1555, eighty-one years before Descartes wrote his *Discours*.

times carried beyond disdain into contempt, is thoroughly characteristic. M. Gilson and others have warned us, however, against accepting Descartes's utterances about his 'independence' and 'originality' at their face value. Yet behind the exaggeration there are clear signs of a love of personal effort and a preference for working out conclusions in one's own way. It is no exaggeration, but simply an expression of preference, when he says, " I confess that my greatest happiness in study has always consisted, not in following the arguments of others, but in discovering them in myself," and nothing more than an added *hauteur* when he writes, " I am not for becoming one of those little artisans who apply themselves only to the restoration of old works, because they feel themselves incapable of achieving anything new " (AT, X, 509).

His experiment of composing philosophical and scientific treatises in his native tongue had far-reaching consequences in philosophy and letters. Scholars came to regard the French language as an instrument worth careful cultivation. Descartes's writing had proved it capable of expressing thoughts far from simple with an extreme simplicity, clearness and elegance that had been attained in no earlier 'reflective' prose— not even in Montaigne's. In choice of words and constructions, Descartes's French is a French French, not a Latin French—it is the French of the great seventeenth-century *prosateurs*. Except in writing to his friend Guez de Balzac, when he inclines to the picturesque and possibly becomes a little too studied, his prose is as good as any that has been employed for expressing philosophical ideas and distinctions. But though vastly superior to Arnauld's, which is heavy and too often encumbered with long clauses, it is hardly so elegant or pellucid as the writing of Malebranche. Descartes certainly took prose composition very seriously, and in the *Correspondence* we frequently read of him redrafting his *ébauches*. And that he readily discerned perspicuity and elegance in the writing of others is evident from his observations about de Balzac. He says, " Whatever my frame of mind when I read these letters, whether I subject them to careful analysis or give myself up to enjoying them, so complete is the satisfaction with which they fill me that I not only fail to find a single fault in them, but, among their many fine qualities, I can scarcely tell which most to praise. There is in them such purity of expression that, like health in the body, the better it is the less is it noticed. There is in them too such an elegance and grace that, like the beauty of a woman who is perfectly beautiful, no one quality may be extolled without risk of imputing imperfection to the others." Though Descartes was not the first to use his native tongue for the expression of philosophical thought, he did adapt its use to a variety of literary *genres*. His first published composition in French assumed the form of "essays," and many of his letters are masterpieces of style ; later he attempted, though less successfully than Malebranche, that most difficult of forms—the dialogue (as Galileo had, in his Italian *Discorsi* and *Dialogo*), while his principal metaphysical work comprises a set of "meditations." There were, of course, precedents and fine models for each of these forms in the philosophical literature of antiquity, but to adapt them to the spoken language of daily life and commerce in France, and, in this way, to create a literary language, was in large measure due to Descartes.

His first printed work then pretends to no more than reporting a series of attempts at formulating and applying a method. It is not an expository treatise but a report, with a discussion of what is reported. It is something tentative, as he himself makes clear : " I do not propose to unfold the nature of the method here, but only to talk it over." But he could hardly discuss its applications without informing his readers in a broad way of the results those applications had yielded. Now these include some of the most central principles of his metaphysics (*Discourse*, pt. iv) : the project of a general doubt, the analysis of knowledge and certitude, the discovery of their criterion, the existence and nature of the self and of God. On these subjects he had already worked, at the commencement of his residence in Holland, but he did not publish his arguments and conclusions in their full length till ten years later, and then as *Meditations on the First Philosophy, in which the existence of God and the distinction between Mind and Body are demonstrated*. Intended primarily for philosophers and scholars, Descartes composed it in Latin, and before publishing took two further precautions against it being misconceived. He besought Mersenne to submit it to the Theological Faculty at Paris to canvass the approval of the " Docteurs en Sorbonne," and to have copies of the manuscript sent to the ablest philosophers with a request for their criticisms, it being a condition that none should have a sight of the work unless he permitted his criticisms to be printed along with Descartes's replies at the end of the volume. This was, of course, a shrewd move to secure that the learned gave really serious attention to his matter, and that the reading public should not be perverted or prejudiced by reviewers' objections to which he could not reply. The best criticisms that came to be collected in this way were contributed by Caterus, a professor in theology at Lyons, Thomas Hobbes, Pierre Gassendi and Antoine Arnauld. The acute and careful annotations of the last Descartes regarded as the most important of the several sets. His other precaution, that of submitting the work to the Doctors of the Sorbonne, had none but gratifying consequences at the time. Father Gibieuf, who examined it with more particular care, communicated his entire approval. This, however, is the very work which, twenty-two years later, Rome was to place on the Index!

Meanwhile, in the very country where Descartes had rejoiced to find such good sense and toleration, he was now to meet his bitterest enemies. Regius (Le Roy), a professor of medicine and warm admirer of Descartes, had introduced certain characteristic principles of Cartesianism into his lectures on physiology at the University of Utrecht. The enthusiasm of the students rose higher daily and at length overleaped itself, regarding all as dross that was not Descartes. The arrogance of this upstart enthusiasm among young and rather raw ' intellectuals ' is, of course, easily matched in university annals, but not so the downright hatred evinced by Descartes's dissenting or envious contemporaries. The most odious of them appears to have been Voët, the President of the University, who eventually succeeded in securing from the Senate an explicit disapprobation of Le Roy's teaching and of Descartes's philosophy. In 1642 the Senate issued this decree : " We, professors of the University of Utrecht, reject and condemn the new philosophy, because : first, it contradicts the old and subverts its principles ; secondly, it makes students averse from studying the old philosophy and so hinders their development, since they cannot understand the terminology of the schools once they have become acquainted with the principles of this so-called philosophy : and, finally, so many false and irrational conclusions follow from it, and immature youths may easily draw inferences from it inconsistent with other sciences, and in particular with the true theology." It would be of little profit to pursue in detail the long, rather tedious and very acrimonious controversy that ensued. Hostility and calumny became so bitter, intrigue and threats so dangerous, that Descartes had eventually to appeal to the Prince of Orange for protection, which was effectively given by an order from the States-General. In the meantime, fearing arrest (for he had been publicly summoned with the ringing of the city bells, to appear before the magistrates as a fugitive to answer charges alleged against him), Descartes sought security at the Hague.

In 1644 Elzevir of Amsterdam published Descartes's third main work, *The Principles of Philosophy*, in four books, in which he resumes his entire system under separate articles or " propositions " in the manner of the college manuals of the time. Five years later, disgusted by his later experiences in Holland, and thinking of retiring to France, he received a request from the Queen Christina, who had been persevering with the *Principles*, to go to Stockholm and instruct her. It was not unnatural that the philosopher, born among the sunny vineyards of Touraine, should have contemplated rather wryly an invitation " to live in the land of bears amongst rocks and ice." He was apprehensive, too, of further unpleasantness from jealousy on the part of courtiers, and of interference with his habits and independence. Exhorted by his friend Chanut, the ambassador of France to the Queen, Descartes departed for Sweden, after sending to the press the manuscript of his last composition, *The Passions of the Soul*. Five o'clock in the morning, unhappily for Descartes, was the hour at which the Queen's mind was most active, and returning from court one November morning in 1650 he contracted a severe chill, to which, after a week of delirium and suffering, he succumbed. So, in his fifty-fourth year and at the height of his intellectual powers, passed away the greatest philosopher of France. " Indifferent to the life of the court, to military glory, to the pleasures of society and the superstitions of social rank ; desirous, certainly, of seeing his philosophy triumph over error, but setting the passion for research and the joy of discovery at a far higher price than the pleasure of publishing and the satisfaction of success, Descartes conceived no other ideal than that of a perfectly disciplined will placed at the service of a perfectly clear reason. 'Seek peace in wisdom' was the profound aspiration of this man who lived by thought alone for thought alone . . . never was an existence more noble than his."[1]

[1] Gilson, *Études*, p. 280.

II

THE INTELLECTUAL CLIMATE OF THE AGE

"The new mentality is more important than the new science."—
WHITEHEAD.

OUR object in the last chapter was to form an impression of the intellectual temper of Descartes by reviewing those proclivities, native and acquired, displayed in his reactions to circumstances that touched him more personally. We shall now consider the spiritual legacy which Descartes inherited, those formative and restrictive influences that composed the intellectual situation in which his work was conceived and developed. It should become evident that Descartes was not the sire of his age but its child; as Dr. Whitehead puts it, "the soil, the climate, the seeds were there."

It is the theocentric thought of the Middle Ages that forms the upper air of his climate. But Descartes was not to breathe this air in its purity. In this late autumn of Mediaevalism new and keener currents were already felt. Philosophical thought was far from being completely emancipated from the tutelage of theology even in the sixteenth century, although the project that had lent it vitality for four centuries had received its death-blow some two hundred years before Descartes's birth. The great mediaeval philosophers were all theologians. The dogmatic teaching of the Church, the common and central term of their discussions, was fixed and final. What varied with thinker and period was the direction of their incessant attempts to reconcile the Church's revelation with the philosophy of antiquity. Such a reconciliation, the ultimate possibility of which was not doubted, called for unusual powers of synthesis and systematisation, and a thinker like Thomas Aquinas, who, besides possessing those powers in the highest degree, had an encyclopaedic grasp of detail and a genius for the clear arrangement and expression of ideas, was evidently most likely to perform the feat, were it possible of performance. So the divergencies and oppositions revealed in the history of philosophy through the Middle Ages centre in this single, absorbing problem of reconciling Revelation with Reason. This is not to say, however, that no element of innovation or originality is traceable, that the experiments, on their philosophical side, reduce merely to stressing now what is Aristotelian in Plato, now what is Platonic in Aristotle. Nor do they resolve into a merely eclectic performance. Until the twelfth century the only work of Plato extant was the *Timaeus* (and that in translation), and of Aristotle, two logical tracts, the *De Interpretatione* and the *Categoriæ*. It was natural, then, that the earlier period —that of Augustine—should have been imbued more with the spirit of Plato and the later Platonists than with anything distinctively Aristotelian. Thomas Aquinas was not the man to leave his materials as he found them. So when eventually the major works of Aristotle came to light in Paris (in Latin translations from the Arabic text), and scholars saw in them the possibility of a completer and more scientific doctrine than the rather fragmentary Platonism hitherto current, Thomas's handling of these acquisitions, directed to furnishing a unified, harmonious body of all truth, human and divine, resulted in no slavish commentary, but in a highly original reinterpretation. In fact, so original was it that the Thomist version ends by being a distortion of pure Aristotelianism. Thomism, in the form it took from Suarez, had become, by Descartes's youth, the standard systematic philosophy, explanatory and apologetic, regularly taught in the colleges throughout France.

Meanwhile, dissent and movement towards freer enquiry had been effective in unsettling acceptance of the Church's doctrine, and even of its dogmas. In the fifteenth century Pietro Pomponazzi, who had studied Aristotle directly in the Greek, vigorously contested the Church's version of " the Philosopher," and the Aristotelians are henceforward divided into two camps. Those following Alexander of Aphrodisias and Pomponazzi hold that genuine Aristotelianism either denies or does not maintain many of the things that endear it to the Church—the soul's immortality, the world's beginning and control by a Divine Providence. Confrontation of the Church with arguments based on an independent interpretation of its own official philosopher naturally opened men's minds as well as their eyes. The desirability of free discussion was clearly seen and often avowed.

THE INTELLECTUAL CLIMATE OF THE AGE 31

So much, however, had already been long prepared by the destructive criticism of the anti-papal William of Occam. He too had struck at the roots of the Church's Aristotelianism, maintaining that the soul's immortality was impossible of demonstration, that the arguments to prove God's existence did not do so, and that the dogmas of the Incarnation and the Trinity were not only undemonstrated but highly improbable. Destructive criticism, inspired and directed by reason, had thus quietly loosened the hold of much questionable doctrine, and predisposed men's minds to newer theories, newer discoveries and a newer method of research. But a little time and men would openly declare for fair hearing and fair answer to reservations they had long made *in foro conscientiæ* and for doubts that had long lain unavowed. But the significance of the revival of Greek learning does not turn merely on the interpretation and assimilation of Aristotelianism. The dissemination of Greek culture that followed on the fall of Constantinople brought to light and made available to scholars, besides the Aristotelian corpus, the principal works of Plato, and certain fragments and records of the early Ionian cosmologists. So we find men of learning, mainly in Italy, assiduously revising this or that pagan philosopher: Nicholas of Cusa among others immersed in Plato and the Neo-Platonists, Berigard and Telesio in the Ionian physicists, Gassendi in Epicurus. Such a situation, in which the individual implicitly claims his right (by overtly exercising it) to seek his own preferred authority, and therewith his own way of salvation, is in itself a long stride towards open enquiry and against the Church's proscription. With the revival of Letters, willingness to find satisfaction either in dogmatic injunction or in exclusive acceptance of some one thinker gives place to a desire to explore adventurously these fresh alluring avenues that seem to offer an inward satisfaction both rational and lasting. Where such a wealth of great work lay open to contemplation, a vast, lost world now recovered remained to be explored, interests naturally divided. How far a second Aquinas might have realised a more durable synthesis with this fresh and fuller material is a problem profitless to consider, for with the realisation that the earlier one was neither satisfying nor rationally authoritative, interest in its reconstruction vanished, and, with it, belief and hope in the possibility. Humanism, at once young and mature, bore another message, and one which could be transfused into a different ideal, and it is Leonardo da Vinci who voices the profounder character of the transition. While for a Pomponazzi the excellence of a science derives rather from the beauty immanent in its objects, for a da Vinci it lies in the truth and certitude of its demonstrations. " So base is falsehood that even in exalting godly things it would divest divinity of its grace, so excellent is truth that in extolling the slightest things it invests them with nobility. Truth, even in contemplating the mean and lowly, infinitely surpasses the uncertainty of sublime and lofty speculations. But you whom dreams nourish, find more pleasure in sophistries about what is extraordinary and unknown than in trustworthy and natural conclusions that do not rise so high."

Philosophically, the Renaissance marks a change in the manner of conceiving truth and knowledge generally. The epistemological transition to be inferred from the scientific attitude of such minds as da Vinci and Galileo is, briefly, from one of unquestioning conviction that truth ultimately relates to a reality transcendent and inaccessible to mind, to an active faith in the essential sufficiency of human powers to discover truth, precisely because knowledge is not ultimately of a transcendent reality. Or, as M. Bréhier puts it,[1] " truth is not disclosed in the form of a systematic and total vision of the universe (whether the vision be due to revelation or reason or both), but is, so to say, distributed in a multitude of propositions." So intense is this reactionary movement that at its culmination in the sixteenth century it declares itself openly in papal Italy and in face of the Inquisition. Seismical rumblings that had long been heard are now followed by volcanic upheavals that leave traces visible long after the era of Descartes. We noticed the tragic ends of Bruno, Vanini and Fontanier, in whom the passion to satisfy rather than still reason was so acute and constant that they counted not the cost. If their aims were diverse, they were at one in the forthrightness with which they strove to compel recognition of the right of every man to seek intellectual satisfaction in his own way. Bruno, a thinker more comprehensive and rigorous than Vanini, tried to work out a consistent pantheism through a synthesis of the conceptions of God,

[1] E. Bréhier, *Histoire de la Philosophie*, Tome 1, p. 759. Paris, 1928.

THE INTELLECTUAL CLIMATE OF THE AGE 33

Intellect, the World Soul and Matter (as he found them in Plotinus), the heliocentric astronomy of Copernicus, the Being of Parmenides and the Atomic Theory of Democritus. Bruno's philosophy, frankly eclectic, original only in the selection of themes and in the manner of their combination, did not influence Descartes in even the limited measure it influenced Leibniz. But Bruno helped to secure that degree of intellectual freedom without which a prudent Descartes could never have thrived. Of strong individualistic temperament, Bruno had no patience with " the harmful and ambitious Aristotle," for " ambitious and presumptuous is he who would persuade others that there is but one way of attaining knowledge of nature." Doctrine good as it was dangerous. Less remote perhaps was the doctrinal influence of Campanella, who insists that self-awareness necessarily accompanies every cognitive act, and that cognition of a common character among known objects is the cause or occasion on which the self comes to contemplate the essences (Platonic Ideas) in which they participate. Revolt against the Church's Philosopher is carried a stage further by Peter Ramus, who followed up his thesis for the Master's degree at Paris (" That all Aristotle has said is false ") with the *Aristotelicæ Animadversiones*, which so annoyed François I that he was forbidden to teach or write for a while, on the ground that his book "showed both ignorance and ill-will, and condemned many things good and true." His later teaching at the Collège de France (for Ramus was primarily a professional teacher) was, however, so brilliant that his fame spread throughout the land, and his method of dialectic was enthusiastically studied in Germany. This dialectic divided into two parts, one treating of the search for arguments, the other the method of rightly marshalling and presenting them clearly and cogently. Each, " discovery " and " exposition," are conceived as separate pursuits, neither influencing the other in any way. There seems little of first importance in this methodology. Ramus emphasises the need of starting with the better known and passing on to the less known (a favourite maxim of Descartes), and stimulates interest in quite general questions concerning order of thought and order of statement. He has nothing like so clear or developed a conception of method as Descartes, and much less still than Leibniz, but nevertheless he did much to accustom minds to

c

reflect on the method of successful thinking in itself. His examples of analysis and illustrations are invariably chosen from what Descartes would have called "merely probably arguments" (namely, from arguments of historians and orators), while Descartes, of course, made it a special point to model his method on the procedure of mathematical demonstration. The worth of Ramus lay largely in his teaching and in constantly insisting on the need of clearness and rigour in thinking. He also carried a stage further the steady undermining of Church Aristotelianism, and therefore of Church authority, by denying Providence and Creation.

Bruno, Campanella, Ramus, then, all passionately believed in the competence of reason to reach knowledge of nature and man, no less than in the individual's right freely to exercise his reason. For them, disagreement among men of science and philosophy argued no radical defect in human powers: it was simply a witness to the difficulty of the task. But there is another and parallel current of thought to be reckoned with, one which, even though it advanced considerably the general movement of liberating and destructive criticism, yet denied to reason competence to satisfy its own incessant claims, and sought to discourage it by a doctrine of morals that was predominantly Epicurean. A new turn is given to the current of criticism; the very foundations of these rationalistic edifices are assaulted and sapped. In this revival of scepticism, the representative figures are Montaigne and his friend Charron—the former died four years before, the latter seven years after, Descartes's birth. Their scepticism seems to have been covertly directed against the Church's doctrine, but it certainly concluded with an avowal of the weakness of human reason, and with a recommendation (possibly from prudential motives) to harmonise our lives with the injunctions of the Church. Superficially, then, it bears the stamp of reaction. Montaigne announces the main theme when he writes: " It is Presumption that is our natural and original malady.[1] Man, the most pitiful and frail of all creatures, is at the same time the most arrogant. He feels and finds himself quartered here amid the mire and

---

[1] Descartes characteristically assigns "desire for knowledge" as man's "incurable malady"—"incurable," for curiosity grows with advancing insight. Cf. AT, X, 499.

THE INTELLECTUAL CLIMATE OF THE AGE 35

dung of the world . . . but, through imagination, he projects himself beyond the rim of the moon, and draws the heavens about his feet." Though we invent rational support for conceptions that are prompted by our aspirations, that support is really indefensible. What induces us to attempt their defence is, in truth, our supreme arrogance and self-satisfaction, which, from their universality and long life, have hardened into conviction. Man's fond idealisation of himself as being at once the purpose and explanation of the universe, his pride of knowledge, his pride in the active possession of its instruments, his pride in the wisdom and justice of his social ordinances—all are vain fancies of his overheated brain, none can withstand a sober, searching criticism. Before crying aloud our superiority to the beasts, let us consider their lives and their works, for both will reveal to us ourselves. Our so-called knowledge but lightens up our ignorance, our mouths mutter what our minds cannot comprehend. Of our own self we know nothing, and the philosophers' accounts of it are as fantastic as they are divergent. We know that if our will be exercised then our body moves, but we know nothing of how will moves body. We know *that* our bodily organs function, but not *how* they function. We do not understand the machine we control. Certain measures we know to be a remedy for its ill-functioning or illness, but why these remedies and not others are effectual we do not know. Yet, in the vanity of much learning we dress out our ignorance in impressive strings of senseless words. Such is our natural science. " In words are its questions asked, in words are they answered. What is a stone ?—'tis a body : and a body ?—'tis a substance ; and a substance ? . . . One word we exchange for another and often another less well understood. I know better what a man is than what is ' animal,' or ' mortal ' or ' rational.' To dissipate a single doubt, three more are created.' Nor is this emptiness of our knowledge but a passing condition Everyone at the moment was busied with reversing what the centuries had regarded as unshakable—" in geometry . . . are to be found rigid proofs that subvert the testimony of experience, a thousand years ago it would have been plain heresy to have declared for the antipodes, while in our very century an infinite extent of terra firma has just been discovered." Montaigne surveys wryly the commotion around him at the rebuilding of vast wings in the edifice of knowledge, and predicts that these too, in their turn, will fall. But what he casts his eye upon most sceptically is the idea of a deductive science that purports to set off from fixed first principles that are certain. There is only one method that could retrieve our rational efforts from a constant renewal of deception and disappointment, namely, one which disclosed an absolutely certain criterion of truth. But such a method Montaigne thinks plainly impossible, for we cannot come by a criterion of truth without already being possessed of some truth, and we cannot know whether that which we are possessed of *is* truth unless we are already possessed of a criterion. And if we cannot secure that our beliefs are certain, no more can we establish greater and lesser probability among them. The probable, *vraisemblable*, is that which *seems* true. But must we not already know something that certainly is true, in order to know whether a given belief does or does not resemble it ? Mediaeval thought neglected and so underestimated the amount of variety and diversity in Nature. It concentrated unduly on the similar and connected, but " resemblance does not make so much unity as difference does diversity." No single, homogeneous and permanent stuff is to be discovered in things. The value of our science then derives not from the objects it contemplates, nor from the certainty of its results, but from its utility alone. Science acquires value only in use, in being actively employed and applied by man. Certain and objective knowledge about the world, man or God, is a day-dream. Nor is mankind's proper subject man. It is, briefly, *oneself*, the self as each alone can know it for himself " independently of external aid, by using only his own faculties, and divested of all divine grace and knowledge." Accordingly, writes Montaigne in the famous *Essays* (III, 8), " I not only dare speak about myself, but dare speak of nothing but myself. . . . There is no description so difficult as self-description, nor any so surely useful." *A priori* constructions from universal principles should give place to impartial, painstaking and prolonged self-reflexion. In this way it is not unnatural that Descartes should have been led to the belief that investigation into the character, extent or limit of permissible doubt, and into the nature of self-awareness, were prolegomena indispensable to any future advance in philosophy.

II

Until the seventeenth century, progress in empirical science runs parallel with increasing recognition of the place and importance of experience in investigation. With a realisation of the need and worth of observation, resort to it is more frequently and pertinaciously practised, and this change in the methodological temper of men of science is displayed in their resolution not to be side-tracked by permitting rational argument to decide issues which, of their very nature, demand inspection of 'brute fact.' This change to a new way of knowledge, inaugurated in England by Roger Bacon in the thirteenth century, and in Italy by Leonardo da Vinci in the fifteenth, seems to have been more 'instinctive' than a result of an explicit theory of method, and its character is clear in da Vinci's admission, " it is quite true that Nature begins by reason and finishes with experience; all the same, we must follow the reverse order." Roger Bacon too had insisted that we cannot be " persuaded " by rational grounds alone to accept scientific theories, but only by rational argument which is enforced and confirmed by the results of observation and experiment. " There are two ways of acquiring knowledge—experience and reasoning. Reasoning alone can convince, but it does not persuade, and does not always exclude doubt." He maintained (in opposition to his scholastic contemporaries, who duly persecuted him for it) that a fecund natural science depended upon uniting mathematics and experimental findings.[1] Thus in the *Opus Majus*, pt. iv, he declares, " All that is necessary for physics can be proved by mathematics, and without them it is impossible to attain an exact knowledge of things." How far, then, did the introduction of observed fact and inference from observed fact change the face of natural philosophy in the century before Descartes?

Until this time mechanics underwent little transformation. Archimedes had developed his statics of parallel forces on a basis that called for no revision, and dynamics cannot be said to have been worked out at all. True, Aristotle had formulated *a priori* a law of falling bodies, according to which their velocities varied directly with their weights, and this formula, we

[1] Cf. the detailed study of R. Carton, *L'Expérience physique chez Roger Bacon*. Paris, 1924.

all learned at our mother's knee, Galileo disproved by the simple device of dropping stones from the tower of Pisa. Apart from this correction of Aristotle's misstatement of observable fact, and the vindication of experience, which acceptance of that correction implies, the methodological 'moral' of the lesson seemed to be that the proper question to ask is *how* objects behave, not *why* they behave so, and the only kind of answer acceptable would result from judicious combination of observation with inference.[1] Astronomy, on the other hand, had been attracting the best minds, and the fifteenth century sees its rebirth. The Ptolemaic theory (that the earth is the centre of the world, and that around it revolves the moon, Mercury, Venus, the Sun, Mars, Jupiter, Saturn and the fixed stars) had enjoyed something like the authority which the Church imparted to its religious dogmas. But as more numerous and careful observations were made, more and more interpolations *ad hoc* were required to 'adjust' the data of observation with the Ptolemaic hypothesis. To a point Ptolemy's suggestion was serviceable enough: it accounted for the celestial phenomena then known within limits of error that had to be allowed at a time when our modern instruments were not available; it also enabled predictions of astronomical events to be cast within those limits of error. But if Ptolemy's hypothesis was serviceable, still more so was that of Copernicus. And it was simpler. Instead of postulating some eighty epicycles, Copernicus required us to suppose only thirty-four. Celestial phenomena could be explained just as satisfactorily by this more economical hypothesis, provided we rejected the assumption that our earth is the immobile centre of the world. There was already a low initial probability in its favour from general grounds of 'economy' or 'simplicity.' It was part of the commonest physics, and almost of common sense, that light travels in straight lines, that projectiles did not deviate from the path along which they were propelled, that falling bodies moved perpendicularly; and the usual comment that nature did nothing "in vain," that things in motion pursued the shortest path, that, in a word, nature was 'economical' of

---

[1] Cf. Whitehead: "Galileo keeps harping on how things happen, whereas his adversaries had a complete theory as to why things happen. Unfortunately the two theories did not bring out the same result."—*Science and the Modern World*, p. 12. See the most suggestive chapters, i and ii, *op. cit.*

ways and means, doubtless recommended in some measure the Copernican alternative, and predisposed men of science in its favour. The real 'knot' over which men bungled was the condition upon which they were permitted to accept this simpler explanation. The transition from a geocentric to a heliocentric physics required no slight readjustment for imagination, whatever it might have involved for conception. The superiority claimed for the heliocentric system, in demanding fewer and more convenient assumptions, could hardly carry, besides assent, such overwhelming approval as would cause men to overlook the enormity of the seeming paradox. Yet they were growing accustomed to the reversal of common beliefs. It was no longer possible to suppose the Mediterranean basin the extent of existent terra firma. Other lands of unimagined vastness, other civilisations of unsuspected beauty, had been revealed, in relation to which their own countries were of minute extent, and their mediaeval civilisation was no longer beautiful in its decay. Plain people could easily perceive that a ship's navigation round the earth and a fly's ambulation round an apple were two instances of movement round something spherical. And the antipodes were known to be inhabited. If, then, the European continent were not "all" the earth they had supposed themselves to know, if the early civilisation of Mediaeval Europe were not the only civilisation, if the Church's utterances were not the only utterances claiming authority, was it not possible that our earth may not be the centre of the physical world? Once imagination could grasp the character of the inversion demanded, intelligence, aided by observation (itself increased in range and precision by the newly invented telescope) could be left to grapple with questions concerning the coherence, consistency and adequacy of the new explanation. The camel to be swallowed, then, was that the sun is really the centre of the world, and that our earth, in common with other celestial bodies, moves round it. So much Copernicus had proposed but not proved. Compatibility with known facts is one thing, however, capacity to absorb new disclosures is another. A further stage in the course of the heliocentric theory had to await the advent of Kepler. He, like its inventor, was first attracted to it by its simplicity and its aesthetic appeal. After his empirical apprenticeship under Tycho Brahé, who had corrected and augmented planetary theory, determined the place of many fixed stars and located regions of space occupied by comets, Kepler succeeded, while Descartes was yet at La Flèche, in reducing the motions of the planets to three primary laws. These laws, which presupposed that the planets moved around the earth in ellipses, he deduced from observations of Mars and our earth. Further, he elaborated two other hypotheses, one explaining the origin of planetary motion (along the lines of the vortex theory later suggested by Descartes in the *Principles*), the other accounting for the behaviour of tides in terms of lunar attraction. About this time, too, an optician of Middelburg made a tube in which lenses were so arranged as to magnify objects seen through it—the optical properties of concave and convex lenses having already been discovered accidentally nearly three centuries earlier. Galileo heard of the tube, conceived its principle, and constructed his first telescope, through which objects appeared at a third of their real distance.

By 1609 enthusiasm for the new astronomy had reached fever heat in scientific circles. Galileo now constructed a more powerful instrument magnifying objects about a thousand times, and by its means Jupiter's satellites, Saturn's rings, the phases of Venus and the mountains on the moon's surface soon became wonders that seized the imagination of the learned and simple alike—discoveries that gave impetus to the growing faith in using one's eyes along with one's brains. New voyages of discovery were begun ; the discoverers had navigated uncharted seas and found unknown lands, Galileo voyaged through space and found unknown worlds. Despite the imperfections of his telescope, he was able to make out the existence of spots on the sun, to ascertain that they moved, and thence infer that the sun rotates about its axis. By the time Descartes left La Flèche, the Copernican explanation had secured the assent of most savants in France, and news of Galileo's discoveries was widespread. Though it had not yet reached La Flèche, it had been reported to the Collège de Bordeaux (AT, XII, 68). The essentials of the Copernican hypothesis had then been empirically confirmed beyond reasonable doubt. Galileo thought to convince the Church of this fact, but he had underestimated the deadweight of prejudice and hatred against him. There was only one sort of truth to which the Church was prepared to listen,

THE INTELLECTUAL CLIMATE OF THE AGE 41

and this was the truth it had itself already uttered. Its summing-up on the Copernican case was, that in relation to reason the hypothesis was absurd, in relation to the Scriptures it was heretical. For were it sound, then some statements in the Bible could not be literally true. So an attempt is made to compromise with the universal enthusiasm at the invention of the telescope. The faithful of the Church adopt the position that as a means to fuller knowledge it was useful when applied to terrestrial objects, but unreliable when directed upon celestial ones! The official attitude of Rome was made explicit, as we saw by the condemnation of Galileo and the public burning of his offending book.

The newly awakened and absorbing interest in observable and ' stubborn ' fact found in Optics a further field for exploration. Its researches were facilitated by the aid of the microscope, which had been invented at about the same time as the telescope. Kepler had applied his main conclusion in optics (briefly, that the angle of incidence is proportional to the angle of refraction) so as to furnish an outline theory of the telescope, and Snell, a mathematical professor at Leyden, formulated definitely the law of refraction, a law which seems to have been rediscovered independently by Descartes in the year of the *Essays*. During these years of Descartes's first residence in Holland, Galileo had also been occupied with hydrostatics. It had not occurred to men of science before him that one causal factor in the behaviour of bodies was the weight of air. The fact that air exerted pressure, and that this could be measured, became the subject of subsequent researches by his pupil Torricelli in Italy, and by Pascal in France, and issued in the invention of that standardised measure of atmospheric pressure, the barometer. Pascal also formulated, in a tentative way, certain laws concerning the pressures exerted by fluids, and Robert Boyle's contributions to the subject in England culminated in the famous law named after him, to the effect that the pressure of a given quantity of gas is proportional to its density. Shortly after, Mariotte in France discovered the law independently. We are also indebted to Galileo for the first thermometer, an instrument which was, however, much improved upon by the end of the seventeenth century. To another Englishman, William Gilbert, belongs the merit of having consolidated the beginnings of a further branch of physics; and his experiments in electricity and magnetism were published when Descartes was four years old.

The impetus to revolt against the thought and spirit of Scholasticism was not, however, wholly an outcome of advances in physics. Medical science also had a part to play, though this does not become evident until well on in the sixteenth century. If the study of physics in the Middle Ages had meant the study of Aristotle, till much later had the study of anatomy meant the study of Galen. Not until Vesalius did medical scientists begin to temper biological erudition by allowing their own observations to inform their thinking. In 1543 Vesalius published a comprehensive theory of anatomy based on what he had himself observed, and not on what Galen was commonly supposed to have observed. Not that Vesalius was the first anatomist to have experimented, for that universal genius, Leonardo da Vinci, among others, had dissected bodies, and had claimed empirical verification for his hypotheses. None before Vesalius, however, seems to have practised dissection sufficiently to have yielded results that were ample enough to reconstruct anatomical science. Physiology had to wait some fifty years longer for an extension of the same kind of procedure —until William Harvey's *Exercitatio de Motu Cordis* performed for Galen's physiology what Vesalius had done for Galen's anatomy. Harvey's first result, after giving his mind to vivisection, was to correct certain mistaken beliefs then generally held about the function of the heart. Galen had laid down that its proper function was to draw air from the lungs, and Scholastic medicine also had connected the heart's movement with respiration. Regarding the heart as a kind of furnace for the distillation of 'animal spirits' and their distribution through the body, a frequent intake of air was held to be necessary for its continued functioning, on analogy with the need of ventilation for a fire. (The notions of the heart as a distillery of animal spirits and a furnace, and of the " faculties " introduced by Scholastic medicine to explain the heart's action, were taken over by Descartes).[1] Harvey banished these features of the Galenico-Scholastic physiology, and substituted the hypothesis that the function of the heart was to pump blood through the

[1] Cf. Ch. VI.

THE INTELLECTUAL CLIMATE OF THE AGE 43

body. Further, from observing the quantity of blood discharged by the relevant ventricle at each heart-beat, and recording the frequency of the beats, he was led to propose that blood was pumped " of a motion as it were in a circle." This new idea of the circulation of the blood, and of the heart as an organ of propulsion and not of suction or respiration, illuminated for him a number of connected problems concerning the behaviour of the heart and blood-vessels and the function of valves in the veins. Descartes, who became Harvey's stoutest defender on the Continent, seems to have reached similar views independently.

Lastly, let us turn from the physical and biological science and consider the state of mathematics prior to the creation of Cartesian co-ordinate geometry. " Mathematics," says Dr. Whitehead[1] " as a formative element in the development of philosophy, never, during this long period (*i.e.* nearly two thousand years from the Pythagoras-Plato epoch till the seventeenth century) recovered from its deposition at the hands of Aristotle. . . . In the seventeenth century the influence of Aristotle was at its lowest, and mathematics recovered the importance of its earlier period." The recovery is, of course, in the main due to the work of Descartes, Leibniz and Newton, but lesser men did much to bring mathematical knowledge to a condition susceptible of these major developments. In algebra, the principal pre-Cartesian innovation, due to Viète, was the device of using letters of the alphabet to denote general or indeterminate quantities. Mathematicians in Germany and Italy had already employed letters symbolically, but none before Viète had used them with the same extensive significance, or had made symbolism an essential instrument of algebraic procedure. This new algebra, which Viète called *logistica speciosa* to emphasise its difference from the old *logistica numerosa*, makes use of exponents and of the plus and minus signs to signify additive and subtractive processes and relations. About this time, too, Thomas Herriot introduced the symbols every schoolboy now uses to signify the relations ' greater than ' and ' less than,' and William Oughtred our common arithmetical signs for multiplication and proportionality. These improvements in symbolism, and what was more important,

[1] Whitehead, *Science and the Modern World*, p. 44.

the attention given to the mathematical ideas that they symbolise, prepared the way for Descartes to investigate and define the properties of curves by the application of algebraic analysis. The assertion frequently made that Descartes was the first to apply algebra to geometry seems mistaken, for Viète and such contemporary algebraists as Cardano and Tartaglia had employed geometrical constructions as aids to the solution of particular equations. Previous to Descartes it had been the custom to attempt the solution of problems by separate *ad hoc* methods. Each solution was thus something of a *tour de force*, and success largely depended on hitting on a promising line of attack. Mathematical problems were thus so many separate puzzles, and their solutions were regarded as testifying to the student's ingenuity rather than as exemplifying certain highly general principles already known. Little or no connexion was perceived between one problem and another. Consequently it marks a real step in advance when, for instance, all curves are so reduced as to be expressible in a common notation, so that the solution of one problem makes straightway possible the solution of all others referring to the same series. Mathematicians before Descartes had not thought of universalising nor of systematising their science. Its several branches, arithmetic, algebra and geometry, were so many more or less independent specialities —Descartes in fact calls them " curiosities "—and their problems were so many enigmas to be solved for amusement. Thus " mathematics " meant little more than the collection of such puzzles along with the rules of solution partly worked out for particular cases. The originality of Descartes's geometry consists in the introduction into traditional geometry of an analytical method presupposing the concepts of ' constant ' and ' variable,' and in having made it possible to express the properties of curves by algebraical equations. This application, it is true, reacted in turn on algebra. He systematically employed exponents, conceived and interpreted the notion of negative quantities, and elaborated his " rule of signs " for determining the number of positive and negative roots in an equation.

The amount of formal or logical analysis presupposed by these improvements and devices not unnaturally opened his mind to the possibility of retaining the method of algebra, without restricting its application to the materials to which it was then customary to apply it. Once he had clearly grasped that the method of mathematics was purely formal and indifferent to the concrete nature of the terms to which it was applied, he could see no good reason why its range of application should not be extended to any sort of subject-matter whatever, provided only that the ultimate characteristics or ' natures ' composing it could be conceived clearly and distinctly. In a word, he sees no reason why philosophy itself should not become a " Universal Mathematics." Descartes certainly reached this conception, but he did not, like Leibniz, work it out in any considerable detail. Examination of the structure of ordinary algebra (which Descartes would have agreed with Leibniz is " nothing else than the Characteristic of indeterminate numbers or qualities ") had suggested the idea of constructing another —a " Universal " Characteristic—of which the former would be simply a special and restricted application. Hence the enterprise (which in our own day has reached a much fuller development in the ' logistic ' or ' mathematical logic ' of Peano, Whitehead and Russell) of creating a " Characteristic " applicable to any possible object of thought, a formal logic whose principles should be expressed in, and their discovery facilitated by, a convenient notation or symbolism.

Had a more lengthy consideration of formative influences been possible we should have found still other factors which can less easily be disengaged from the labyrinth of connected doctrine. One such factor is the history of the Stoic idea of 'right' through the Middle Ages down to Descartes—the " sense of order " it diffused and from which arose piecemeal the impressive body of Roman law, worked out not inductively, by examining customs and institutions historically, but deductively, from certain abstract principles of right taken over directly from Stoicism. Again, there are the very considerable contributions of the Renaissance to political theory, hardly less momentous indirectly, for they provided intellectual justification, negatively, for the secession of State from Church, positively, for the recognition of civic rights and duties as being secular and independent of ecclesiastical sovereignty.

Yet the sixteenth century was far from being wholly emancipated either from ecclesiastical authority or from animistic and magical superstition. Alongside mathematics, medicine and physics, the pseudo-sciences flourished. Or, perhaps it is more correct to say with M. Cohen that the genuine sciences " were almost all falsified " in being turned from the search for truth towards ends that were primarily utilitarian. Thus, despite Copernicus, Kepler and Galileo, astronomy is still being applied to deciphering the issues of human destiny from the stars, chemistry to discovering the secret of transmuting metals into gold, while physics and physiography not infrequently lapse into a species of magic. And M. Leroy has suggested that Descartes, in his connexions with the Rosicrucian fraternity, was at times intrigued and stimulated by these pseudo-sciences little less than he was by the genuine ones.

These innovations and new accentuations we have reviewed rapidly change the face of natural science, and thence the stock of elementary science that forms the background of everyday belief. " Few of us realise," says William James,[1] " how short the career of what we know as ' science ' has been. Three hundred and fifty years ago hardly any one believed in the Copernican planetary theory. Optical combinations were not discovered. The circulation of the blood, the weight of air, the conduction of heat, the laws of motion, were unknown ; the common pump was inexplicable ; there were no clocks ; no thermometers ; no general gravitation ; the world was five thousand years old ; spirits moved the planets ; alchemy, magic, astrology imposed on everyone's belief. . . . No one could have dreamed of the control over nature which research for concomitant variations would give. ' Laws ' describe these variations : and all our present laws of nature have as their model the proportionality of v to t, and of s to t^2, which Galileo first laid bare. Pascal's discovery of the proportionality of altitude to barometric height, Newton's of acceleration to distance, Boyle's of air-volume to pressure, Descartes's of sine to cosine in the refracted ray, were the first-fruits of Galileo's discovery. There was no question of agencies, nothing animistic or sympathetic in this new way of taking nature. It was description only, of concomitant variations, after the particular quantities that varied had been successfully abstracted out."

[1] *Some Problems of Philosophy*, p. 20.

III

Outwardly the very various procedures of men of science in the sixteenth century exhibit little in common beyond an unwillingness to accept conclusions about what *must* happen, deductively inferred from first principles speculatively reached, and an insistence on first closely observing what actually *does* happen, and the inferring inductively the laws of those happenings. So far, then, there was no detailed theory of scientific procedure, nor clear ideas about what could be inferred from the empirical method so successfully practised concerning the conditions under which natural knowledge can be acquired, the character of that knowledge itself and the limits within which such procedure was likely to be fruitful. And it is a little curious that the first person to advance any considerable theory about the general character of natural knowledge and the constitution of the natural objects known, should be one who had had no first-hand experience in empirical investigation, and indeed conspicuously lacked that ' instinct ' for selecting and extorting from nature just the " right sort " of facts—so essential a part of the empiricist's equipment. In 1620, the year Descartes made his " wonderful discovery " and seventeen years before he published the *Discourse on Method*, the *Novum Organum* of Francis Bacon appeared. In it he explained the principles that should guide experimentation in any branch of physics and the rules by which the results induced should be tested. Bacon, too, was inspired by the idea of a vast and single science of all nature, a science having for its field of appropriate objects everything that can be known to exist in space and time. His attempts to co-ordinate different methodological devices into a uniform ' method ' was intended to furnish, immediately, a stimulus to renewing and concentrating interest in science, and, eventually, an instrument for producing a single vast body of unified natural knowledge.

Bacon, to be sure, shows himself in practice liable to accept facts on insufficient evidence, an error against which he never wearied in warning others. But he also shows great originality in the use he makes of his remarkable grasp of general principles, even though he fails in applying them to particular cases, and underestimates the practical difficulties besetting the discovery of natural laws—defects due to his lack of first-hand experience, and to his naïve faith that a law will complaisantly stand out from its contexture of particular instances ready to strike the eye of an attentive observer. The construction of this single science of nature is not conceived, of course, as a plausible programme for any one investigator, but as a co-operative undertaking for many. In the initial stage, at which no special aptitude or training that cannot be inculcated by instruction are called for, the immediate object is to amass extensive bodies of empirically certified fact. Some of these facts will be discovered simply by discriminative selection and careful observation, others will yield only to deliberate experiment, which, by " taking off the mask and veil of natural objects," will force nature to yield secrets not disclosed to uninformed inspection. Thus posterity is to inherit a whole storehouse of empirical facts —facts carefully described, qualitatively and quantitatively, their authoritative evidence recorded along with them, and, if they have been determined by at all complicated experiment, accompanied by an account of that experiment, for future checking and criticism. The guiding aim in making this accumulation of facts, which Bacon calls a " Natural History," is not, then, either the immediate use or the intrinsic interest of the information itself, but its suitability for suggesting, or for rendering probable, inductions that may be made later on. We should collect as much as possible about as many things as possible, for we can never tell what may prove of service ! Indeed, so impressed is Bacon with the value and indispensability of experiential aid in the construction of a unified natural knowledge that he went to lengths that are indefensible and somewhat extravagant. He imagines a community of scientists devoting their whole life, some to carrying out innumerable observations and experiments at random, the others exclusively to weaving out of those findings explanations of them. Here certainly the reaction against rationalism is extreme. Too impressed with mere quantity and repetition of observations, Bacon carries his empiricism *à l'outrance* and even ' shies ' at the idea of introducing tentative hypotheses to guide in the discrimination of relevant facts.

What is of more, and perhaps the greatest, moment in Bacon's work is his theory of the constitution of the natural world. This assuredly marks him out as an inaugurator of modern naturalism, and shows how unplausible is the supposition that he is merely the last of great Renaissance minds. There is much, indeed, on the surface of his writing to suggest a preponderance of Scholastic influence over native originality. His choice of terminology easily misleads. But though the bottles are old, the wine is new—often indeed " un vin qui n'a pas de bouteille " ! Analogy of formulæ does not establish analogy of doctrine. It was obviously a dangerous procedure to retain the *vocabula antiqua* (in the hope of securing a wider and more ready reading) and simply change " the sense and definitions " of its terms, as he expressly says he often did. The natural world, Bacon proposes, is a vast collection of bodies, each characterised by many sensible qualities or " natures " that are ultimately reducible to quite a few " simple natures." (He even hints at the possibility of an " alphabet " of these elementary characters.) The object of science (or, for Bacon, " metaphysics ") is to discover the *forms* of these " simple natures " (*e.g.* ' red,' ' white,' ' hot,' ' hard,' ' transparent,' etc.) out of which the complex natures of things are composed. These " forms " are " natures convertible with the given (*i.e.* sensibly disclosed) natures," present or absent when they are present or absent. They are ' ontal,' generic properties corresponding to the sensible qualities, related to them as their " causes," so that knowledge of the " form " of a nature carries with it knowledge of how that nature *may be produced* in an object physically capable of manifesting it. Thus, to discover " the form " of heat, enables the discoverer to produce heat in anything capable of being made hot. " Knowledge is power," then, in the sense of power to cause or produce changes in nature, and hence power " over " nature. Indeed, ' practical ' knowledge, knowledge that can be *applied* to bodies (as in experimentation), so as to change or transform them from their *de facto* condition, is limited to two kinds. We can discover how to cause bodies either to change their places or to change their states, *i.e.* cause them to alter by coming to possess different " natures " successively. Such a view of the constitution of natural objects is evidently already ' mechanistic ' in essentials : it awaits only the advent of a Descartes to extend and ' geometrise ' the conception in order to reach that full form of mechanism which continues through Newton and is conserved in present mathematical physics.

A more minute examination of Bacon's natural philosophy[1] and his view of scientific methodology would show that many of these ideas are to be found developed by Descartes along his own lines in the Method. It is beyond doubt that Descartes was acquainted with Bacon's work,[2] and a number of characteristically Baconian conceptions reappear in the *Regulæ*—the emphasis on experience and experiment, the indispensability of a scientific methodology (first adumbrated in a meagre way by Ramus), the essentials of a mechanistic hypothesis (cf. Bacon's " tables "), and the ' rule ' on the necessity of arranging natures serially in order of their complexity and beginning with the simplest (foreshadowed by Bacon's " ladder "). Though, unlike both Descartes and his other great English contemporary, Hobbes, the English Chancellor allowed too little to mathematics in the construction of natural knowledge, he certainly formed a juster estimate than Hobbes of the importance and rôle of experience and experiment. As Professor Taylor remarks, " Kepler and Galileo, while fully sharing Bacon's reverence for the factually and directly given, had understood, as Bacon never did, that mere acceptance of the given will never of itself gave birth to science, but needs to be quickened by the fertilising influence of mathematics, the very type of strictly rationalistic thought." Certainly Galileo had abnormally clear insight into the need of setting his data in a form susceptible of mathematical treatment, and Bacon lacked his passion for applying measurement to observable objects, so as to render his material and problem suitable for solution by geometry. Yet, with both, experiment and induction replace *a priori* deduction.

Descartes was far more indebted to his predecessors than is

[1] For admirable brief statements of Bacon's Inductive Philosophy and what is still of value in it, cf. C. D. Broad's Bacon Tercentenary Lecture, *The Philosophy of Francis Bacon*, Cambridge, 1926 ; and A. E. Taylor's Henriette Hertz Lecture, " Francis Bacon," *Brit. Acad. Proc.*, 1926.

[2] Cf. the parallels established by A. Lalande, " Sur quelques textes de Bacon et de Descartes," *Revue de Métaphysique et de Morale*, 1911 ; Milhaud, *Descartes Savant*, ch. x, Paris, 1921 ; and Descartes himself in a letter to Mersenne (AT. I, 109)—" I thank you for the ' qualities ' you have abstracted from Aristotle. I had already made a longer list of them, some drawn from Verulamius, some from my own head, and they are one of the first things I shall attempt to explain."

THE INTELLECTUAL CLIMATE OF THE AGE 51

usually supposed or than the philosopher himself would have us believe. Nor were all his results the complete novelties he had presumed, though it is improbable that he knew at first-hand the work of his precursors. First his rationalistic method in metaphysics—deduction from primary propositions of compelling evidence—is a clear inheritance from Scholasticism.[1] Not only so, but some of Descartes's most cherished conclusions had been reached before him along different lines. In the twelfth century, Nicholas of Amiens had proposed syllogistic proofs for God's existence, very like Descartes's, based upon what were claimed to be self-evident primary principles, and Hagues de Saint-Victor, a more important mind of the same period, inspired principally by St. Augustine, had reached certain metaphysical conclusions analogous to those Descartes was to maintain five centuries later—more particularly, (i) that the self's existence is a primitive idea (*première connaissance*), (ii) that the self cannot but know of its existence, (iii) that it is not a body, (iv) that it did not always exist, but had a beginning, (v) which beginning is due to God, and (vi) that God does not will things because they are just, things being just because God wills them. Again, two centuries later, Descartes has a precursor in Nicholas Oresme, the illustrious president of the College of Navarre, who proposed two important discoveries in physics (the law of falling bodies, the diurnal motion of the earth) and the main ideas of analytical geometry.

Of non-Scholastic philosophers contemporary with Descartes, the greatest was Hobbes, whose long lease of ninety-one years of life began eight years before Descartes's and ended twenty-nine years after. Hobbes's first visit to Paris fortunately brought him into contact with Mersenne, who was at the moment busied with procuring criticisms of Descartes's *Meditations*, prior to their publication. Hobbes's criticisms (the *Third Objections*), however, were of little use to Descartes, for Hobbes differed from him too fundamentally. It is true they were at one on the deductive character of the method of metaphysics, on the importance of mathematics both in its method and its conclusions, on the soundness of mechanical explanation of

---

[1] Cf. E. Gilson: "The whole history of mediaeval philosophy is one of a rationalistic movement that develops slowly, but with continuity in the midst of obstacles and resistance of every kind."—*La Philosophie au Moyen Age*, p. 167. Paris, 1925.

physiological phenomena and on the ' subjectivity ' of sensible qualities. Hobbes was, however, of all materialists and determinists, the most thorough-going and consistent, and could therefore find no room for a substantival self, for activity that is mental, nor for " an idea of God " (for the strange reason that he can have no image of God). Neither seemed to profit in any way from the other, but to be mutually a cause of friction. After Hobbes had offered his further objections to the *Dioptric*, Descartes wrote to Mersenne that he would have no more of the Englishman.

The more direct philosophical influences on Descartes were those operative during his college studies. At La Flèche the prevailing theology was doubtless Thomist, as the official philosophy was Aristotle's as interpreted by Thomas. After five years of letters, Descartes passed into the *classe de philosophie* for his last three years. In philosophical subjects La Flèche provided a full course (a *cours entier* not a *cours abrégé* as in the lesser colleges in his day). Of these three years, the first was devoted to logic and ethics, the second to physics and mathematics, and the last to metaphysics. Descartes's professor, Father Véron, M. Gilson describes as a " great disputant, ardent controversialist, but in no degree concerned with the renovation of philosophy, or with reconstructing, however slightly, the indestructible work of Aristotle." There is then no trace of distinctively Cartesian ideas to be found in the teaching of Véron, nor in that of Descartes's *répétiteur*, Father Noël, whose allotted task was limited to commenting faithfully on the teaching of the professor. And it was in these times the practice to exact that the professor himself should depart from sound Aristotelianism only where it was incompatible with the Faith. The college manuals of philosophy used at La Flèche show that, from the programme of instruction, a pupil like Descartes, who followed the three years' course, could hardly fail to be well versed in the essential theses of Thomas Aquinas, though he would not necessarily know much or anything of other philosophers, even Scholastic ones. It was, of course, not a period in which there existed a philosophical public distinct from a public of theologians,[1] and M. Gilson's masterly studies

---

[1] " Descartes claimed to inaugurate this distinction," M. Gilson points out, " but time-honoured habits of thought are not broken with in a day, and his

THE INTELLECTUAL CLIMATE OF THE AGE 53

show that Descartes himself was probably the last to recognise an influence of Scholastic teaching on his thought, even where its presence is indubitable.

rupture with the past is perhaps less perceptible in his work than in his intentions." The elucidation of Cartesianism by a minute examination of the theological milieu in which it arose, M. Gilson has presented with more brilliance than any other Cartesian scholar, and the fruits of applying this genuinely historical principle to different parts of Descartes's philosophy are published in his *La Liberté chez Descartes et la Théologie* ; *Index Scolastico-Cartésien*, Paris, 1914; and *Études sur le rôle de la pensée médiévale dans la formation du système cartésien*, Paris, 1930.

PART II

III

THE ART OF RESEARCH IN SCIENCE AND PHILOSOPHY

"L'humanité désormais va méditer en vue de la vérité, non plus à partir de la vérité."—BRUNSCHVICG.

I

THROUGHOUT our study of Descartes we shall, from time to time, find it convenient, and in fact imperative, to distinguish between what he calls, (i) " Metaphysics " and " Theology " ; (ii) " Metaphysics " or " First Philosophy " and " Philosophy " simply ; (iii) " Philosophy " and " Physics " or " the sciences" ; and (iv) the " Method " on the one hand, and " Metaphysics " and " Physics " or " Philosophy " on the other. And to begin we can hardly do better than consider these differentiations in a general way, and so put ourselves in a position to appreciate what is distinctive in Cartesianism.

(i) The separation of Theology from Metaphysics Descartes regarded as clear, absolute and final. The distinction—instituted not by him as is sometimes asserted, but by Albert the Great—is based on a difference not so much in their subject-matter as in the kind of certification regarded as warranting the final acceptance of their conclusions. Both theology and metaphysics contain propositions about God and His relation to the world. What decides which of such propositions belong to theology and which to metaphysics is the mode of their certification. Those belong to metaphysics which have been demonstrated by reason and their acceptance enjoined by reason, those belong to theology which have been disclosed through revelation and their acceptance enjoined by faith and authority.[1] Thus we find Descartes describing his *Meditations*

---

[1] Cf. Descartes's dedication of the *Meditations* to the Faculty of Theology in Paris : " I have always considered that the two questions respecting God and the Soul were the chief of those that ought to be demonstrated by philosophical rather than by theological argument " (HR, I, 133).

as "a little book which deals with First Philosophy or Metaphysics," for he claims to *prove demonstratively* the conclusions he reaches in it. And the material character of those conclusions show that his view of the proper scope and enquiry of metaphysics is not very different from that entertained by St. Augustine[1] some twelve centuries earlier.

Thus (ii) metaphysics is described as "containing the principles of knowledge, an explanation of the principal attributes of God, of the immateriality of our souls, and of all the clear and simple natures in our minds," and further, as "the first part of the true philosophy," its second part being "Physics." Descartes then uses the term "Philosophy" in a very wide sense, in which "metaphysics" and "physics" are parts. Or, to fall back on his favourite metaphor, philosophy is "like a tree, whose roots are Metaphysics, whose trunk is Physics, and whose branches, which issue from this trunk, are all the other sciences."[2] But we shall see that he also uses this term in a narrower sense, as short for "Natural Philosophy" where this is distinguished from both metaphysics (which is a part of it) and from "Philosophy" in this present, wide significance. The distinctive mark of what is 'philosophical' lies in its method—in starting from self-evident propositions as its certain, primary and undemonstrable principles and in deducing all its conclusions from them. So, like Aristotle,[3] Descartes suitably calls an enquiry that aims at disengaging such primary or first principles a "First Philosophy."

(iii) Evidently, then, what Descartes calls "Philosophy" is not what we to-day refer to by that name. In its narrower sense it includes all the physical doctrines presented in the *Monde*, and these are certainly not philosophy nor metaphysics in the sense these words have been employed during the last century and a half. His Physics is intrinsically a deductive system claiming to be a certain body of knowledge that is open to no subsequent revision. None of these characteristics could be rightly ascribed to contemporary physics. Commentators are

[1] Cp. with Augustine's view in the *Soliloquies* : "Deum et animam scire cupio. Nihilne plus ? Nihil omnino"—lib. I, cap. ii. Cf. also N. K. Smith, *Studies in the Cartesian Philosophy*, pp. 10–11. London, 1902. Gilson, *Études*, p. 199.
[2] Cf. letter to the French translator of the *Principles* (the Abbé Picot), which letter serves as a preface to the work (HR, I, 211).
[3] *Met*. iv, 1003, a, 26.

THE ART OF RESEARCH IN SCIENCE

by no means agreed, however, on the order of logical dependence between Descartes's "Physics" and his "Metaphysics." According to Liard, the former is both historically and logically anterior to the latter, although he admits Descartes's original intention was to construct a metaphysics.[1] Against this view, Hamelin maintains[2] that Descartes's Philosophy (and therefore his Physics) derives logically from his Metaphysics. He admits that Descartes was occupied with particular problems in physics before he worked out his Metaphysics, but affirms (as against Liard) that he elaborated his systematic Physics (the *Monde*) after the Metaphysics. Again, Liard urges that the primary propositions of his Physics all appeal for their justification to the criterion of clearness and distinctness, and this is the cardinal principle of Descartes's Method, from which it follows that the Physics does not derive logically from the Metaphysics. The argument, Hamelin points out, obviously assumes that the Method is independent of the Metaphysics, and this he gravely doubts.[3] That the historical order in the development of Descartes's thought is from the invention of the Method to the elaboration of the Metaphysics M. Gilson allows, but that the Metaphysics follow with necessity from the Physics he denies for two reasons. Descartes could have dispensed with metaphysics altogether and still have proceeded with his Physics. Again, setting off from the same initial data, he could have elaborated quite a different metaphysics from the one he did elaborate. These facts together show that, whatever Descartes may have supposed or intended, the Physics is in fact separable from the Metaphysics. Their synthesis, M. Gilson adds,[4] " appears to us indissoluble because it is worked out before our very eyes, but history has undertaken to prove to us that it is dissoluble and even that it could never be realized." Although Descartes's mathematical physics " do not contain the sufficient reason of his metaphysics, it must none the less be allowed that

---

[1] Cf. Liard, *Descartes*. Paris, 1882. He argues (p. 101) that Descartes could not have derived one of the primitive principles of his Physics from his Metaphysics. Extension, the essential characteristic of matter, is not deducible from God's perfection, neither are the laws of motion. For it is not incompatible with divine perfection that the essence of matter should be something other than extension (*e.g.* force), nor that movement should be other than in a straight line (*e.g.* circular). See also, *op. cit.*, pp. 93, 103, 106-8.
[2] Cf. O. Hamelin, *Le Système de Descartes*, ch. ii. Paris, 1921.
[3] *op. cit.*, pp. 28-9. For reasons to show that it is *not*, see Ch. V.
[4] Cf. Gilson, *Études*, p. 175.

the metaphysics alone could really enable Descartes to transform that mathematical physics into a physics, or, as he called it, a " Philosophy."[1] Reasons will be proposed in Chapter V to show that the connexion between natural philosophy (or what Descartes calls simply " Philosophy " in the narrower sense) and his " Physics " is not simply that the former contains the latter as a part. The relation between them is a subtler one than that of whole and part. It is one in which both are equally ultimate and essentially such that the " Philosophy " (as comprehending the " Physics ") can claim to be a body of certain and final knowledge, whereas the " Physics " (independently of the " Philosophy ") cannot make this claim.

(iv) Nor is it easy to state briefly what sort of connexion holds between Descartes's Method and his Metaphysics on the one hand, and on the other his Physics. The difficulty arises partly because he, like most philosophers who stress the importance of their method, is by no means as precise as he should be in stating what he understands by the term. As with the term " Philosophy," he seems to use the term " Method " with now a wider, now a narrower, signification. In its barest meaning (as in the *Discourse*, pt. ii, where he sums up his method in four " rules "), the word " Method " stands for a set of ' imperatives,' precepts or recommendations on how to act in certain circumstances with a view to attaining a certain end, and they are proposed to the investigator for his free acceptance and habitual adoption. But this would be too restricted a description of his Method to apply fairly to the contents of the *Regulæ*. Here, besides such methodological recommendations, we find a great deal of material which is in no sense hortative, but is pretty plainly explicative. Such are the statements about the character of the ultimate entities ingredient in the very different pieces of knowledge that are possible of attainment, and about the nature of the mental operations by which that knowledge is attained. So in its wide sense, the term Method comprehends a number of statements about certain elements and facts which combine to give the universe its ultimate constitution, and about certain activities of our minds concerned in the discovery and synthesis of those elements, as well as a number of practical recommendations

[1] For fuller discussion, see pp. 119-28.

THE ART OF RESEARCH IN SCIENCE 61

concerning the course we should pursue in conducting research. The assumptions of fact, ontological and epistemological, alleged in theoretical justification of these practical rules, require demonstration. But this the Method cannot of itself afford, so the onus of demonstration we shall see (pp. 73-82) falls on Metaphysics.

The deduction Descartes incorporates in his Method is not that of Aristotle's treatises. He neglects the syllogism as useless for aiding in discovery and useful only for expounding and stating convincingly what we have already discovered. The logic of deduction that *is* of practical value is that which he calls the " method of mathematics." Insight into this kind of deduction and expertness in its performance is not to be had by studying its principles in their formal purity, but only by analysing typical specimens of mathematical proof, and better, by constantly applying those principles to solve particular mathematical problems. Mathematics provides the most suitable material for such exercise, since the terms in which its problems are set can be grasped clearly and unambiguously. Constant practice of this kind will tend to form a habit of accurate thinking, which, once familiarity and confidence in its employment has been acquired, can be profitably applied to other materials, Accordingly we do not find Descartes composing a treatise on formal logic to replace Aristotle's or the scholastic manuals, for in his view a really serviceable ' logic ' would be one of discovery, and this cannot be studied in separation from its embodiment in some material.

Descartes never wearies of reiterating the importance of orderly and cautious procedure. " So blind," he observes, " is the curiosity possessing mortals that they often direct their minds along routes quite unexplored without any reason to hope for success, but prepared to take their chance of the truth they seek lying there. As well might a man, consumed with a desire to find treasure, wander continually through the streets, looking for anything a passer-by may chance to have dropped. This is the way, however, that most chemists, many geometers and not a few philosophers conduct their studies. Nor do I deny that in these wanderings they are sometimes lucky enough to light on a truth. But I do not allow that this argues greater diligence but only better fortune." Often, too, people " investigate the most difficult questions with so little regard to order that they behave like a man who tries to leap in a single bound from the basement to the roof of a building, not noticing or not troubling to use the ladder placed at his disposal." And since the order of fruitful research is usually " so obscure and intricate that not every one can clearly make it out," the more is it necessary to proceed slowly and cautiously.

II

The fullest statement of the Method and its presuppositions are found in the *Regulæ*.[1] This little treatise on scientific method is not simply a compendium of recommendations or injunctions, but also an attempt to explain their grounds, so we find along with them a good deal of discussion on the character of knowledge and the general structure of what is knowable. What is mainly practical and exhortative is summarised, usefully though inadequately, in the second part of the *Discourse*. His success in the solution of scientific problems, Descartes there points out, is solely due to having followed these four simple precepts :—

(1) " Never to accept anything as true which I did not know to be such : that is to say, carefully to avoid precipitation and prejudice, and include nothing more in my judgments than what was so clearly and distinctly present to my mind that I had no cause for any doubt about it."

(2) " To divide each of the difficulties under examination into as many parts as possible and as are requisite to solve it completely."

(3) " To conduct my thoughts in an order, beginning with those objects that are simplest and easiest to know, and so gradually rise, step by step, to an understanding of the more complex, even supposing some order among those which do not precede one another in a natural sequence."

[1] Descartes intended the *Regulæ* to comprise thirty-six ' rules.' The first twelve were to guide us in any investigation, whatever the subject under investigation ; the next dozen were to aid in solving those problems which, though perfectly comprehensible, have not yet been resolved, and the last twelve were to indicate how to proceed with problems of which not even the import is wholly clear. Only half of this programme was carried through. From the titles of the second set of eighteen rules it seems that they would have referred to purely mathematical problems.

THE ART OF RESEARCH IN SCIENCE

(4) " In every case, to make enumerations so complete and reviews so general that I might be certain that nothing was omitted."

At first sight these rules appear so simple and straightforward that we are surprised Descartes should have expected so much from them. But their observance in practice turns out to be anything but easy, and on closer inspection, comparing them with what he has to say in the *Regulæ*, we see that they depend on a most detailed and important theory concerning the conditions under which knowledge is attainable. And if later we find reasons for doubting certain points of this theory, and have to part company with Millet, who asserts that the *Regulæ* " is the profoundest and most wonderful logical treatise extant, not excepting even the *Organon* of Aristotle or the *Logic* of Hegel,"[1] we shall at all events have to agree that, besides being indispensable for an understanding of Descartes's philosophy, the work is one of great and permanent value. Let us, then, consider how Descartes understands these four injunctions, each in turn, asking what led him to propose them, and what information he adduces concerning our knowledge and its objects that could explain their effectiveness in practice.

(1) Only that which we *know* to be true is ever to be accepted or asserted. But how does it happen that we should ever accept anything else ? Why do we sometimes assert to be true that which we later retract as false ? The ' pathology ' of error shows that at bottom there are two causes responsible for this : precipitate judgment, due to insufficient care, and prejudiced judgment, due to the bias of habit or strong feeling. We may be unwilling to take the trouble of thinking out and stating clearly what exactly *is* the difficulty, or the character of the fact, under contemplation, and so we acquiesce too readily in passing judgment upon what is only ' more or less ' clear.[2] Thus our judgment expresses not knowledge but mere conjecture. And this hasty conjecture is erroneous precisely because it misinterprets the real character of what is given in thought or perception, misinterpretation being due to a vague, unclear

---

[1] J. Millet, *Histoire de Descartes avant 1637*, p. 162. Paris, 1867.
[2] For vagueness, unlike " clearness and distinctness," *is* susceptible of degrees.

awareness of what is given for interpretation, whilst knowledge is due, at least in part, to a clear discernment of it. The trouble comes, then, from our being so constituted that we can affirm without restriction as often as we choose, even on those occasions, far from rare, when we do not clearly understand 'all' or exactly 'what' we *are* affirming. Our only security plainly lies, then, in refusing to affirm as true whatever is not clearly and distinctly discerned. Or we may be unwilling to suppose we lack knowledge of common matters that the majority of men unhesitatingly claim to possess. Or we may be reluctant to accept a proposition which really is true, because we recognise it to be incompatible with some belief we hold with conviction and should be displeased to find false or groundless. A very strong inclination to believe a proposition true, even when it is confirmed by the generality of mankind, or has been rendered familiar through years of acceptance, is quite insufficient to justify its assertion as true. For other people are probably no less precipitate than ourselves, so their concurrence is worthless. And our long acceptance of a belief merely refers us back to an infancy when, we can now see, it was acquired and accepted uncritically, and this again is worthless. So we must take arms against these insidious forms of rashness and bias in judgment, never affirming what we do not know to be certainly true, or what is even capable of being doubted.

From this it follows that Descartes regards "probable knowledge" a contradiction in terms, and declares it a waste of time to study matters that are so difficult and complex that the only conclusions we can even hope to reach about them would be at best no more than probable. This, it might seem, would seriously proscribe our range of legitimate studies, for mathematics alone had satisfied this stringent requirement of certainty. But, far from proscription, Descartes intends just the contrary. By finding out *how* it is that mathematics has been so successful in reaching truths that are certain, we may discover how certainty may be reached in other sciences whose proper subject-matter appears vastly different. So, insistence on the need for certainty should really result in an extension, not in curtailment, in the range and variety of our knowledge. No there is much certain knowledge already lying at hand, though it is usually neglected as being uninteresting and trivial; but really it is not so, for from it much more than that is equally certain can be derived. These elementary certainties are valuable not for the information they impart, but because, starting from them as premises, we can demonstrate with certainty other propositions which hitherto could not be seen to be more than probable. And it is the currency of so much merely probable belief that explains the frequency of disagreement among even talented men. Now the existence of this disagreement is conclusive evidence, Descartes argues, that neither disputant really has knowledge respecting the point in dispute. For both parties cannot be in the right, and neither need be. Nor in fact can either of them be possessed of knowledge, for its possession presupposes it to have been reached by clear and cogent reasoning. But neither disputant could have reached it by this means, for if he had, he could have expounded that reasoning point by point, convinced his colleague at each step, and so in the end have compelled his agreement. Thus, from the fact of their eventual disagreement alone, we may infer an absence of relevant knowledge in both disputants.

Since certainty in knowledge is so extremely important and its attainment so easily frustrated, we cannot do better than dissect some considerable body of belief that is demonstratively certain and elicit the conditions under which its certainty is demonstrable. There can be no fairer samples of such knowledge than those found among the principles of arithmetic and geometry. The success and rapid development of these sciences Descartes traces to three characteristics, two possessed by their data, the other by their method. Their initial principles and data are simple, they cannot therefore be understood without being discerned to be certainly true. And these principles are very few in number. The peculiarity of the method of these sciences consists in deducing as much as is possible from these primitive principles, and in refraining from introducing additional ones so long as it can be avoided. In this way we come to understand complex truths about properties of figures or numbers through understanding how they are formally derived from a few simple ones each of which we clearly and completely grasp. The revolution Descartes sought to bring about through the whole domain of human knowledge was to result from an extension of this method—whose essentials are so elegantly exhibited in mathematics—to all other sorts of data. He did not doubt, we shall see, that the extremely different materials studied in other sciences were, in their logical form or structure, essentially like those proper to mathematics. So methodological precepts must be quite general: they must be applicable indifferently to *any* subject-matter and to *any* type of problem.

(2) All research presupposes a problem, often a highly complex and general one. So these " questions " or problems (" *Quæstiones* " in the *Regulæ*, " *difficultés* " in the *Discours*) must first of all be split up into so many departmental ones as may be necessary to expel vagueness or indeterminateness of meaning from our thought, and each of these simpler and clearer problems must be attacked separately. Descartes is therefore led (*Reg.*, xiii) to investigate the general character of " difficulties " or problems on its own account. Being complex, though the specific character of their complexity does not appear on first inspection, what exactly is asked in such questions is ill-determined, and so only imperfectly understood. Familiarity with the use of language enables us to know the meanings of several words which express the difficulty proposed and so to gather some vague impression of meaning from the whole expression, but we do not see ' all that is involved ' in, the implicit ' reach ' of, the problem under investigation. So any problem imperfectly expressed must first be reduced to a set of others whose meanings are quite clear. Now every problem contains a *quæsitum* or " unknown "—a factor of whose intimate character we are ignorant at the beginning (otherwise there would *be* no problem) and which is to be discovered and exhibited in its relations to what *is* already known. But though we cannot at the outset identify this factor, we must ' know ' it in *some* way, or else there would be no sense in saying that *this* it is which we are investigating. We ' know ' it in the sense that we know certain descriptions of it in terms of some of its external connexions with other factors in the total datum. So our procedure must plainly be to describe as determinately as possible how far the unknown factor is limited by, and in what respects it is connected with, other factors that *are* already known. Obvious examples of *quæstiones* are exercises in textbooks of algebra and arithmetic, or geometrical riders, though of course there are multitudes of them that are not mathe-

matical at all. To discover the causes of, say, influenza or war, to construct an apparatus for television, to devise means of manufacturing an article more rapidly, economically and efficiently—all would be " questions " to be attacked in this way in their early stages. For solution of them all depends essentially on seizing what is relevant to the problem and ignoring the rest, and to do this presupposes we have made sure what exactly is the character of our data, neither adding nor omitting surreptitiously any factor in observing or interpreting them. And this is partly why mathematical exercise is such an invaluable propædeutic to other sciences. " How superior mathematics is in utility and simplicity to all those sciences that depend on it is evident from the fact that it applies to all the objects with which they deal, and many more besides, and that any difficulties it contains are also found in them, as well as many others due to the peculiarities of their subject-matter, whilst these difficulties are not likewise found in it " (*Reg.*, iv).

(3) Not only must a complex problem be so divided as to exhibit its dependence upon subordinate ones, and these attacked first of all, but our thoughts, when directed to explanation, must be so ordered that each is deducible from some other, until every step of the explanation is filled in, any single step in the series being shown to follow from some second and to imply some third. Now our problems and explanations can exhibit such dependence and order only because the data they are concerned with, and the mental activities operative in their analysis, have a certain definite constitution.

Let us then first consider the constitution of ' data '—knowable objects in the widest sense—about which questions can be raised, and of which explanations can be given. What is factually given consists in a complex unity of what Descartes calls " simple natures." The vast variety of character we perceive among natural objects is solely due to many different combinations of " simple natures." These ultimate, unanalysable ' kinds ' are few in number, compared with the extremely numerous types of unity they make up. Now since a complex is *de facto* composed of simples, it follows, Descartes thinks, that whenever we apprehend a complex we *eo ipso* apprehend the simples composing it. But such apprehension is only implicit. The most it makes possible is *recognition* of the total object, but this, though biologically and socially useful, does not constitute scientific knowledge, since it presupposes only bare acquaintance with the constituent simple natures, and not knowledge about them. To have genuine knowledge of a complex object we must discriminate (i) its several constituent natures, and know each in isolation so as to intuit its intimate character or intrinsic *quale*; and (ii) the mode or order in which they are connected so as to form together that composite whole we began by apprehending. Research proceeds by conjectural hypothesis. When confronted with a phenomenon to be explained, we know in advance that it consists of a certain few simple natures combined in certain ways, and we know that we are already familiar with those natures as ingredients of other phenomena. What we do *not* know is just *which* out of the whole range of simple natures are the ones present in this particular phenomenon and about which we have this descriptive knowledge. We know *that* certain natures are involved without knowing *which* they are; we can describe them but not identify and name them. So from the general knowledge we already have about the simple natures present in other combinations, and how they combine to make up other complex objects, we now try to deduce which are those natures that would, when combined in certain ways, form a complex unity characterised as the one under investigation is characterised. The aim of explanatory research, then, is to discover which particular natures conjoin so as to yield each type of empirical fact, and to specify their typical modes of conjunction. To perceive clearly and distinctly certain natures in such determinate connexion as to constitute the complex object in question is to have full knowledge of that object, in the only sense of 'knowledge' that can and must be final.

We shall do well here to examine Descartes's doctrine of simple natures, in view of the decisive rôle it plays in his subsequent philosophy of nature, mind and knowledge. And we must be careful to distinguish between simple natures as they " really are " (and " really " they are not isolated, but necessarily conjoined), and as they " are " separately present to thought and severally related in knowledge. Really, " simple " natures are opposed to " complex " natures or composite objects. In our knowledge (which presupposes alternate abstraction from, and synthesis of, these ultimate reals), natures are ordered in series. The initial terms of a series are its " absolute " terms, and these may or may not be also " simple natures." Where the problem to be solved or the datum to be analysed is highly complex, or where the analysis has not been carried far enough to bring us to ' indefinables,' the absolute terms of the series will not be simple natures. And it is quite legitimate and satisfactory to stop short at such ' relatively ' absolute natures, always provided we know that they have been, or can be, exhaustively explained by others that are simple and ultimate. The distinction of " simple " and " complex," then, is, as we should now say, an ' ontological ' one, whilst that of " absolute " and " relative " is epistemological. It is thus a peculiarity of our knowledge that the object given to be known is, *in* being known, partitioned into distinct elements (elements not separated in reality but discriminable in thought), and these perceived as so conjoined that they form a unity of specific kind.

Descartes nowhere pretends to give a complete inventory of these simple natures, though he indicates a number by way of illustration. The characteristics of being independent, universal, one, equal, like, straight, a cause, are all simple natures. Contrasted with them, yet sharing in their ultimate character, are their correlatives : being dependent, particular, unequal, unlike, curved, an effect. And the " relativity " of these latter natures varies in degree. The inequality between a pound weight and a ton is greater than that between a pound and two pounds. Such " relative " terms are variable natures, but simple natures are neither : one straight line cannot be more or less straight than another, nor one weight more or less equal to another, but either simply equal, or unequal in greater or lesser degree. These examples of simple natures (cf. *Reg.*, vi) seem, then, to have the common character of being ultimate limits to formal analysis and of being correlated with certain relative natures from which issue most types of variation and deviation. A second set of examples that Descartes gives (*Reg.*, xii) illustrates not so much these formal properties of simple natures, but their concrete character, as ultimate ' kinds ' materially constitutive of the real. So regarded they fall into three classes : natures that are (i) purely mental,

(ii) purely physical, and (iii) common natures. The first class (*e.g.* that referred to in each case by such words as ' knowing,' ' doubting,' ' willing ') have the peculiarity of being directly or intuitively seized or never seized at all. We cannot represent such natures to our minds indirectly, through imagery or sensation, as we can natures of the second class (*e.g.* those of ' shape,' ' movement,' ' dimension '). These latter can be both perceived and imaged, but always as characterising physical bodies or images of them. The third class are natures incidental to both mental and physical natures (*e.g.* ' existence,' ' duration,' ' unity ') and such " common notions " (*i.e.* relations) as ' likeness,' ' diversity,' which are " links connecting together *other* simple natures, and on the evidence of which all our inferences depend."

All such then are simple natures. If we know that to which each of these words refers, we know it directly and completely by a single intuitive act, not analytically and progressively through knowledge of its parts or factors, for it has none. All these natures are indispensable for knowledge. For our knowledge is to be of this *actual* world, and the actual world is made up of complex unities composed of these ultimate natures, and these unities would not exhibit the various characters they do if there were no simple natures of just these kinds. This seems to be what Descartes particularly desires to emphasise.

From his views on the constitution of knowable objects we may now turn to what he has to say about the mental activities involved in knowing them and operative in the solution of problems. Descartes specifies three distinct operations : " enumeration," " deduction " and " intuition," the first being dependent on the second and the second on the third. The peculiarities of intuition, that " undoubting conception of an unclouded and attentive mind," we have already noticed. Its function is to apprehend simple natures by a single operation and in their complete essentiality. Deduction is simply a succession of these intuitive acts, through which we progressively come to see the dependence of one relative term upon another, and in the end reach that simple nature from which they all follow. For instance, suppose we deduce that line A is longer than line C, from the fact that A is longer than B, and B than C. Here are involved three separate intuitions, namely, that of A being longer than B, that of B being longer than C, and that of A being longer than C. The whole inferential passage here is a deduction, but it is composed of nothing but intuitions, the results of the first two being retained in memory so that the third arises from their being held conjointly before our minds. Now the outstanding mark of intuition is its exemption from error,[1] but deduction, though it consists of a series of intuitions, is nôt certain in its results. For our intuition of what is disclosed in any such " third step " of a series depends on our having held over in memory what *was* (but is no longer) intuitively disclosed at the two preceding steps. But memory is not infallible. We may at this moment *believe* that what we perceived a moment ago was clearly and distinctly perceived, when it was not. Or, what we now remember may be very like what we did intuit, and yet not be precisely ' it.' Indeed, to call those intervening acts ' memory-acts ' begs the question. To assert that an idea now present to mind is ' remembered to have been intuited ' implies that the same idea was previously present and actually intuited. But illusions of memory occur as well as illusions of perception. There may have been no idea previously present, and my present claim to '*remember* having intuited it ' may be merely a false belief that I now have about my present idea. Acts of memory then, unlike intuitive acts, are uncertain, and therefore need some guarantee. To ' remember having intuited so and so ' is not an intuition, and need not be a true memory. Hence the results of deduction are less certain than the disclosures of intuition. All the same, we must accept both, for we have no infallible source of knowledge but intuition, and this alone will acquaint us only with simples, and will not exhibit the structure of all the combinations into which simple natures enter. Nor is Descartes's reason for asserting fallibility of deduction a trivial one. For deductions are seldom so short and elementary as that of our illustration : they usually consist of more than three—in fact, of a vast number—of such intuitive steps, and the greater the number the greater the risk of our ' making a slip '—the more are our

[1] Intuitive acts are ' infallible ' operations. But we must be careful to distinguish what really is disclosed in intuition from what is asserted in a judgment purporting to report what intuition disclosed. We may unwittingly include ' more ' in the interpretation than is given in what is interpreted, so error *is* quite possible in judgments asserted *about* what we intuit.

memories liable to jump over a step or misinterpret through unclear ' memory ' what exactly *was* intuited earlier on.

(4) Our only safeguards against falling into error on this count are summed up in the fourth rule. We should, especially in long arguments, make a general review of its whole course, and so minimise risk of error through tricks of memory. " I would run over the steps from time to time, keeping the imagination moving continuously in such a way that while it is intuiting each fact it simultaneously passes on to the next, and this I would do until I had learned to pass from the first to the last so quickly *that no stage in the process was left to the care of memory, but I seemed to have the whole in intuition before me at the same moment*. . . . And, we must add, this movement should be nowhere interrupted " (*Reg.*, vii ; HR, I, 19). A general review, then, is insufficient, for we may again fail to see, and so repeat, the error, and " wherever the smallest link is left out, the chain is broken and all the certainty falls away."

The four rules of the *Discourse* are not intended to be a compendium of instructions that can be immediately, unhesitatingly applied, automatically so to say, for the production of certain knowledge. Their object is rather to describe a kind of intellectual habit that we should form. The method is emphatically a *reconstruction*, reached by scrutinising and generalising certain procedures *after* their adoption had been found successful in solving problems in mathematics. It is essentially wisdom ' after the event. The method seems to assume that in any particular piece of research we are, or easily become, possessed of the simple natures relevant to our problem, but their discovery (when indeed they are discovered at all) is usually made very late, nearer the end than the beginning of the research, or, rather, of many connected researches. Neither Descartes nor anyone else can provide a recipe universally applicable for unravelling the simple natures embedded in vast ranges of complex phenomena. No rule can replace that ' instinct ' for the right line to follow up, peculiar to really great scientific minds. Descartes himself, in a letter to Mersenne (1637), disclaims any intention of *teaching* a method, for it is not to be learned from any formal instruction, but to be acquired only by persevering, individual effort and practice. Yet summarisations of the course of his own successful practice can be useful in preparing the minds of others by indicating the general lines along which particular researches might fruitfully be prosecuted, especially when those recommendations are illuminated by an explanation of why they should have proved successful.

III

We have already noticed that there is, in Descartes's Method (in the wide sense of the term), an abundance of theory, epistemological and ontological, intricately mixed in with the elaboration of practical "rules for guidance." The four rules briefly summarising the art of research presuppose, like the rules of any other art, certain ' theoretical ' knowledge, namely, information about the constitution of cognisable objects and cognitive operations. The very universality claimed for the method (that of being applicable indifferently to any subject-matter and to solving any problem) itself raises a difficulty, the answer to which may enable us to understand more clearly how Descartes's Method is related to his Philosophy. The method is an art ; its purpose is to aid the investigator in realising certain conditions, given certain contexts and occasions, so that he may procure certain consequences that would be unattainable unless those conditions were fulfilled. Like any other art, the art of research presupposes insight into the structure of facts and certain funded experience, for it is these that determine the character of its prescriptions. According to Descartes, the entire domain of knowledge or "Wisdom" covers two overlapping areas, Philosophy and Metaphysics—for these are not alternative names for the same thing. Where then does the Method fit into this scheme ? It plainly assumes some certain knowledge to have been attained, since its recommendations *are* ' recommendable ' only because they have facilitated its attainment. Had they not proved successful in use they would lack their mandatory character and thereby any claim on our attention. Now the knowledge that certifies the method's utility must be certain and not merely probable. But the method is not exclusively an art of discovery, it also proposes a criterion of certainty. xDescartes claims that a body of results constitutes certain knowledge *because* it satisfies the method's criterion. He also claims that the method containing that criterion is trustworthy *because* its adoption leads to certain knowledge. Can both these claims be advanced without circularity ? I think they can. Descartes would have argued in a circle had he maintained *both* (a) that it is impossible to have any knowledge that is certain without having first of all acquired a criterion of certitude and having seen that our knowledge satisfies it, *and* (b) that it is impossible to come by a criterion of certitude without having first of all acquired some knowledge that is certain. But Descartes does not make both these assertions, he accepts the latter, but would deny the former. To maintain that (i) some propositions are known to be certain because they are seen to satisfy a criterion of certitude, is quite compatible with maintaining also that (ii) other propositions are known to be certain without being seen to satisfy that criterion, although they do in fact satisfy it. And these two assertions exactly express Descartes's position. To state the matter in general terms, the Method in its *ensemble* is logically neither anterior nor posterior to the Philosophy. It develops piece by piece, *pari passu*, with certain more and more fundamental and general stages of the Physics and Metaphysics—philosophical conclusions now stabilising and justifying some procedure of method, a precept of method now extending further the range of assured philosophical knowledge. And when we examine those of Descartes's works that are not professedly or primarily occupied with methodology, this is just what we find. The *Meditations* is one sustained effort of Descartes to extricate himself with rational justification from a general doubt on the possibility of any certain knowledge at all, and from particular doubts on specific matters. But it would seem that any method (and not only Descartes's) that insists on literal universality of application must, like Descartes's, sooner or later seek justificatory support from metaphysics. The first and third rules of the *Discourse*, as explained by the *Regulæ*, cry out for this support. Take the first rule. It formulates a requirement and proposes a criterion by which to judge whether that requirement has been met. It exacts certainty in knowledge, rejecting probability however high, and proposes ' clearness and distinctness in conception ' as the condition to be satisfied. Now there is an implicit inference contained here, namely, that if the condition is satisfied then certainty is attained. But what right

THE ART OF RESEARCH IN SCIENCE 75

has Descartes to assert this ? Even supposing the criterion be satisfied, and—what is to suppose much more—that when it is satisfied we never fail to *know* this, it still remains for Descartes to produce justification for asserting that what is thus known to be clear and distinct is also certainly true. For, far from being impossible, we seem only too often to have conceptions which, though perfectly clear and distinct, give us no knowledge about the actual world, much less certain knowledge about it. Therefore Descartes's assertion that clearness and distinctness on the part of an idea entails that it is a piece of certain knowledge requires justification from his metaphysics. For the truth of the dogma is not self-evident ; grounds for it are not provided by the other rules of the *Discourse* or the *Regulæ*, and it cannot be deduced from his views about the constitution of knowable objects or about our cognitive operations, since proof of these views has not been given, but is also awaited from the Metaphysics.

Lastly, turning to the third rule of the *Discourse* we find that it depends on a theory which, unless independently supported, must render our search for strict certainty in knowledge hopeless from the start. For the greater part of our knowledge is reached by inference, but Cartesian " deduction," though a succession of intuitions that are certain, cannot complete itself without the aid of memory, and this, we saw, is anything but certain. Though review and enumeration of steps may diminish our risk of error, such diminution can never bring certainty. Hence independent support is needed here too.

All this Descartes himself recognises. He must now concentrate on the foundations of his method to find " ground of assurance " and ascertain that it is " built on rock or clay " and not on " mud or sand." Science, in the only sense of the word that interests him, cannot establish for itself the legitimacy of its own procedure, methodology cannot of itself demonstrate that the character, connexion and order of our thoughts exactly represent, correspond point for point with, the character, connexion and order of independent fact. So if certain knowledge about the ultimate character of parts of reality is to be attained by science, science must be guaranteed by something more radical than can be supplied by inference from its own procedure. Accordingly Descartes plainly intends his Metaphysics to be no mere appendage to his Method, nor to his Physics. Without a supporting metaphysics the Method would be no more than an elaborate speculative hypothesis, and it would be foolhardy to expect certain knowledge from it with any confidence. Again, without a supporting metaphysics we should have no right to believe that the Physics resulting from application of the Method—however comprehensive and consistent that Physics may be, however satisfying its explanations may seem—really is a body of certain knowledge about *this actually existing natural world*.

This appears to underlie that foreshortened statement of Descartes which strikes us as so curious at first sight—that an atheist cannot possess knowledge in the strict sense.[1] "Atheist" in this connexion stands for one whose 'knowledge' is not supported by a suitable metaphysic. And a metaphysic 'suitable' to guarantee knowledge, Descartes is to show, is one that centres in a God whose nature and existence are knowable. We may express the point in a more modern way, thus: the scientist pure and simple—physicist who is only physicist, mathematician who is only mathematician—cannot be said to "possess" certain knowledge in respect of his science. For though from time to time he has a clear intuition of this or that proposition, or of its logical entailment by others, and therefore *is*, at just *those* moments, possessed of particular pieces of knowledge, yet at other moments, when no longer intuiting those propositions, but only remembering that he has intuited or proved them in the past, he nevertheless *still* affirms their truth, or assumes as certain and uses without reflexion a whole body of such interconnected propositions. But his assertion or assumption is groundless. At those other moments he is *not* possessed of knowledge and is not entitled to regard those propositions as certainties. In other words, to ask whether the scientist who is not also metaphysician 'possesses knowledge' is ambiguous. The question refers to at least three very different sorts of occasion: (1) at any moment in which he perceives the proposition clearly and distinctly he is *then* possessed of knowledge; but (2) at some moments in which he

---

[1] Cf. *Prins.*, I, 13 (AT, IX, 30; HR, I, 224); *Meditations*, V (AT, IX, 55; HR, I, 184); *Reply to Objections II*, AT, IX, 110-1; HR, II, 38-9. Also: AT, IX, 152; HR, II, 78 : AT, IX, 190; HR, II, 115 : AT, IX, 230; HR, II, 245.

claims the proposition to be certain he is not intuiting it, but remembering that he intuited it earlier; while (3) at still other moments, without making a *détour* to prove it over again, he employs it, or unwittingly presupposes it, in a course of reasoning, and would justify doing either on the ground that he already ' knows ' the proposition to be certain. Thus any such proposition stands to the scientist in three distinct relations on those three occasions : (1) it is directly present to mind and intuited ; (2) it is indirectly present to mind and remembered (the ' secondary ' statement, to the effect that the proposition had been intuited by him, being what is then airectly present to mind and believed); and (3) it is either indirectly present to or absent from mind, but is, in either case, logically supposed by what *is* then directly present to mind. What Descartes wishes to maintain is that though the scientist in question does have knowledge in the first case, his claim to its possession in the second and third cases is baseless. Yet in order to possess knowledge in a sense having scientific or philosophical interest he must be certain of the proposition on *all three* sorts of occasion. On the other hand, the scientist whose science is supported by a suitable metaphysics *does* possess knowledge on all three kinds of occasion. It is evident, then, that the ' support ' awaited from metaphysics must be such as to confer validity on propositions quite *independently of the various relations in which they stand to our minds at different times*. Felt conviction is no criterion of their objective validity. Thus, if we ask the scientist *why* he is certain that the body of knowledge he claims to possess *is* absolutely certain information about the character and structure of some part of reality, he cannot reply. There is need, therefore, of a common guarantee for the propositions that he accepted because they seemed clear and distinct, no less than for the principles of reasoning which he employed, probably ' unconsciously,' in reaching them. In other words, the first principles of " Physics " and the criterion and injunctions of the Method all depend on metaphysics for a common guarantee. Further, that certainty in knowledge *is* attainable—which is assumed but not proved in the *Regulæ*—must itself now be demonstrated with certainty. That is to say, metaphysics must establish with certainty that certainty is attainable, both within and beyond its own field. Descartes must now find guarantee for three tacit assumptions of his Method: (1) that certainty in knowledge about what exists is not an unrealisable desideratum, but really is attainable; (2) that the dogma, ' What is clear and distinct is certainly true,' is itself certainly true (this *does* require proof since it is synthetic;[1] it is not self-evident, it has been doubted by some thinkers and has been denied by others); (3) that our unavoidable dependence on memory in the progress of deductive inference can be so guaranteed that inferred conclusions may, in general, have the same certainty as single intuitive acts.

Of these three demonstranda the first plainly stands in a special position. If it cannot be proved, proof of the other two need not be attempted. If Descartes fails to establish that there can be some certain knowledge, it would be futile to trouble whether ' clearness and distinctness ' is a genuine criterion of certainty, or how uncertainty of memory can be strengthened in the interests of certainty.

These appear to be the more immediate reasons for Descartes's transition from methodological preoccupations to the study of metaphysics. To metaphysics falls the responsibility of conferring validity, by means of some certain knowledge it contains, on the Method. But the premises and conclusions of the metaphysics current in his day were extremely dubious and anything but pieces of certain knowledge. Where so much is asserted with such assurance but so little justification, reconstruction is possible, Descartes decides, only through a reform of method or procedure even more radical than that already proposed.

Required to find a belief that is certain: this is Descartes's first *quæstio*. He sometimes speaks as though he were indifferent to what the belief is about, and cared simply that it should be certain. But from the turn his argument takes we shall see that really he does care what it is about—and requires it to be about ' something *existent*.' This then is really his problem. We may now conveniently adopt Descartes's favourite device of supposing it solved so as to elicit the conditions to be satisfied in order that it should *really* be solved. The conditions to be fulfilled by the belief that it is acceptable as a piece of certain

---

[1] Cf. *Reply to Seventh Objections* (AT, VII, 520; HR, II, 312). " To perceive clearly is one thing, to know with certainty is another."

knowledge seem to be three: (1) It is insufficient that its certainty be confirmed by this or that particular person, whatever his competence. Its certainty must be such that everybody is in fact agreed and is justified in being agreed. And the only belief that everyone will accept and will be rationally justified in accepting as certain is one in which it is just impossible for anyone to disbelieve. Its 'necessity' must be self-evident. (2) The belief must not depend on another more ultimate, for then a further guarantee would be required to certify that latter one. It must be a belief fitted to stand as an "absolute term" in any series of deductive inferences. And though it may be implied by none, it should be such as to imply others. (3) The belief must be about something actually existent. It must not be about, say, relations between merely formal properties such as those studied in algebra and geometry, for such a belief does not establish cognitive contact with this actual world of concrete existents. What he requires, then, is some existential proposition that is certainly true. And though Descartes does not himself describe the object of his search in precisely these terms, this way of formulating it brings out what he really has in mind. Briefly, then, the belief must be such that (i) it is impossible to doubt of its truth; (ii) it is directly (intuitively) and not indirectly (deductively) known; and (iii) it contains essentially a reference to something actually existing. But here again it is one thing to make demands and another to satisfy them.

Descartes's next step must evidently be to devise means of discovering, if possible, a belief possessing these three characteristics. The precepts already elaborated are insufficient to direct us to a belief of this kind. Even the *Regulæ* do not contain his last word about certainty in knowledge; in fact, they were composed, he tells us, as 'memoranda,' in case he should forget later the kind of steps by which he had proceeded so successfully in solving problems and making discoveries. So he must supplement the precepts of the Method by a new injunction fitted to meet the peculiar requirements of his present problem. This supplement is the decision to practise doubting systematically— *de omnibus dubitandum*. Now we should be quite clear about the character of the doubt referred to here. It is possible 'to doubt' in two senses, each distinguishable by reference to its 'cause' or origin. There is first of all that doubt we 'feel' in regard to the truth or even the plausibility of an assertion because what is asserted is itself dubious, or 'appears dubious,' when considered in connexion with other relevant knowledge we have already. And such doubt is susceptible of degrees of intensity, so that we say we feel more doubtful or less doubtful about this than about that belief. And there are three things to notice concerning such *experiential* doubt : (i) it is directly experienced or ' felt ' by us as being mild or intense ; (ii) it is regarded as caused by, or expressly due to, the character of what is asserted or proposed for our acceptance ; and (iii) the experience and its intensity are independent of our volition. Doubt in the second sense, however—that with which Descartes is concerned when he says he is going to doubt of everything that can be doubted—is something very different. Here we do not undergo an experience which could be strictly called ' feeling doubtful,' for the assertion doubted need not appear to us at all dubious, and may even seem to be true. And since there is no genuine feeling of doubt, there cannot be 'more or less' of it in respect of different assertions. This is the ' *methodical* doubt ' which Descartes practises in the *Meditations*, and it differs from a ' state of doubt ' in (i) not signifying any experience directly lived through by us ; (ii) in not being regarded as caused by, or expressly due to, the character of what is proposed for acceptance ; but (iii) in being caused by our volition. Thus ' experiential doubt ' refers to a certain state of mind or attitude which we do *not* voluntarily originate ; ' methodical doubt ' refers, not to a feeling but a decision or volition which we *do* purposively originate.

Further, in view of this distinction, it is plain that 'methodical doubt ' is vastly different from scepticism, while ' experiential doubt,' if of frequent or habitual occurrence, contributes the most characteristic feature of a ' sceptical frame of mind.' To illustrate the point of the difference, we need only to recall that mathematical conclusions, according to the *Regulæ*, are free from the slightest suspicion of doubt, while in the *Meditations* they are, one and all, subjected to doubt. There is no inconsistency here, for they can quite well all be doubted though no one of them is dubious. All may usefully be subjected to ' methodical doubt,' though none inspires ' experiential doubt.' So, in adopting the maxim *de omnibus dubitandum*, Descartes is not asserting that whatever can be doubted is false, or even that it is improbable, he is only *supposing* it false. He is going to test all manner of common beliefs—those derived from the consensus of opinion in society, those supposedly formed by himself, those encountered in studying natural science and philosophy—all, in fact, except those concerning morals and religion. Methodical doubt is thus the general decision to doubt ' on principle ' any particular belief or class of beliefs that can be doubted. It is, in Liard's words, " a *parti pris* by the will against one of the most natural and powerful inclinations of human nature," namely, that of ascribing the content of our thought or contemplation to the actual world, and so conferring on that thought an existential reference to which it may not be entitled. The decision to doubt systematically is to operate as a check on this tendency. It is to restrain us from imputing existential reference to any thought unless the thought is itself of such a character as compels us to do so, a refusal on our part rendering it meaningless and ourselves self-contradicted.

Methodical doubt is therefore other than what has commonly been meant by ' scepticism.' Scepticism is essentially a *conclusion* about knowledge, the conclusion either that there is none or that there can be none. Methodical doubt, however, is not a conclusion about knowledge, it is an injunction to be obeyed in the hope of attaining knowledge. But though not the same as scepticism, its adoption might easily lead us into scepticism, for we may fail ever to find a proposition that cannot be doubted.

This last direction, to doubt persistently everything that can be doubted—a fifth to be added to the four already noticed—has a specifically metaphysical application. Its nature will be considered in the early pages of the next chapter. Meanwhile, we should notice that Descartes does not propose to apply this extremely restrictive check to beliefs that arise in the course of daily conduct. For though those beliefs may often be far from clear and distinct, though we uniformly act as though they were literally and completely true transcriptions of facts of the actual world, yet Descartes considers they have a ' moral certainty ' which justifies our *using* them and trusting to them in practice. These common beliefs are useful and sufficient for the needs of daily life, they are biologically valuable in enabling us to minister to bodily wants and to the preservation of our organism, so that even should any or all of them turn out to be rationally unjustifiable, their pragmatic worth would not be thereby impaired.

IV

RECONSTRUCTION IN METAPHYSICS

" Much philosophy inspired by science has gone astray through preoccupation with the *results* momentarily supposed to have been achieved. It is not results, but *methods*, that can be transferred with profit from the sphere of the special sciences to the sphere of philosophy."—
BERTRAND RUSSELL.

I

DESCARTES'S immediate problem, we saw, is to show that there is really attainable some belief which (*a*) is clear and distinct, (*b*) essentially refers to something existent, and (*c*) can be known with certainty. We further saw that the methodology of the *Regulæ* cannot lead us right up to a belief of this character. But it can prepare the way, assisting us to carry out a methodical survey of the miscellaneous stock of beliefs commonly held and acted on by us. Hence the introduction at this juncture of a more radical test—*de omnibus dubitandum*[1]—resolutely to doubt whatever *can* be doubted.

Now to examine singly all our beliefs would be an endless undertaking, and fortunately an unnecessary one. For, noticing that particular beliefs are connected with more general ones, under which they may be classed on account of logical dependence or similarity in their subject-matter, it will be sufficient to investigate certain among them as being fair representatives of their class. If irremovable objections can be preferred against any of these typical beliefs, then the whole class of which it is typical will be *eo facto* condemned. " The ruin of the foundation necessarily entails the downfall of the whole

[1] I am indebted to my friend, Dr. R. Leet Patterson, for drawing my attention to a singular parallel to Descartes's *de omnibus dubitandum* in the *Deliverance from Error* of Al Gazali (1058–1111). While for Descartes methodical doubt is eventually stilled by the discovery of a truth that is both intelligible and certain, for Al Gazali it leads to a state of mystical illumination. Relevant parts of the *Deliverance* are translated in the appendix of Léon Gautier's *La Philosophie musulmane*, Paris, 1900, pp. 78–94, and arranged opposite extracts from Descartes's *Discourse*. For fuller information of Al Gazali's criticism of sense-experience, and his ' universal doubt,' consult Baron Carra de Vaux's *Gazali*.

superstructure." So we shall pass from one belief to another, each typical of some class, until we encounter a belief that resists our most deliberate and persistent attempt to doubt it. That belief, besides disproving the possibility of scepticism, may, in some way, lead us on to others that are equally sure.

The *locus classicus* for this investigation is the first *Meditation*. " Several years have now elapsed," Descartes there tells us, " since I first became aware that I had accepted from my earliest youth many false opinions for true ones, and that what I had afterwards based on them was in consequence highly doubtful. And from time to time I was convinced of the necessity of undertaking once in my life to rid myself of all the opinions I had adopted, and of beginning afresh the work of building from the foundation, if I desired to establish a firm and abiding superstructure in the sciences." Like everyone else, Descartes had been in the habit of accepting as knowledge beliefs based on what is disclosed in sense experience. Yet they had not infrequently led him into error. It is common enough, for example, when perceiving a distant object, to misjudge its shape or size, or mistakenly ' recognise ' it for what it is not. And even when the object perceived is near at hand, we may mistakenly judge it to have a character which it does not exhibit on closer inspection, say, through a microscope. The phenomena of illusions, hallucinations, the visual and auditory experiences of disordered minds are collectively the evidence from which Descartes decides that as media of certain knowledge, the senses are untrustworthy. For all such experiences, and indirectly the beliefs based on them, depend on the operations of one of our senses or of several jointly. Now what has once deceived us may do so again, and, what is worse, it may deceive us in such circumstances that we cannot discover, then or thereafter, that we *are* being deceived. Indeed, if we cannot affirm, neither can we deny the possibility of a regular and continuous deception of this sort. So far as certain knowledge is in question, then, such a source of experience can only be condemned as radically defective, from which it follows that no opinion derived from or dependent on materials sensorily given can be accepted as true. Every opinion of this kind is, by its very origin, exposed to legitimate doubt, for we cannot

RECONSTRUCTION IN METAPHYSICS

tell in any fresh instance whether the senses are, or are not, then deceiving us. Are we, however, entitled to condemn the whole class of beliefs based on sensations because we find certain subclasses of them untrustworthy? What shall be said of those common beliefs, in part dependent on sense-experience, which we all accept from habit and implicitly, beliefs that are so familiar and whose evidence we consider so obvious that we do not trouble to formulate them explicitly, but ' take them for granted ' ? Is not the evidence patent and overwhelming for my present belief that here and now I am seated by the fire reading ? Is such a belief to be rejected because I sometimes make mistakes about what I see in the distance ? Clearly not. Yet, Descartes answers, if we are to act rigorously on our decision to doubt, this, as all other opinions, must be subjected to it. For *is* it really impossible that I should be mistaken even in believing myself to be now seated by the fire ? Have I, for instance, never dreamt of being in some place in which I certainly was not at the time ? And is not the erroneous dream-belief just as convincing ; is not its genuineness just as much ' taken for granted ' when I am dreaming as when I am awake ? How, then, can we decide, beyond possibility of error, whether the truth of any belief, about where I am or what I am doing, not only *seems* undeniable but really *is* undeniable ? Is there some criterion I can apply to any unexpressed conviction I may have while dreaming, which can show that the conviction is groundless and will hold sway over me no longer than while my dream-state lasts ? There seems to be no such criterion. Beliefs about my present condition or situation must, then, go by the board as well, for I cannot *know* with certainty at any moment that I am not dreaming, but only ' believe ' that I am not. And the mere liveliness of feeling or conviction attending belief is no evidence that the belief is true. Nor are these cases essentially different from the earlier ones we noticed. The content of the dream-belief consists mainly of imagery, just as the content of a belief in waking-life is mainly composed of sensory-factors. But over and above these factors of sense and imagination there is in both cases the tacit assertion that this content genuinely represents, say pictorially, an actual situation in the real world. It is, then, our reference of this content to the existent world (or, conversely, our assumption that the content presents, literally and without distortion, the character of some real situation) that, by the very nature of the case, could never be justified by considerations about our activities of sensing or imaging alone. Sensation and imagination often do seem to yield us information about present or absent existents, but neither can assure us in any particular instance that the character cognised does, in fact, belong to something really existing. They cannot validate the 'existential reference' in our belief. Some sense-beliefs may be more probable than others, almost all seem convincing, but that even one of them is certainly true we have, as yet, no grounds for believing and strong grounds for doubting. Nor is imagination exempt. It might be argued that image-objects which appear to us while sleeping must be 'counterparts,' in some sense, of objects actually perceived in waking life. For even 'free,' 'creative' imagination cannot produce a quality never previously sensed by us, or an 'object' whose parts, at least, are not representations of objects actually perceived by us at some time. In other words—the objection might run—what is unreal about sirens and satyrs is not that the several parts and qualities each is imagined as having do not exist, but that there exists nothing which is a unity or combination of those parts and qualities, and therefore that error lies precisely in ascribing existential reference to the content imaged. But this argument, far from supporting the claim of imagination, furnishes the ground for its rejection. Since even the 'genuine' factors of objects imaged in dreams are derived from what was previously sensed, the argument which concludes for the rejection of sensation, concludes *a fortiori* for the rejection of imagination too. Indeed, so far we have found no adequate reason to believe there really exists an external world or any material things at all. It would therefore be a waste of time to carry our search into the 'empirical' sciences like physics, astronomy or medicine, for these all " have for their end the consideration of composite objects " disclosed through the senses, and these, we have seen, " are very doubtful and uncertain."

Shall we succeed any better if, turning from beliefs based on sense-experience, we consider those seemingly 'solid' conclusions reached in the 'exact' sciences, arithmetic, algebra and geometry? Sensory experience, far from providing contradic-

RECONSTRUCTION IN METAPHYSICS

tions to their principles and results, would, were it possible, tend to strengthen them. For, " whether I am awake or dreaming, it remains true that two and three make five." Beliefs about relations between numbers, or between geometrical properties, seem to be more promising for several reasons. In the first place, it is not by the senses that we become aware of these properties. Again, of all data they are the simplest and most general, not highly complex and specific like chemical compounds, or individuals of the mineral, vegetable and animal kingdoms. Further, in studying these mathematical objects, "little trouble is taken to ascertain whether they really exist or not," Descartes here suggesting (what has since been established) that the conclusions of mathematics would still be certain, though they had no application to the actual physical world. Lastly, what is particularly noticeable about them is that they do contain " a measure of what is certain and indubitable." Most mathematical conclusions, then, have every appearance of being items of absolutely certain knowledge. But even mathematicians are not infallible ! It is possible for them to be sometimes mistaken; is it not possible they are always mistaken ? Is a systematic deception, due to some radical and undiscovered defect common to all minds, beyond possibility ? Descartes himself feels quite convinced about mathematical propositions. But *ought* he to be, he asks himself. Is it literally impossible to doubt of such propositions ? Now, it would scarcely be profitable for him to investigate the cognitive operations that furnish them in order to satisfy himself about their trustworthiness as he did with beliefs derived from the senses, since any theory of the mental activities involved in knowing ' two and three make five ' would inevitably be more tentative and less probable than that proposition itself. On the other hand, he cannot see that it *is* literally impossible for those beliefs to be false. So, for want of finding a reason for doubting them, he makes one. The resolution to doubt is now to be invoked in its extremest form, under the figure of a god who causes me on every occasion that he can to deceive myself unknowingly when I make an assertion. Not, of course, that Descartes seriously believes in the existence of such a being, for that would be to accord to creative imagination the very credence that we saw, a moment ago, he must deny to it.

This "malignant demon, no less cunning and deceptive than powerful, who uses all his artifice to deceive me," is simply a literary device for expressing in all its rigour the decision ' to doubt whatever can be doubted ' concerning the whole intellectual constitution of man, or the constitution of objects commonly supposed knowable, or both. Underlying this figure is the supposition, though not the assertion, that our faculties are such that we never *can* reach certain knowledge, or that the universe and its parts are such that they never *can* be clearly understood by us. Thus Descartes has reformulated his methodological doubt in an hypothesis which is *the most unfavourable* to the possibility of certainty in knowledge that can be devised. Consequently, if a single belief can be found to withstand it, we shall be assured that this belief can never be overturned in the future ; for that which can destroy the strongest possible doubt must *eo ipso* be itself of the greatest possible certitude. And from such an absolutely certain truth Descartes thinks he may reasonably hope to pass to further propositions of equal certainty.

To this devouring doubt mathematical propositions fall a comparatively easy prey. Is there any belief that does not ? Descartes affirms that there is. There is the belief in his own present existence. He, the doubter, exists while he is doubting. Of this he feels absolutely convinced once for all, and, more importantly, is justified in feeling so, for unless he existed, even an all-powerful deceiver could not deceive him. If I am deceived, there must exist an " I " who is deceived. " Let him deceive me as much as he may, he can never cause me to be nothing so long as I think that I am something . . . the proposition ' I exist ' is necessarily true each time I assert or conceive it." Whether or not deception involves an existent deceiver, it assuredly involves someone existing and capable of being deceived. For it is only ' me,' not ' a thought of me,' that can be deceived. It is impossible that I should doubt or be deceived and yet not exist at the moment of doubting or being deceived. Hence the general formula ; *cogito ergo sum*. Descartes has attained this piece of certain knowledge and thereby shown that certain knowledge is attainable.

There are two questions which should be sharply distinguished and separately considered if we are to appreciate the full import

RECONSTRUCTION IN METAPHYSICS

of the *cogito*, namely: (1) What is the importance of this proposition? (2) How is it to be interpreted? In answer to (1), plainly the piece of knowledge is not in itself very startling, there is no novelty in the information it conveys. All the same it is of the very greatest importance for Descartes on account of the ' strategical ' position it occupies in his Metaphysics, and because it *does* satisfy the three requisites stipulated, viz. : (*a*) it *is* " clear and distinct," (*b*) it *does* essentially refer to something existing (myself), and (*c*) we cannot contemplate it at all without knowing that it is certainly true.

(i) The *cogito* is an instance of an indubitable truth of whose certainty we are absolutely assured on every occasion of self-inspection. So, if we compare it with any of the propositions previously rejected, we shall see in what respect it differs from them, and so discover in precisely what consists this element of certainty in knowledge. The difference lies in this : the ' *cogito* ' proposition provides *its own* evidence of clearness and distinctness, but the others do not. This differentiating character may therefore be taken as a universal criterion by which to judge every other belief we shall entertain in the future. So the test of ' clearness and distinctness,' first proposed tentatively (in *Reg.*, iii), is now asserted categorically. It is not the character of the test proposed that has changed in the meantime, but *our attitude* towards it. Earlier, we were in a position only to enunciate it hypothetically ; now that it is confirmed we may accept it finally and apply it with confidence. And it should further be noticed that the validity of the general criterion is secured by a *single* comparison of the *cogito* with any rejected proposition, for what is disclosed in that single comparison is really universal and not merely particular in its import. Thus the criterion is not deduced, but intuitively induced, from a single instance.[1] And Descartes stands in immediate need of such a criterion, for without it he cannot advance to certain knowledge about anything that is not disclosed immediately in the *cogito* itself. Now, it does not seem

---

[1] The derivation of the criterion is an instance of what W. E. Johnson would call " intuitive induction " of the " experiential type." What Johnson has to say in his *Logic*, II, ch. viii (especially pars. 4, 5), is perfectly applicable here, and illuminates brilliantly the question of how Descartes derives his criterion of certainty from the *cogito*. For further instances of ' intuitive inductions ' on Descartes's part, see pp. 89, 93-4, 101.

plausible to suppose that from experiences of our own self-existence we can derive information about anything beyond our self and its states. So if we are to reach knowledge of objects in the material world, we must introduce beliefs other than that of our own existence. But these beliefs, like it, must be certain; so it is clearly of vital importance for Descartes to have discovered a criterion by which to test them.

(ii) The *cogito* is neither a 'first principle' nor a premise of Descartes's Metaphysics. Its proper function is to determine the fundamental situation from which strict knowledge is to begin and to render definitive the context from which further strict knowledge can be developed. Thus it marks the first limitation to that agnosticism which follows from applying methodical doubt, and constitutes a sufficient answer to any form of agnosticism which would rule out *ab initio* every effort to attain certain knowledge. The transition from the *cogito* to the metaphysical conclusions proper is made, we shall see (pp. 166-7), by means of what Descartes takes to be an implication of what is disclosed in the *cogito*, namely, that I recognise doubt to be an imperfection in me only because I already possess the idea of perfection.

(iii) The *cogito* is not merely a 'clear and distinct' deliverance, but a clear and distinct deliverance of something existing. Now if the final conclusions of a philosophy are to be truly descriptive of this actual, existent world, then clearly some of our premises must assert 'existence,' and not merely " essence " or 'character.' For though Descartes thought we could attain knowledge of existence in one unique case (namely, God's) from premises not asserting existence,[1] he did not consider that such *a priori* arguments could be used in general to establish the existence of quite specific things. So his philosophy can in the end give an account of the character of existing selves and existent natural objects if, and only if, his arguments include certain premises asserting their existence, in addition to premises asserting " essences " or " attributes."

(iv) The *cogito* is the expression, not of a 'simple nature' but of a fact composed of certain simple natures. The fact is an ultimate one, and the proposition expressing it is not deducible from any other. And in perceiving this ultimate fact

[1] Cf. the account of the 'Ontological Argument,' pp. 107-8.

(which is necessarily complex) we *eo ipso* come to intuit certain simple natures. Euclid had prepared the way by which we may easily intuit the simple natures of geometry, but metaphysics had only now found its Euclid in Descartes. Which are the simple natures into which he resolves this fact we shall see from his analysis of the *cogito* (pp. 93-6).

(v) In the *cogito* experience we are acquainted with certain fundamental qualities that must be intuitively known if they are to be known at all. The general, pervasive character of all those states of our self that we denominate ' conscious ' is known in this way, likewise those more determinate and differentiating characteristics of these states (" modes ") that we call ' thinking,' ' doubting,' ' denying,' ' asserting,' ' believing,' ' willing.' The qualities peculiar to all these states necessarily call to be examined, since it is part of the business of philosophy to reach the completest knowledge possible about selves that have such states and the consequences of their having them. Acquaintance with just these simple natures is also indispensable for Descartes's later argument, to prove that selves and their states are qualitatively different from, and independent of, physical objects and their properties : that neither minds nor bodies depend on one another for their existence or for their nature. The whole of Descartes's Natural Philosophy presupposes this qualitative difference and existential independence of minds and bodies.

(vi) Lastly, a fuller investigation of what is disclosed in the *cogito* situation enables Descartes to intuit certain " common notions " and " principles," which are essential for acquiring any further knowledge (see pp. 100-102). Thus certainty, objectivity and ultimacy can be asserted of those primary principles upon which the organisation of knowledge and the validity of inference alike depend.

We shall have ample occasion, in the present and three succeeding chapters, to consider the consequences that follow from our assertions under these six heads. For the moment it is enough to notice that they resume conveniently six respects in which the experience and knowledge summed up in the *cogito* formula are ' strategically important.'[1]

---

[1] That Descartes is well alive to the necessity of distinguishing in philosophy between the order of logical demonstration and the order of effective exposition

Let us pass to the second question we raised : How is the *cogito* belief to be understood ? How does Descartes himself interpret it ? For, even though it be clear, distinct and certainly true, it is still significant to ask precisely *what* it is in the belief that is so. Now everyone will agree that in *some* sense of the word " I," it is true that I exist, and that in some sense of the word " think," it is true that thinking implies the existence of something. But just what connotations does Descartes assign to these words, and are they such that the *cogito* is certainly true when interpreted in terms of them ? Evidently we are here concerned, not with the *uses* that Descartes makes of the belief, but with his *analysis* of it. In interpreting the import of a belief at once so fundamental and familiar as this, it is very easy to make mistakes. There is an extremely strong tendency to be biased by preconceptions, to introduce considerations which, though commonly associated in our minds with the thought of the datum under analysis, are nevertheless not really constitutive of it. The form of language or ambiguity in the words we use in communicating a belief may easily cause us to be deceived concerning the real character of the fact the belief expresses.

In his criticism of the *cogito*, Gassendi,[1] like many of his betters, allowed himself to be misdirected by language. Fastening on the word " therefore " in the dictum " I think, therefore I exist," he thought he had scented a step of inference. In his view, *sum* was a conclusion syllogistically deduced from the minor, *cogito*, and a suppressed major, *qui cogitat est*. Had this been so, Descartes would, of course, have needed for the major premise separate evidence that is both certain and independent of that which warrants the joint assertion of *cogito* and *sum*. But he

is apparent from his letter to Mersenne, 1640 : " It should be observed," he says, " that in all my writings I do not proceed according to the order of subjects (*matières*) but only in the order of grounds (*raisons*) ; *i.e.*, I do not undertake to say in one and the same place all that appertains to a subject, since it would not be possible for me to demonstrate it there—some of the grounds (for such a demonstration) having to be deduced one from another much farther on. Rather, by reasoning in the order *a facilioribus ad difficiliora*, I deduce at each step whatever is deducible, now on this subject, now on that. . . . To proceed in the order of subjects (*matières*) is good only for those for whom all the grounds have been extricated and who can say as much about one problem as about another " (AT, III, 266–7).

[1] Cf. Gassendi, *Objectiones quintæ* and *Disquisitio metaphysica* (AT, IX, 198–9 ; 200–1 ; 205 ; HR, II, 125, 127).—The same error was made by Kant and by Reid : cf. *Critique of Pure Reason*, trans. N. Kemp Smith, p. 378 ; Reid, *Works*, ed. Hamilton, sixth edn., Vol. I, p. 100.

offered no such independent evidence. The assumption of that
" major " would thus have been due to pure prejudice. Or
had he argued that in knowing the evidence available for the
general major we necessarily know that available for the particular minor, it could rightly have been urged that such a syllogism is circular. But Descartes points out[1] that, in asserting
" I think, therefore I am," he is propounding no argument
whatever, but simply expressing a fact which he ' reads off '
by a direct act of intuition. " It is a primitive act of knowledge
derived from no syllogistic reasoning." Language is ambiguous ; " therefore," it is true, does sometimes mark an inferential step, but it also sometimes symbolises a relation of necessary
connexion between terms. In his dictum it is the latter, not
the former, that " therefore " expresses : a relation of entailment that so connects consciousness with existence that that
to which the characteristic of ' being conscious ' applies, must
exist. The fact in question is that in which one simple nature
connects two others—the former one being a ' necessary ' relation, the latter ones being characteristics or qualities it relates.
And it is precisely those simple natures in that connexion
which constitute the fact we directly intuit and express in the
cogito formula.[2] There is no need of any deductive step at all.
No reasoning is required to pass from the knowledge that I am
now doubting to the knowledge that I am now existing ; on
every occasion that I perceive I am doubting I also perceive
that I *am*—my present doubting involves my present existence.
Nor can I think of my own existence (since this involves my
being conscious) without at the same time believing in it.
Doubtless Gassendi's general proposition, ' Whatever thinks,
exists,' is certain, as is the particular proposition, ' I who think,
exist.' But the second is not deduced from the first. Indeed,
the factual evidence for both is the same, and we may say
that the general proposition is ' intuitively induced ' from the
latter in the same way as the general criterion of certain truth
was intuitively derived from a particular instance of its fulfilment. ' Intuitive induction ' is immediate, not discursive.

[1] Cf. *Reply to Second Objections* (AT, IX, 110 ; HR, II, 38–9).
[2] Spinoza (*Principia philosophiæ cartesienæ*, I) does not make this blunder
of supposing *sum* to be reached deductively, and points out that the immediacy
of the *cogito ergo sum* can be brought out by expressing it *"ego sum cogitans,"*
thus avoiding any possible ambiguity from " *ergo*."

Which, then, are the simple natures composing the fact expressed in the statement ' I who think, exist ' ? These natures, being simple, can of course only be indicated, not defined. But the fact of which they are constituents, being complex, can be analysed. Of ' existence,' all we can say is that it is an ultimate quality[1] of the third class of simple natures (cf. pp. 69-70). Next, what does the symbol " I " symbolise ? First of all, we can be sure, that since the whole proposition is certain it must be made up of constituents whose genuineness is indubitable. " But I do not yet know clearly enough what I am, I who am certain that I am, so I must be careful that I do not rashly take some other object instead of myself as being myself." (*Med. II.*) " I " then cannot refer to my body or any part of it, though in common speech it is sometimes used, and by materialism usually understood, with such a reference (viz., to my brain). For no certain grounds have yet been advanced to warrant our affirming any physical bodies to exist, much less for asserting that " I " am one of them. For the possibility of deception has by no means yet been banished, but only restricted, in favour of the single belief in my own existence. I can be intuitively sure that what exists is " a thinking thing, a thing that doubts, understands, conceives, affirms, desires, imagines and senses." For although I often make misjudgments about the character of what is experienced, I do not judge falsely when I judge no more than that I am now experiencing. I judge truly provided I stop short at that point and do not go on to ascribe the qualities sensed or imaged to something supposed existing in the outer world. That is to say, I am justified in being more certain of the existence of my states of awareness (acts of intuiting, thinking, imaging, etc.) than I am of the belief that the various things we commonly suppose ourselves to know in those states really exist independently of us. Even if the material bodies we all ordinarily suppose to exist, did not exist, still the ' seeming ' or ' appearing ' would be no less genuine, or, conversely, my states of awareness would nevertheless exist.

But can nothing more be said about this " thing that thinks " than that it exists ? The nature of the self is to be determined

---

[1] " Quality," for that is how Descartes regards existence in the ' ontological ' argument.

RECONSTRUCTION IN METAPHYSICS 95

progressively through the metaphysics.[1] At this stage only two statements can be made of it, a negative and a positive one. Whether the " I " refers to my body or a part of it, cannot be decided until we know what are the defining properties of body. " I do not at all deny," says Descartes to the materialist Hobbes, " that the thing which thinks may be corporeal. I have left the question entirely undetermined until the sixth *Meditation*, and there my answer is demonstrated."[2] What, however, I *can* know at this stage, and by simple inspection, is, that " the thing which thinks " is a " substance." That Descartes *does* maintain this is placed beyond all doubt by his *Reply* to the third *Objections* proposed by Hobbes, who reproaches him with having confounded " the thinking thing " with " thinking," which is simply activity.[3] To this charge Descartes replies that he is far from intending the words ' mind,' ' soul,' ' understanding ' and ' reason ' to mean " the faculties alone, but the things that are endowed with the faculty of thinking. . . . Nor did I say," he continues, " that understanding and the thing which understands are one and the same if ' understanding ' is taken for a faculty, but only if taken for the thing itself that understands. . . . It is certain that thinking cannot exist without a thing which thinks, or generally, that any accident or activity cannot be without a substance of which it is the activity."[4] The " thing which thinks," the ' ego,' is, then, a substantival existent or persistent particular. Not that such a question of fact can be settled simply by considering the usages of language. " It is quite in accord with reason," Descartes points out, " and usage indeed requires that we call by different names substances we know to be subjects of acts or accidents that are entirely different. It is afterwards that we enquire whether these different names signify different things or one and the same thing."[5] Intuition thus gives knowledge of the existence of a substantival self and certain knowledge about its essential nature, but no detailed information about its determinate nature. Its existence is disclosed through its activity : if we could never be aware of our own activity, we could never be certain of our existence. In a word, I cognise my activity *as*

---

[1] Cf. Chs. VI, VII, VIII. [2] *Reply to Third Objections.*
[3] *Ibid.* (AT, IX, 134). [4] *Ibid.* (AT, IX, 135–6).
[5] *Ibid.* (AT, IX, 137).

being 'mine.' What we know intuitively, then, is not the determinate character of the substance that thinks, but the fact of its existence. "We do not know substance immediately in itself, but only because it is the subject of certain acts."[1]

II

All that is certain so far is, that I am an existent substance, and that it is my nature to have thoughts, ideas, or conscious states. So far, these beliefs and these alone are known to be exempt from error. For they afford no ground for supposing that I cannot be deceived in all judgments I make about anything other than my own existence and my present mental state. My own existence cannot secure for me the truth of mathematical propositions, nor can it be seen to imply the existence of a physical world or of physical bodies. There can be no certain knowledge on these heads until the possibility of the "malignant demon" (or what he represents) has been finally disproved. That possibility has not yet been destroyed; we have only fixed a limit to its range of application. How can we pass, then, from certain knowledge of our own existence and of our present experience to certain knowledge of the existence and nature of anything else? Or is solipsism to be Descartes's last word?

Evidently we cannot make a transition from our present knowledge to that which, though knowable, is as yet unknown, without some idea of what are the sorts of things which may be knowable. And, once clear about *what* we want to discover, we shall further need to know by which *means* we may hope to make the discovery.

How to make a transition from knowledge of our selves to knowledge of other things constitutes the second *quæstio* in Cartesian metaphysics, and the method of its solution will be essentially the same as that of the first. We must at once get clear on what we want to prove, and what principles would be presupposed in a proof, supposing proof possible. Now, we can only know what we want to prove by reviewing ideas we previously held but have now set aside from lack of reasons for believing them. We shall, therefore, take back certain of the more general and important of these beliefs, not, however, as

[1] *Reply to Third Objections* (AT, IX, 136).

RECONSTRUCTION IN METAPHYSICS

pieces of certain knowledge, but merely as hypotheses, the acceptance or rejection of which awaits demonstration. It is significant that out of the vast number of beliefs Descartes could have re-entertained, he selects only those having direct reference to existence, and therefore no mathematical ones. There are, he finds, plenty of his former beliefs which do contain something that is clear, though this ' something ' is, in every case, ' complicated ' with other factors that are unclear, so that their joint import is far from being clear and distinct. The clear and confused factors must therefore be sorted out, and the latter, if possible, replaced by something clear. This selective review of his past beliefs first suggests ideas of material objects, e.g. the sun, the stars, the earth and material bodies of all sorts upon it—the belief in the existence of a physical world. Now if we scrutinise these beliefs we see that all that is clear and distinct in any of them is simply that " thoughts of those things are present to my mind." But accompanying these clear " thoughts " present to mind, and intimately connected with them, are two *judgments*, namely: (i) that the " thought " is " *of* " an object other than it, and existing independently of it; (ii) that this independent existent possesses the same characteristics as are found in my thought of it. That is to say, we ordinarily judge, without hesitation or reflexion, that our ideas are ideas *of existing things*, and that these ideas convey faithfully, however incompletely, the real nature of those existents. Now, in many cases that part of the belief which consists of " idea " is clear, but the part which consists in the two judgments is quite unclear and alone cannot withstand a resolute effort to doubt it. The " idea " of the earth as that of ' a spherical body which revolves ' is clear, and doubtless that of a possible existent. Indeed, there is, says Descartes, no difference between ' my idea of the earth ' and ' my idea of the earth as existing '—but a difference there certainly is between thinking of the earth as existing and asserting that the earth exists. So, to state the case quite generally, it is one thing to conceive x as existing, and another to assert its existence. Should x, as a matter of fact, not exist, in the former circumstance we have fallen into no error, but in the latter we have. And it is precisely to assertions of existence that our commonsense beliefs about the material world commit us. Here, then,

G

is a question of fact to be examined : *ought* we to permit ourselves to be committed to such assertions of existence simply on the strength of our clear " thoughts," and if not, can additional support be found to justify those assertions, and, hence, our common beliefs ?

We have only to examine the reasons ordinarily adduced in their favour to see that these beliefs are highly uncertain. Our assumption of the independent existence of material objects certainly *seems* to be caused by things independent of our minds. When I burn my hand, I do not believe that it was I who caused my painful sensation, but some independent external body that really exists and is hot. Some ideas, however, do seem to be caused by my mind and not by things existing independently of it (*e.g.* my ideas of the other side of the moon or of a mermaid). These can be accounted for as due to my combining in mind other ideas not caused by my mind, so then all that is due to my mind on those occasions is the *synthesising* of certain elements into a unity, not the elements that are synthesised. Now if we are asked what justification we have for claiming that beliefs of the former kind really are caused by things existing independently of our minds, and things which are in nature essentially like our ideas of them, the answer usually returned is, that we have a strong impulse to believe in their existence, and that this impulse is approved when we reflect that our ideas of those things occur in mind quite independently of our will. This answer, however, is plainly inadmissible. As for the first reason, our strong natural tendency or " blind impulse " may be nothing more than a constantly operative *bias*, of which we are ignorant and for which we are in no sense responsible. Indeed, this might well be just the form our " continuous deception "—our radical incapacity to reach knowledge about anything except our selves—would assume. Nor is the second reason any stronger. That these ideas occur in mind independently of our will is no ground for asserting that there exist independent external bodies causing them. For, in dreams the ideas occur independently of our will, but we never adduce this fact as a ground for asserting them to be ideas of real objects existing then and there in the external world. What has to be established then is tolerably clear. It is our right *to affirm the existence* of what our idea refers to when it is an idea of some material object. But before considering how Descartes tries to establish it, there is a second important belief, taken up from the general review, which must be subjected to scrutiny.

All clear " thoughts," like those of material objects and certain others such as the elementary propositions of arithmetic and geometry, had been set aside only because " it came into my mind that perhaps a god might have endowed me with such a nature that I may have been deceived even about things which seem most evident." Hence, if ever we are to place confidence in the evidence of our thoughts, we must find grounds that definitely refute that supposition. Now whether or not we believe that a God exists, we certainly have an *idea* of one. This idea, Descartes maintains, is clear and definable. And like other clear ideas, so long as " we consider them only in themselves, and do not relate the thought to anything beyond themselves," it cannot be false. But here again, men not only have the " thought " of a God, but further, on the strength of it, proceed to assert that God *exists, i.e.* to assert that this thought is one of an actually existing being, whose nature is faithfully, if not completely, presented in that thought. The problem of justifying the existential reference in beliefs that assert existence is, then, a general one. The belief in an existent God, or in an existent material object, is simply a particular case falling under it. The clearness of the " thought " itself does not warrant our affirming the existence of a counterpart or corresponding object. ' To have an idea of God ' is one thing, ' to believe in God ' (*i.e.* to assert that God exists) is another. Can reasons justifying this belief be discovered ? Descartes's choice of the belief in God's existence as the second proposition to be entertained hypothetically with a view to its demonstration is not a haphazard selection, but a strategical ' move ' whose consequences are as far reaching and important as those of the *cogito*.

The upshot of Descartes's survey of the beliefs he had accepted in the past, then, is to select two, one asserting the existence of material bodies, the other the existence of God, both of which give rise to the same problem, namely, that of justifying the passage from awareness of what is thought to asserting the existence of what is thought.[1] The " thoughts " those two beliefs contain, being clear, are *ipso facto* ideas of possible objects ; but before we can know whether they are also ideas of actual existents we must discover one or more certain propositions of a character suitable to be employed as principles of demonstration. Where should such principles be sought ? Now at first sight it might seem futile to begin such a search, for if the " plain truths " of arithmetic are still uncertain, surely the principles of demonstration would be no less so ? Descartes, however, does not take this view. Since the required principles must be certain, they will be found, if at all, by the same operation that disclosed our earlier certainties, that is to say, by intuition. And to what more promising field could intuition first turn than that which has already yielded the only certainties we yet possess ? So Descartes returns to the *cogito* situation, to see whether still more cannot be extracted from it.

" When my mind, which knows itself but still doubts of everything else, looks around in order to extend its knowledge," says Descartes, " it discovers certain common notions. From these it constructs various demonstrations that carry within them such conviction that their truth cannot be doubted so long as we concentrate attention on them." (*Prins.*, I, xiii ; AT, VIII, 9.) Now the simple natures we intuit may be assigned to two classes, (i) those which are " things or affections of things " (*Prins.*, I, xlviii), including such factors as are indicated by " substance," " existence," " thinking," and (ii) those which are neither, but are what he calls indifferently " eternal truths," " maxims " and sometimes " common notions " (though unwisely so, since some " common notions," *e.g.* existence, duration, diversity, unity, are not strictly of this type). But the *cogito* situation not only contains several natures of the first sort (" the thing " which is " I," " existence," " thinking "), it further exhibits these natures as *connected* in that definite, intelligible way that may be expressed by saying ' my present

[1] Descartes's Metaphysics, we shall see, develop from an analysis of the *cogito* situation, which yields three central conceptions : those of mentality, materiality and divinity, for self-awareness yields knowledge of our self as cognitive, and a review of our cognitions discloses ideas of material bodies and of God. It remains then to demonstrate the existence of objects corresponding to these conceptions, and to determine so far as may be the detailed character and relations of those objects.

RECONSTRUCTION IN METAPHYSICS 101

conscious state entails the existence of that substantival self which is me.' The several distinct natures are thus connected into a unity of characteristic structure. The formulæ that together express this structure separately express the second sort of simple natures, *i.e.* those *principles* that Descartes calls " eternal truths," or, when employed in inference, " the *vincula* of knowledge." They are " bonds for connecting together the other simple natures, and on the evidence of which depend all inferences obtained by reasoning " (*Reg.*, xii ; AT, X, 419) They are objective or factual, in that they are seen to constitute the structure of what exists, and therefore, once abstracted *in thought* from their concrete setting, they may be used *by thought* as principles to reach more extensive and determinate knowledge about what exists.

Which are these " vincula "—irreducible, elements *of form* that give the *cogito* fact its structure ? There are three of particular importance that Descartes indicates. In the first place, there is the necessary relation of attribute to substance. We are acquainted not only with our conscious states and with our self as their subject, but through them also become acquainted with ' what it is to be an attribute ' and ' what it is to be a substance or thing.' This ultimate difference in type between substance and quality is clearly exhibited in that concrete fact which is ' my self being conscious.' By intuiting that particular fact we can also intuit the further quite general principle that every quality belongs to some or other substance —that it is of the nature of qualities to inhere in existing things.[1] So the concrete fact is both the experiential ground that certifies this general principle and a particular exemplification of it.[2] Secondly, for whatever exists or ' is,' there is some cause or some ground explanatory of it.[3] This principle, we

---

[1] " That all the objects of our knowledge are to be regarded as things or the affections of things ; or as eternal truths with the enumeration of things " (*Prins.*, I, xlviii) ; also, " to nothing no affections or qualities belong ; accordingly, where we observe certain affections there a thing or substance, to which these appertain, is necessarily to be found " (*ibid.*, I, xi).

[2] " When we apprehend that we are things which think, this is the first principle which is not drawn from any syllogism ; and when one says, ' I think, therefore I am,' he does not conclude his existence from his state of thinking by the constraint of any syllogism, but, as something known of itself, he sees it by simple inspection of his mind."—*Reply to Second Objections* (AT, IX, 110).

[3] It is doubtful whether this maxim, in the negative form that Descartes states it (" *ex nihilo nihil fit* "—*Prins.*, I, il ; lxxv) is, as he asserts, " an

shall see, is compound; it includes the principle of causation and that of sufficient reason or ground, both of which Descartes is to employ in his proofs of God's existence. And, lastly, as a third " vinculum," there is the principle of contradiction. These together, according to Descartes, are the necessary and sufficient principles for demonstrating the truth of the two beliefs selected and entertained hypothetically, viz., that God and material bodies really exist. And Descartes claims that those principles are as certain as the *cogito*.[1]

If we reflect on the occasions on which Descartes applies his methodological doubt, we shall notice that, though he regards it as a preventive measure against error of any sort, he thinks of it especially as counteracting error of one particular and insidious kind. He practises it primarily in connexion with beliefs that imply an affirmation of the *existence* of objects corresponding to our ideas, and only secondarily to the ideas themselves.[2] The purpose of his next enquiry, then, is to discover whether there is any reason for being certain that the thought of God, besides being clear and distinct in itself, is an idea of something that really exists and really possesses the properties assigned in the thought. But before entering on this investigation it is desirable to notice a preliminary analysis of " ideas " that Descartes works out, for the demonstrations to follow turn upon certain distinctions which that analysis provides.

---

axiom." And it does not seem to be a principle ' intuitively induced ' from a particular perception of my own existence as " a thinking thing," but rather an hypothesis that reflexion on my existence suggests to my mind, or a postulate tacitly assumed in any attempt to explain changes of state the self undergoes. Descartes himself seems to recognise a difference, for he does not say that it is disclosed in our states of self-awareness, but vaguely speaks of it " having its seat in our mind " : cf. " When we apprehend that it is impossible for a thing to arise from nothing, the proposition ' *ex nihilo nihil fit* ' is not to be taken as an existing thing or as a mode of anything, but as an eternal truth having its seat in our mind."—*Prins.*, I, xlix (AT, VIII, 23 ; HR, I, 238–9).

[1] They are " so transparent and at the same time so simple that we can never think about them without believing them true. . . . For we cannot doubt them without thinking of them, but we cannot think of them without at the same time believing them true, hence it follows that we can never doubt them without at the same time believing them true, which is really to say that we can never doubt them."—*Reply to Second Objections* (AT, VII, 145–6 ; HR, II, 42).

[2] " We shall doubt in the first place whether of all the things that have fallen under our senses or that we have ever imagined, there are any that really exist in the world. . . . We shall doubt also of other things we previously held as most certain, even of the principles of mathematics. . . ."—*Prins.*, I, iv, v.

RECONSTRUCTION IN METAPHYSICS

Descartes employs the term "idea" in several senses (cf. also pp. 161-2). It is a general name denoting immediate apprehension of : (i) simple natures, that are 'units,' (ii) complex natures composed of simples (both simple and complex natures are objects of true belief), and (iii) the products of various cognitive activities, viz., sensa and percepta, and 'images' (in one of the three senses assigned to the word), as well as 'thoughts,' where this stands for both concepts and propositions. And, as we have seen, there is the very general distinction between "idea" in the sense of 'item apprehended' simply, and the wider sense in which we are said ' *to have* ideas,' the ' *having* ' (*i.e.* apprehending) rather than ' what is had ' (*i.e.* ' item apprehended ') being uppermost in mind. Again, " idea " in both these senses is sharply discriminated from assertions of existence, by which we judge or believe there *exists* something corresponding to our " thought " or " idea " in the former of the two last senses. Now clearly in some sense ideas are ' real,' for we are continually ' having ' ideas about all manner of things. Descartes decides that they are real in two senses. They are real as occurrent states of the self that is said to ' have ' them, and they are real in being that about which assertions and suppositions can be made at different times. That which I think is real in one sense : the act of (or the fact of) my thinking ' it ' is real is another. What is true of both is that they require " causes." We know by direct self-inspection that we are at this present moment apprehending so-and-so ; our ' apprehending ' really *occurs* at this moment, and therefore exists. This sense of ' real ' Descartes calls ' formal reality,' and it may be truly asserted not only of ideas, but (he is going to show) of physical bodies, of God, and of many things which would, in ordinary parlance, be said simply to exist. The second sense of ' real,' however, applies exclusively to " ideas " or ' items apprehended.' It is that in which an idea could not ' purport to be about,' or ' claim to represent ' something unless it had being. This sense of ' real ' Descartes calls the " objective reality " of an idea. Everything that exists, then, has " formal reality " (this is but an analytic statement), ideas alone have " objective reality." Thus in any situation in which someone is thinking or believing something there are two kinds of ' real ' factor to be distinguished and explained separately. What 'accounts for' or 'explains' each is called indifferently, in Cartesian language, the " cause " of that factor. To explain the above situation, then, is to assign the ' formal ' cause of the ' thinking ' or ' believing ' referred to (*i.e.* to state what caused that act of thinking to occur just ' then and there ' in just that person's mind), and to assign the ' objective ' cause of the ' something ' thought or believed (*i.e.* to show how an idea of the sort thought or believed should be *thinkable* at all, by anyone).[1] So, to state Descartes's problem in his own terminology : We are certain of the formal reality of the thought of God, and the idea contained in it is quite clear. Can we, however, be certain of the formal reality of God ? To ask if belief in God is rationally justified is to ask what reason we have to assert that the idea of God has for its ' objective ' cause something having the same formal reality as the idea has objectively ; *i.e.* whether there exists something really possessing the characteristics that conjunctively constitute our idea of God. Now we should notice that in the single instance of the *cogito* belief, awareness of the " objective reality " of that idea and awareness of the " formal reality " which is its ' objective ' cause are *both* disclosed in a single inspective act. In perceiving that idea we also intuit the fact it is ' about,' and in intuiting that fact we perceive the truth of the idea. But with our beliefs in the existence of God and of a material world, the relevant ideas are not similarly certified by an intuitive or immediate disclosure of any corresponding formal realities. So if ever we are to know that a God or a material world exists, we shall not know it by direct intuition of the formal reality that is the objective ' cause ' of the idea, but by some indirect, discursive proof. And such a proof must start from relevant *ideas*, since there is nothing else from which it can start. So then, in order that the " objective reality " of an idea should not express merely the outermost limit beyond which we cannot pass, in order that we may be able to work outward from the objective reality of idea to something really existing independently of it, some further principle must be found to justify this passage from

[1] The relation of ' objective cause ' is *not* the inverse of that of ' objective reference,' for every idea has objective reference, but there may be no one formal reality which is its objective cause and which it represents, though there must, of course, be formal realities that are severally the ' objective causes ' (or objective cause-factors) of its separate constituents.

conception to affirmation of existence. If our ideas are to be instrumental in establishing a contact between our mind on the one hand, and existent realities that are not ideas on the other, then the establishment of such a contact depends on our discovering some relation which is both objective (or factual) and which really does relate the existent to our idea. We have already examined one situation in which such a relation *is* exhibited—the *cogito* situation. The proposition ' I exist ' is certainly true. The *formal* reality of that thought or belief is accounted for by *my* formal reality as an existent self: that *act* of thinking or believing I can cause, because I do exist and because I am essentially a thing that thinks and believes. The *objective* reality of that thought, on the other hand, is accounted for, because there is a formal reality (myself) that really possesses the qualities present in, and constitutive of, my idea of my self. Evidently, then, we may proceed analogously in dealing with the idea of God. Here, again, two things have to be considered—its formal and its objective reality. Hence, one of Descartes's proofs for God's existence starts from the fact that there certainly is, at any rate, *an idea* of God in men's minds. And its " formal " reality raises no difficulty, for " all ideas," says Descartes, " considered as modes of thought, have the same reality." My own reality as a " thinking thing " being sufficient to enable me to think once, is sufficient to enable me to think any number of times. I can ' cause ' myself to think so often as I choose. But can I also cause the thoughts I think on those occasions to have just the objective import they do have ? Clearly I can when my self or my states are the formal realities which those thoughts are ' of ' or ' about.' But plainly not when the thoughts I think are about something quite other than my self and my states (*e.g.* God or material bodies), for the formal reality which is my self is neither a material object nor God. So the very possibility of thinking such a thought requires explanation. And Descartes's answer to the question, ' How can there be such thoughts as these ? ' will, we shall see, also reply to the further question, ' How can we know that those thoughts are thoughts of things that exist independently ? ' The possibility of there being ' such a thought to think ' in any particular instance cannot be explained by the *non*-existence of a real object corresponding to it. But neither ought it to be explained in all instances by the actual existence of a corresponding object; otherwise, from the fact that we can 'think of' a hippogriff, we should rightly assert the independent existence of a hippogriff. Thinking and knowing would then be interchangeable terms; there would then be no problem of error, because there would be no error, for all ideas would be 'of'— all that they can be 'of'—namely, actually existing and resembling counterparts. But there *is* error; to think the idea of a hippogriff does not entail that a hippogriff exists. How, then, are we to distinguish those ideas which do, from those which do not, have existing objects corresponding to them? To return to the idea of God; the idea is certainly thinkable, for we often think it. That it is a clear idea of a possible existent is plain from the fact that we can define what we mean by " God."[1] How could I have come by an idea of just this kind, an idea having just this " objective reality "? Descartes replies that it is impossible that this idea should be thinkable unless there exists a substance possessing its defining properties. This, however, requires to be proved. The very problem presupposes, and its solution depends upon, the principle of causality which he takes as having been previously guaranteed by intuition. It also depends, however, on a theory concerning the *character* of all causality[2] and of terms causally related. Not only must those terms be "real" (for " nothing cannot cause something "), but their reality must differ in degree, such that it is significant

---

[1] Cf. " By the name God I mean a substance that is infinite, eternal, immutable, independent, omniscient, omnipotent, by which I myself and everything else, if indeed anything else exists, have been created."—*Meditation III* (HR, I, 165).

[2] Cf. " That there is nothing in the effect that has not existed in the same or a higher degree in the cause is a first principle, and there is none clearer. This is the same as the popular saying, 'from nothing comes nothing,' for if we allow there exists something in any effect that did not exist in its cause, we must further allow that this something has been created by nothing. But it is not evident why nothing could not be the cause of a thing except that such a cause would not contain what exists in the effect. . . . It is on this (principle) alone that we wholly depend when we believe that things outside mind really exist, for what should have made us suspect their existence except the fact that ideas of them come to our minds by means of our senses ? "—*Reply to Second Objections* (AT, VII, 135). See also axioms iv and v in same *Reply*: " Whatever reality or perfection exists in a thing, exists either formally or eminently in its first and adequate cause. Whence it follows that the objective reality of our ideas requires a cause in which the same reality is contained, not merely objectively, but formally or eminently. Admission of this axiom is absolutely necessary, since knowledge of all things, sensuous and non-sensuous, depends on it alone."

and true to say that one term is more real than some other. And the degree of the reality of any cause can never be less than that of its effect, though the degree of the former may well exceed that of the latter. So in order that " an idea should contain some one certain objective reality rather than another, it must derive it from some cause in which there is at least as much formal reality as this idea contains of objective reality" (HR, I, 163). But the idea of God as defined by Descartes is that of an existent substance possessing all positive qualities in their most " eminent " degree, in their " perfection " or fullest degree of reality. Now, for this thought to be thinkable it follows that there must be some cause of it. But the ' cause ' cannot be less formally real than its ' effect ' (the *idea* of that cause) itself is. It may be more real, in which case the objective reality present to thought will be " less perfect " (*i.e.* less real) than the reality that causes it. Nothing could cause this idea of God, *as defined*, that had not as great a degree of formal reality as the idea has of objective reality. My self, therefore, could not be its cause, for I am far from omniscient, omnipotent, etc. My formal reality then, being not nearly so great as the objective reality of my idea, is not adequate to ' cause ' that idea. So something else must have caused it, something whose reality *is* adequate to do so, *i.e.* something that possesses formally those perfections which my idea possesses objectively.[1] A ' something ' possessed of such perfections answers exactly to that idea which is our definition of ' God.' Therefore, God really exists. Thus, in general, all ideas having existential reference, and in particular my idea of God, are instrumental in establishing a contact between existents that are not ideas (*e.g.* my self and God). In this way Descartes thinks to pass beyond the circle of himself and his states, and attain to knowledge of other existents and their qualities.

In *Meditation V* he gives a second demonstration of God's existence, similar to the ' ontological argument ' of St. Anselm. This proof does not proceed from the fact that men have an

---

[1] Cf. " I admit that we could form this idea (of God) though we did not know that a supreme being existed, but *not that we could do so if such a being were in fact non-existent* . . . the whole force of my argument lies in the fact that the capacity to form such an idea could not exist in me unless I were created by God."—*Reply to Second Objections* (AT, VII, 133 ; HR, II, 33)— my italics.

idea of God which they were unable to construct themselves, but consists in inferring from the defining qualities alone (present in the idea) to the necessary existence of something possessing them. God is defined as the most perfect being conceivable. Now for such a being not to exist would be for it to lack a " perfection " or completion. But the *most perfect* being could not lack any perfection, much less that of existence. So, given the definition of God, the assertion of God's existence could only be denied on pain of self-contradiction.

III

The existence of God, Descartes's second principal existential conclusion, occupies a 'strategical' position at least as important, retrospectively and prospectively, as the *cogito*. Alternatively to the defining qualities enumerated in *Meditation III*, Descartes attributes to God (*Discourse*, pt. iv) " all the perfections of which we can have any idea," including all those positive excellences, each in its highest degree, which we find present in ourselves in some low measure (*e.g.* veracity, volition). Now it follows that an existent God possessed of every positive quality in its completest degree cannot be the objective cause of deception, for deception must proceed from an imperfection of nature. Deception is incompatible with omnipotence and complete veracity and with omnipotence and complete goodness. And since the god proved existent has both these pairs of perfections, it doubly follows that he is not deceptive, and, further, that there cannot exist a second god who is so. The fact of God's veracity can therefore be used as a general principle to prove that whatever depends on God for its existence or nature cannot be " deceptive," unreal, 'ungenuine,' and hence that our clear and distinct ideas are true. So there is no longer any reason to continue our enquiries under the restrictive hypothesis that we may be so constituted intellectually as to be unable to reach certain knowledge. Provided we assert in our judgments and beliefs nothing that is unclear and indistinct in its conception, we are immune from deception and error. Hence, the propositions previously rejected in the absence of this assurance (*e.g.* those of mathematics) may now be reaffirmed with confidence, not as propositions about which we

RECONSTRUCTION IN METAPHYSICS

merely feel conviction, but as principles of whose truth we are rationally justified in being convinced, since now we *know* that they cannot be false.

Retrospectively, there seem to be four important consequences of having established the existence of God.

(i) Descartes's initial refusal to accept as knowledge anything ' probable,' however high its probability, has not resulted, it follows, in his having defined knowledge in such a way as to render its attainment an unrealisable ideal. That is to say, '*sum*' and '*deus est*' are two pieces of certain knowledge which secure for us for all time the possibility of attaining knowledge of innumerable other propositions whose truth is certain.

(ii) That " what is clear and distinct is true " is no longer a methodological dogma, but an absolutely certified truth which may be employed as a criterion to judge of particular ideas we shall contemplate in the future.

(iii) What formerly appeared as a defect besetting all inferential thought, depriving its conclusions of the certainty that uniformly accompanies single acts of intuition, is now shown to be only apparent. Those unavoidable stages in inference, at which memory must intervene to hold over results we believe ourselves to have intuited before,[1] are likewise, Descartes thinks, guaranteed by God's veracity.

(iv) And since my idea of my self as that of a continuous and identical existing substance is clear and distinct, I may trust and affirm it too. Previously, so much as this was not certain. All I was previously entitled to claim to know was that I existed on every occasion that I perceived myself to do so. But each particular intuition, though a necessary condition, is not a sufficient one to warrant my asserting that I continue

[1] A present act of remembering ourselves to have intuited so-and-so is not an intuitive act but a memory-act, and therefore did require a ' guarantee.' In saying at some present stage of a reasoning process that ' I remember ' some just past intuition, I may fall into error for three reasons. It may be untrue (1) that the idea in question *was* present to my mind in the past, or (2) that it really was *intuited* even though it *was* present, or (3) that what was then intuited *is* exactly the same as the idea now present and said to be ' remembered.' So to call any non-intuitive step in a deduction ' a memory ' begs the question. Vividness or clearness of what is now said to be remembered does not secure infallibility for that memory-act, for, before divine veracity was established it was precisely the truth of that which *is* clear which was in question, and now, after divine veracity is established, it is precisely ' what is clear ' that God is known to guarantee at times its truth is not being intuited.

to exist through all those periods when I am not intuiting my self's existence, nor for asserting that the " I " intuited on one of those occasions is the same as the " I " intuited on another. But ordinarily I do assert both these things ; the proposition ' *sum* ' can be understood in both the wider and the narrower sense. But since the idea of an identical substance persisting throughout alterations of state is a clear and distinct one, and since I now know that what is clear and distinct is ' guaranteed,' I may assert as a piece of certain knowledge that I am now the same self as the self I remember at different dates in my past history, and that that identical self has continued to exist through the several periods between those dates at which its existence was intuited. Thus, the *cogito* asserts no more than that the self is a ' logical substantive ' (that to which an introspected present state belongs as its ' predicate ') ; it is God's veracity which establishes further that the self is a ' metaphysical substantive '—a continuously, identical existent.

Prospectively, there are two particularly important consequences following from our discovery of God's existence :—

(i) Knowledge of God's nature and existence is indispensable in two ways. Without it there can be no knowledge of any body of science, nor even of single, isolated propositions belonging to science or metaphysics. Without it we can come by knowledge of nothing but our self and its states, and even of those only intermittently, at such isolated moments as we happen to intuit our own existence or our present mental state. Without it we can have nothing more than ' opinions ' on matters appertaining to mathematics, physics or metaphysics, which opinions, however satisfying to us personally, cannot be known to be well founded, and cannot therefore rank as knowledge. It is plainly one thing to know a single, isolated proposition, say about certain properties of triangles, and quite another to possess an interconnected knowledge of the whole corpus of Euclidean geometry, just as to know only the *cogito* proposition is vastly different from knowing the whole system of Cartesian metaphysics. But constituted as our minds are, it is impossible to have *all* the interrelated propositions of a science together present to mind as one complex ' object ' which can be completely seized in a single intuitive act. If, however, it be granted that we have knowledge of God

RECONSTRUCTION IN METAPHYSICS

(or more particularly, of divine veracity), then knowledge of a whole science *is* theoretically possible. For knowledge of its constituent principles can be attained piecemeal and progressively. And once each has been proved it can be employed subsequently without re-proof; there is then no need to marshal all the propositions on which it depends and intuit afresh its dependence upon them, for each proposition that is once intuited by me as being certain is guaranteed true at times when I am not thinking of it no less than at times that I am employing it without re-proof.[1] Thus the way is opened out for the acquirement of extensive bodies of certain knowledge, and my limitation to a few particular ' private ' truths so removed. He who does not know of God's existence can nevertheless have clear intuitions and therefore certain knowledge at the moment of intuiting, *but only at those moments*. Now this limitation is serious. It rules out the possibility of that person ever acquiring knowledge of a corpus of science. For to do so presupposes introducing at later stages of reasoning propositions proved earlier on, and this in turn presupposes the intervention of memory. What the ' atheist ' *remembers*, however, is not ' evidence.' To remember a proposition is not to intuit its truth, and, *ex hypothesi*, the ' atheist ' does not know that the truth of what he remembers and employs has already been guaranteed by divine veracity. Hence, though he may often reassert what is true, he can never *know* what he is reasserting is so, therefore he can never acquire, even progressively, a body of certain knowledge. Knowledge is thus an individual's private possession. Though two persons assert the same proposition, and though that proposition be true, it does not follow that both or either are possessed of certain knowledge. Knowledge, Descartes insists, is always a person's private possession, privately striven for and divinely vouchsafed.

(ii) Proof of his third principal existential proposition (viz.,

---

[1] Cf. " Though I am of such a nature that from the moment I understand something very clearly and distinctly I am naturally led to think it true, yet, because I am also of such a nature that I cannot hold my mind constantly fixed on one and the same thing, I often recollect having judged that it is true, after ceasing to think of the reasons that impelled me to judge it so. Now it may happen in the meantime that other reasons offer themselves which would easily cause me to change my opinion, if I did not know that a God existed. Thus I should have no certain and true knowledge, but only vague and fluctuating opinions."—*Meditation V* (AT, IX, 55 ; HR, I, 83).

that there exists a natural world of physical objects) is possible only from the basis of the two existential propositions already established. The assertion of neither our own existence nor that of God needed any general guarantee, but at the moment the second is established a general guarantee of truth is *eo facto* established with it. The third argument, to prove that matter exists, does however require us to resort to some guarantee. That is to say, the argument proper for God's existence (as distinct from explanations of terms used in it) is so short that both premise and its entailment of the conclusion can be intuited together in a single act, without falling back on memory. But the argument to prove the existence of a material world is longer. Since it contains more premises, we must avail ourselves of the help of memory in the later stages to hold over in mind results we had intuited earlier on. Hence the guarantee of divine veracity is indispensable if we are to know our final conclusion is certainly true.

It is one of Descartes's merits that he consistently distinguishes questions of ' essence ' from questions of ' existence.' Thus we saw that in *Meditation III* he is careful to define what he means by the term " God " before beginning to demonstrate that there *exists* something of a nature corresponding to that described in his definition. So here too, in *Meditation V*, he first seeks a clear idea of what the term ' material thing ' is to *mean*,[1] before attempting to prove that such things *exist*. And this is all in line with his radically new, anti-scholastic procedure of passing from the perception of a clear idea to affirming with certainty of knowledge the existence of something corresponding to it. Thus it is never the existent that confers certainty on the idea, but always the certainty of the idea that guarantees the existence of the thing : *du connaître à l'être la conséquence est bonne*.

Have we any reason to be certain that material bodies really exist, as distinct from being certain that we can, and normally do, *think of* material bodies existing ? Let us attack this problem by easy stages, following that rule of method which enjoins us to summon before our minds whatever we already

[1] Cf. " But before examining whether there are any material things such as I conceive exist outside me, I must consider the ideas of them in so far as they are in my thought, and see which of them are distinct and which confused." —*Meditation V*.

suppose ourselves to know about the matter in question, without regard to the source from which the 'knowledge' comes. This commonly received 'knowledge' of a material world turns out to consist of a number of ideas, intricately intermixed, some of them clear and others confused. We ordinarily suppose that we know very many truths about individual bodies by seeing and touching and hearing them, and that we come by highly general and important knowledge about the purely formal determinations of all bodies or of matter in general by studying geometry. But the former sort of evidence adduced to justify our certitude of the existence of matter consists of ideas that are far from being clear and distinct. Yet careful analysis of that evidence shows that, even beginning from such unclear ideas as a basis, a clear meaning *can* be found for the term 'material.' This meaning Descartes works out in his famous analysis of the essential character of a piece of wax, in *Meditation II* (HR, I, 154). The argument presupposes that what constitutes the 'materiality' of a material thing is *that* (whatever it turns out to be) *on account of which* the body is "*the same* body" after undergoing change as it was before it changed. So it follows that no determinate character the object manifests at one moment, but fails to manifest at another, can be, or be part of, what is meant by 'being material,' for we declare the thing to be '*the same* material body' when such transitory character is absent from it no less than when it is present in it. Now, Descartes decides, the only character that belongs to the thing throughout the whole history of its changes, and despite its alterations of state, is the determinable, though not uniquely determined, character of being spatially extended. It is the capacity to assume, under certain and different conditions, this or that determinate size and this or that determinate shape, and, further, the capacity to move, when caused, and so to occupy different places at different times or to have its parts differently arranged at different moments. These determinable properties of being outspread in space and being capable of movement are all that Descartes sees clearly and distinctly to characterise permanently the material body. Therefore they must be the defining characters of 'matter.' They are the characters on account of the possession of which we call a thing 'material,' and those which serve to differentiate material

H

existents from existents of other kind. This property of being extended can be *imagined* only vaguely and confusedly as, say, a more or less indefinite ' spread ' of some coloured, homogeneous medium, but it can be *conceived* with perfect clearness and distinctness, and is precisely what geometers call ' space.' So from studying geometry we can reach a fuller knowledge of it, discovering its derivative properties and their relations, and come to conceive it as three-dimensional, and are thus enabled to define ' surface ' and ' solid ' in terms of it. Likewise by studying kinematics we acquire more detailed knowledge about the other property (capacity to move) which presupposes extension, and so come to acquire many more perfectly clear ideas about the ultimate constitution of material bodies, and about the real character of their behaviour, as distinct from those unclear ideas we also have which relate only to the ways those changes appear in sense-perception. So the confused ideas acquired through sense-experience which we accept in daily life, as marks of the ' materiality ' of objects we perceive, are replaced by a set of clear and distinct ideas acquired through mathematical study. Mathematics, however, only brings us to see that these geometrical and kinematical properties are such as *could* belong to material objects, if they existed. Mathematics provides no warrant for affirming that there actually exist objects to which they *do*, as a matter of fact, belong. The idea of a material body is doubtless that of a material body as existing, just as the idea of God is that of God as existing. But the idea of God as existing is not an existent God, nor is the idea of an existing material object a material existent. To have a clear idea and nothing more is simply to think of a possible existent, and not to intuit infallibly the existence of something really existing. So the problem confronting Descartes is to adduce reasons that prove that our clear ideas of bodies as existing *do* enable us to know with certainty that material bodies actually exist.

If it be granted that we have a clear and distinct conception of what is meant by ' material ' when we ask, ' Do material bodies exist ? ' and if it be allowed that the principle of causality interpreted in Descartes's special way is true, he is then in a position to demonstrate that an existent possessing the defining properties in question is (and that nothing other than this could be) the 'cause' of an idea having just the 'objective reality' that is contained in our idea of 'material body.' Some ground for the 'objective reality' of that idea there *must* be; Descartes's business is to show that actually existing matter is the ground that in fact it *does* have, because it is the only one that it *could* have. The attempt to prove this is an argument by exclusion of alternative possibilities. First, could my self be the 'formal reality' that is the objective cause of this idea? True, my volition can cause me to have images of material bodies whenever I choose, so my formal reality is amply sufficient to produce *these* ideas. But images give only confused ideas of bodies, and the presence of confused ideas never entitles me to assert that there are formal realities corresponding to them. Secondly, I am constantly perceiving by my senses appearances of bodies, and these appearances I instinctively refer to existent bodies as their causes. Unlike my images, these sensible appearances I am certain of not causing by my volition. They come and go independently of it, and I cannot by any effort of will perceive a body that is *not* locally and suitably present to my senses, nor, on the other hand, can I, by any effort of will, avoid perceiving what *is* suitably situated in relation to my sense-organs. This complete independence of my volition, characteristic of the occurrence of sensible appearances but not of the occurrence of imagery, is significant. That peculiarity might plausibly be explained as due to the fact that bodies actually exist in an external world independently of me, and that, under conditions yet to be discovered, they are capable of causing those sensible appearances of themselves which are present to my mind. For these " appearances of bodies " do not depend for their occurrence on my volition or on my self or on God. If I were to cause them I should know myself to do so,[1] whereas precisely what I do know is that I do *not* cause them. Nor are our sense ideas of bodies due to

---

[1] Geulincx (1625–69), a follower of Descartes, employs this idea along with the *cogito* as the primary principles of his ethics; cf. Γνῶθι σεαυτόν, *sive Ethica*. We are the cause of all our mental states of which we know not merely *that* they occurred, but also *how* they occurred. " If you do not know the means by which a thing is produced, it is not you who produced it," *i.e.*, unless you are acquainted with the entire course of events that led up to the occurrence of the state in question, it is a state caused by something other than yourself. See Ch. IX, and the section on Geulincx in my article ' Cartesians ' in *Encyclopædia Britannica*, 14th edn.

God, for the idea caused by that formal reality is one of an existent having all perfections and no limitations, not an idea of an existent of limited dimension and shape. The characteristics composing God's nature then, being so vastly different from those constituting my idea of a material body, it follows that God could not be the cause of the latter idea. He could not be the formal reality of which we are in search, unless he were deceptive. But God has been proved veracious, so it follows that the formal reality which my clear idea of matter is ' of ' must be an independent existent actually possessing those determinable properties, geometrical and kinematical, which form my concept of matter. Thus the proof proceeds, negatively, by eliminating two of the three possible alternative ' causes ' (the three being assumed exhaustive), namely, the alternatives—my self, God, material bodies; and positively, by recourse to God's truthfulness and his consequent endorsement of any idea that is clear and distinct. Thus we are entitled to claim certain knowledge, Descartes maintains, of the actual *existence* of a world of particular material bodies and of their most pervasive and intrinsic properties. It only remains to acquire further knowledge, as extensive, as detailed and as exact as possible, about the *constitution* of natural bodies, and we shall take a first step in this direction in the succeeding chapter.

Surveying the ground we have covered, we see that Descartes's incessant preoccupation has been to reach certain knowledge of the main types of *existent substances*. In order to accomplish this he was committed to certain highly general conclusions concerning the *nature* of those existents as well, but these conclusions, though valuable ' by-products,' were subsidiary to his main project. It now remains for him to make what was a secondary *détour* the principal object of his investigation, and determine more fully the nature of the self and its states, and the nature of matter and its properties. God and his relations to man is regarded as a spiritual problem that falls rather to theology for treatment than to metaphysics, since its discussion depends upon revelation of certain *vérités de foi*, dogmas that can be neither discovered nor confirmed or refuted by rational argument.

To sum up, then, Descartes claims that the three principal

RECONSTRUCTION IN METAPHYSICS

existential conclusions reached follow from premises and principles that can be extracted from the *cogito* situation.

From the fact that we have (1) a number of clear and distinct ideas, including those of our own existence, of certain formal principles of inference, and of certain simple natures in terms of which we can form defining ideas of what the terms ' God ' and ' material ' signify ; (2) certain insight into the character of causality, namely, as ' efficient ' (where one formal reality causes another formal reality) and as ' sufficient reason ' (where an independent existent of an intelligible nature is possessed of sufficient formal reality to explain ' formally ' or ' eminently ' the possibility of our having ideas of that reality) ; and (3) an assurance of divine veracity which is our ultimate and sufficient warrant for asserting the independent existence of things corresponding to those ideas whose character we clearly and distinctly understand, and which we distinctly perceive to have ' existential reference ' beyond themselves.

Descartes's Metaphysics, though usually described as a ' dualism,' may be quite as correctly accounted a ' pluralism.' It is an existential pluralism, since the universe comprises very many particular existents that are selves, a far greater number of particular mental states that are owned by those selves (for these too are ultimately real, and not mere appearances), a single substance that is ' material ' or spatial, and the existent that is God. Qualitatively, it is a dualistic metaphysic, for there are two irreducible attributes—determinable spatiality and determinable consciousness—one of which characterises every substance and both of which jointly characterise none. Again, within Descartes's epistemology a hard and fast distinction is drawn between two kinds of cognitive experience, the possession of the one constituting in itself certain knowledge, the possession of the other constituting not knowledge but at best working belief that is pragmatically justified by its biological or social efficacy. By the method of his metaphysics, Descartes initiates a complete reversal of Scholastic procedure. Starting from the certainty of an existent world, Scholasticism attempts to infer as a consequence a knowledge of God's existence. Descartes contrariwise proceeds from " ideas " and attempts to reach knowledge of an existent world as a consequence of a knowledge of God. From first to last knowledge is sought of that which is other than idea through the intermediary of idea. His ceaseless scrutiny of " ideas," his examinations of their import, of their clearness, of their distinctness, of their relations one to another and of the order of their dependence, all of which is through and through epistemological in emphasis, does not entail, however, that what we have knowledge *of* must be, in the end, " idea." So far, at any rate, Descartes's philosophy is more accurately described as a ' realism ' than as an ' epistemological idealism.' And lastly, because of his rigorous adherence to the view that only through intuition and deduction (" pure thought ") can certain knowledge be acquired, and that sense-experience forms, at most, only the occasion for their operation and never a criterion of their conclusions, Descartes's philosophy may fairly be called *a priori* and deductive, or ' rationalistic.'

V

THE NATURAL WORLD AND OUR KNOWLEDGE OF NATURE

"Qu'on me donne l'étendue et le mouvement et je vais refaire le monde."—DESCARTES.

IT was the object of Descartes's Metaphysics to establish two conclusions which should guarantee the certainty of all other knowledge we can attain ; namely, that God exists, and that the defining attributes of self and body are completely disparate. We have now to see what more detailed knowledge that is perfectly certain can be reached about the world of animate and inanimate bodies, and about selves and their states. Our knowledge of the existent natural world will be considered in this chapter, the next will be devoted to his account of the constitution of minds and their knowledge. The two bodies of science here distinguished (knowledge of nature and knowledge of selves) might appear to correspond with what are nowadays called physics and psychology. But such an identification would be quite inaccurate. The resemblances between them are so superficial, and the differences so radical, that to regard Descartes's " Natural Philosophy " as equivalent to physics in our modern sense, or his doctrine of self as substantially what is now meant by psychology, would not only be mistaken, but would prevent us from understanding aright his philosophy or his metaphysics, and cause us to miss the somewhat subtle consequences that proceed precisely from their differences. First, what Descartes calls " Physics " is not what we call physics nor what he calls " Philosophy " or " Natural Philosophy." A person competent to discuss in what sense modern physics is " knowledge " (which is far from saying " any physicist ") would not claim that physical science is " a system "—would he indeed go so far as to say that physics even " aspires " to become one ? For Descartes, however, there is no question that his " Physics " is a system.

Again, a modern physicist who was also a philosopher would, I fancy, claim that physics does contribute independently of any metaphysics to our knowledge of the existent natural world, though he would not claim that such knowledge were certain, but admit that the best of it is no more than highly probable. Descartes, however, maintains that Physics alone does not give us knowledge of the existent natural world, but that his Natural Philosophy does, and, moreover, that it gives us wholly certain and never merely probable knowledge of it. His Physics is the result of applying the "mathematical method" to certain non-mathematical objects; it is a corpus of interconnected results, highly general, mainly about distinct classes of natural objects.[1] Physics is not differentiated from geometry by its method, but by the fact that geometry treats only of certain natures (the properties of Euclidean space), while physics treats of others ('physical constants'). Physics is "another kind of Geometry, which proposes to itself the explanation of natural phenomena." "My whole Physics," he says, "is nothing but geometry"—a geometry he describes to Mersenne (letter, 1638) as "concrete," in distinction from "abstract" (Euclidean) geometry. And he adduces his researches into the constitution of salt, snow, light, the rainbow, and the various discussions in the *Dioptric* and the *World* as further examples of his "Physics." It is, then, the totality of such results, co-ordinated and arranged so as to exhibit the deducibility of one from certain others that constitute "Physics." Such a science of physics is knowledge of a possibly existent world, but Descartes is satisfied with nothing less than knowledge of this actually existing one. To show that no proposition of his Physics is incompatible with any other is to show that such a world is "logically possible," or, in Cartesian language, that it is such as would be actual had God chosen to make it so. But the important point for Descartes is to discover whether God *has* caused such a world actually to exist, *i.e.* to discover whether the natural world proved existent in the Metaphysics is a world having the character and constitution described in the Physics, or—to state the issue inversely—

[1] Notice Descartes's criticism of Galileo on this point. True, Galileo investigated physical data by a "mathematical method," but not having considered "the first causes of nature," and having restricted his enquiry to seeking explanations of only certain particular effects, he "built without foundation."

THE NATURAL WORLD

to discover whether the Physics is, as a matter of fact, descriptive and explanatory of the natural world that actually exists. Now we can be clear that no constituent proposition of the Physics itself can warrant our affirming the whole Physics to be a true description of all Nature actually existing. But the Metaphysics, if we accept it, *will* warrant such an affirmation, Descartes thinks, and his science of Physics, together with the demonstration that it is deducible from the Metaphysics, is precisely what he means by " Natural Philosophy " or " Philosophy." It is nothing other than the Physics presented as in indissoluble connexion with the Metaphysics. So, Descartes would say, no physicist who was not also metaphysician can have knowledge of the existence and constitution of the *de facto* natural world. He will have a knowledge of physical science, but he cannot infer from it that it is also a true explanatory description of actually existent Nature. It is, then, mainly the researches between 1619 and 1628 that constitute Descartes's Physics. The Metaphysics, first drafted in 1629, and definitively stated ten years later, confers once for all, on the Physics already elaborated, an *existential reference*, which in itself it does not contain. Such " existential reference " is established by showing that the most general principles of physics (hence that all other and less general ones) are deducible from the conclusions of his Metaphysics. So Descartes's Natural Philosophy is a part of his Metaphysics in a sense in which his Physics is a part of neither.

It follows from such a view that Descartes is not here embarrassed by any problem of the relation between appearances and the reality of which they are appearances, for his Natural Philosophy is not a Phenomenalism that requires to be related to an ultimate, ontological theory, but is itself an ontological theory—an essential *part* of that systematic and ultimate account of the Universe which is Metaphysics.

In this chapter, then, we shall consider his Natural Philosophy and not simply his Physics. For we shall consider what he has to say about the constitution of this existing material world. And to this end it will be convenient to review separately (i) his theory of the structure of our natural knowledge, (ii) his theory of the constitution of the existent Nature.

Modern readers of Descartes's Natural Philosophy are usually astonished to find him insisting that our knowledge of natural laws can and must be final and certain. And they are inclined to feel there is some inconsistency in his maintaining both that natural philosophy is strictly deductive, and yet that it is of the utmost importance for the naturalist to resort to observation of particular objects and occurrences, and even to resort to experiment on certain occasions. The use of observation and experiment suggests a procedure predominantly inductive, and therefore that conclusions reached by it would be at best highly probable and never certain. Is it not likely that Descartes has muddled the matter? Has not his desire for certainty in knowledge led him to believe prematurely in its possibility, through ignorance of the real conditions under which knowledge of Nature is attainable? And, further, has he himself not acted inconsistently with his own view in having performed experimental investigations?[1] Descartes considers himself neither mistaken nor inconsistent. And whether he is right or wrong in this we are certainly not entitled to judge until we have assembled and weighed what he has to say in various places concerning the character of natural knowledge and the rôle of experience and experiment in its production.

There can be no question that Descartes does suppose his Natural Philosophy to form a system of knowledge that is both certain and demonstrable,[2] and his Physics alone to be neither.[3]

[1] Descartes was much impressed by the value of experiments. He urged Mersenne (letter, 1632) to attempt them, and, though frequently complaining of insufficient time and money to engage in more, he managed to investigate experimentally many widely different kinds of phenomena (the weight of air, 1631; the laws of light and sound, 1633; the differentiating characteristics of oils, spirits, common waters and salts) and dissected the heads of various animals to discover the functioning of memory and imagination.
[2] Descartes speaks of the " foundations " of his Physics (*i.e.* those ultimate and most general principles of the system that are logically independent of each other) as being " nearly all so evident that it is only required to understand them in order to accept them, and . . . there is not one of them which I do not consider myself able to demonstrate."—*Discourse*, vi (AT, VI, 68 ; HR, I, 123). Cf. also his two letters to Mersenne, (i) 1629 : " I am resolved to explain all the phenomena of nature, that is to say, the whole of physics. And this project pleases me more than any other I have ever made, for I believe I have found such a way of expounding all my thoughts as will satisfy some and leave others no opportunity of contradicting them " (AT, I, 70) ; (ii) 1640 : " As to physics, I should consider I knew nothing about them were I only able to explain how things might be, and were unable to demonstrate that they could not be otherwise. For, having reduced physics to the laws of mathematics, such demonstration is possible " (AT, III, 39).
[3] This distinction between Descartes's Physics and his Natural Philosophy (*i.e.* Physics as " guaranteed " by Metaphysics) follows from the point made

Natural Philosophy is throughout general in character. It contains no proposition directly about just this or that particular body or particular state or particular event. It is not a history of the actual succession of natural changes and occurrences, but a statement of the laws that are collectively sufficient to explain the more pervasive characteristics of innumerable natural objects and events of definable kinds. So, from beginning to end, Natural Philosophy consists of none but general propositions. But the laws these express are, some of greater, others of lesser, generality. And they are so connected that from a knowledge of one of them, knowledge of some certain other can always be deduced. The most general of these physical principles (the laws of geometry and mechanics) are directly deducible from our certain knowledge of the existence and nature of God and other conclusions of the Metaphysics, and any less general law of physics is mediately deducible from these metaphysical results through the immediately deduced laws of mechanics. In this way we can know in advance, quite generally, that any particular state of a natural object *can* be explained by reference to some or other physical principle or principles, that is to say, before we are in a position to determine *which* principle or principles are relevant, and so to complete the explanation. In other words, granted suitable laws, we can show that the state of the particular body we are investigating is a necessary effect of some further natural state, of that body or another, and of nothing else. Thus Natural Philosophy can be em-

earlier, viz., that results reached by application of the method stand in need of a " guarantee " before they can be accepted as knowledge about this existent world. And this distinction I have inferred receives explicit confirmation in a letter by Descartes to Mersenne, dated 1638 : " You ask whether I hold what I have written on refraction to be a demonstration. I think I do —at least in so far as it is possible to give a demonstration *without having previously proved the principles of physics by metaphysics* . . . and in so far as any other question of mechanics or optics or astronomy, or one that is not purely geometrical or arithmetical, ever has been demonstrated. But to demand from me geometrical demonstrations of matters which depend on physics is to ask me to perform the impossible. And if you restrict the name ' demonstration ' to the proofs of the geometers, you will be compelled to say that Archimedes demonstrated nothing in mechanics, nor Vitellion in optics, nor Ptolemy in astronomy, and so on—which is not customarily said. For one is content in such matters, the authors having presupposed certain things that are not plainly contradictory to experience and having besides argued cogently and without fallacy, even though their assumptions are not exactly true " (AT, II, 141-2)—my italics.

ployed to explain particular occurrences, in the sense that knowledge of natural laws is indispensable for enabling us to decide *just which*, among various events independently known to us, *is* the particular one that accounts for the occurrence in question. Explanatory use of laws is one thing, however, discovery of them quite another. Their explanatory ' use ' is to enable us, in particular cases, to elicit and identify that particular fact, out of a multitude of others intimately connected with it, which is the cause or explanation of the phenomenon we are investigating. But our immediate concern is with what Descartes has to say about the discovery of natural laws, not about their explanatory use.

Now to say, as Descartes does, that every natural law is deducible from the primary propositions of Metaphysics, by a lesser or greater number of intermediary steps, is not the same as to assert that this or that natural law *was so deduced* : " to be deducible " is not " to have been deduced." And when he says that all physical principles are deducible from metaphysical ones, he does not mean that all of them were so deduced by him. But those which he did not deduce he none the less claimed to be deducible, given the time and care required to carry out a protracted deduction. Those more concrete, less general physical laws, which, though deducible, were not deduced, from metaphysical propositions, could not, however, be received as certain knowledge, but only as hypotheses. Hence, though they are constituent parts of Physics, they are not constituent parts of Natural Philosophy—not until they have been shown to follow directly from those ultimate and independent principles of Natural Philosophy, and indirectly from metaphysical first principles. How, then, may laws of Physics, as distinct from laws of Natural Philosophy, be discovered ? Descartes's answer may be drawn from two sources, namely, from what he explicitly tells us in various places about the function of experience and experiment, and from an analysis of his own procedure in the resolution of particular problems in natural science. Writing to the physician Plemp in 1637, he says, " I practise that mode of philosophising in which there is no principle that is not mathematical and evident, and that does not lead to conclusions which are confirmed by true experiment " (AT, I, 420-1), and in the *Regulæ*, ii, he admits there are "two ways of reaching a knowledge of facts—by experience and by deduction," even though he has resolved to set aside (*Regulæ*, iii) "the fluctuating testimony of the senses" and "the blundering constructions of the imagination."

Descartes thus recognises that perceptual experience is in some sense indispensable for scientific knowledge, and that yet, in another sense, it is ineffectual, except in producing error. What he appears to mean is this: that 'sense-experience,' when its disclosures are focally attended to as in purposive observation and experiment, is never purely sensory. It always includes 'interpretation' of what is experienced. And the danger is due to our normally trusting and accepting such *interpreted* experience, without prior criticism of it, and without disengaging the sensory factor from the accompanying element of interpretation due to the intervention of judgment. The "testimony of the senses" is "fluctuating" in two respects, the one harmless, the other harmful. The purely sensory factor in a flow of sense-experience is "fluctuating" or changing according as we sense different sensa at different moments. Such fluctuation is neither true nor false, but simply occurrent and so factual. The "harmful" sense in which the testimony of sense "fluctuates" is that in which we put different *interpretations*, some positively false, others mutually incompatible, *upon* our sensa, then, failing to distinguish the experiential factor from our interpretation of it, proceed to regard *the whole* as 'sensory'—as experientially and immediately given, therefore as factual and indubitable. Voluntarily and involuntarily we refer qualities sensed to objects existing in nature as their causes, and it is this act of reference which is erroneous. There are three common types of such illicit existential reference, viz., that in which (i) a sense quality is transferred to an externally existing object, as really belonging to it, when it does not, but is merely judged by the uncritical to do so; (ii) different sensa, having incompatible characters, are all referred to the same object at different times, each as unconditionally characterising it; and (iii) sense qualities are referred to and located in non-existent objects (*e.g.* the continued 'localisation' of felt pain in a limb that has long been amputated). On all such occasions the source of error is the same. Falsity lies wholly in the existential reference, tacit or explicit—not in the sensum that is sensed and referred. So it is not strictly " the senses " that " deceive " us, but *judgment* by its illicit reference of what is disclosed in sensation. It is *criticised* sense-experience alone, then, which is safe and indispensable for Natural Philosophy. But even this is limited and negative in its function. For sense-experience, as operative in purposive observation and experiment, never contributes the constitutive premises of Natural Philosophy. These, we have seen, must be certain, so they cannot be inferred inductively from even criticised sense-experience. It *is* possible to infer general principles *of Physics* in this way, and Descartes himself, in fact, frequently does so ; but such inductions are of minor importance *for Natural Philosophy*, since they are only " probable knowledge." What, then, is the part of criticised sense-experience in his Natural Philosophy, as distinct from its ancillary rôle in his Physics ?

Deduction from principles that are universal yields only what is universal, so we can never become aware of this or that particular instance by deduction alone. But it is precisely the instances or particulars of experience that suggest or ' set ' most of our problems in the early stages in the development of a science, and it is to them again that a fully developed science must revert if it is to explain ' the concrete ' and be ' applicable in practice.' Now even if criticised experience alone could yield certain knowledge about particulars, it could not yield certain knowledge of general laws.[1] And even though deduction could yield certain knowledge of general laws, it alone could never bring us into contact with concrete particulars or ' instances.' Descartes is fully aware that he cannot, by deduction, pass from the most general laws of his Physics to this or that particular occurrence. The difficulty, then, is to see how to pass deductively from those few highly general independent principles of Natural Philosophy (the primitive propositions of geometry and mechanics) that are secured by the Metaphysics to one and another of that vast array of particular

---

[1] This he makes clear in *Regulæ*, xii, saying that we fall in error " so often as we judge it possible to deduce anything general and necessary from a fact that is particular or contingent " (AT, X, 424 ; HR, I, 45). This does not, of course, deny the possibility of ' intuitive inductions,' since their experiential facts are not contingent but necessary.

experiential facts, such as we commonly class together and call, say, the behaviour of magnets, the circulation of the blood, the transmission of light, magnification by lenses, etc. It is at just this juncture that sense-experience is apposite. The transition depends upon the intervention of sense, though sense alone can contribute no law of even the meanest generality,[1] any more than deduction alone can yield knowledge of any existent particular. Now it is often possible to formulate several alternative hypotheses, each of which is compatible with the primitive principles of Physics and each of which, *prima facie*, could account for the production of the phenomenon under investigation.[2] Deduction alone, however, can afford no ground for our choosing one rather than another of these alternatives as being ' the ' explanation we are seeking: so far as ' reason ' is concerned, they are equi-probable or equi-possible. So sense-experience intervenes here to justify rejection of one and another of these alternative possible explanations, until we are left with one which sense-experience also is seen to confirm. Thus its function is to negate all the alternants but one of the alternative proposition that sums up the *a priori* possibilities deducible. Descartes brings the points well into focus in the *Discourse,* part vi. : " Passing over in mind all the objects that have been presented to my senses, I venture to assert that I have not observed anything which I could not explain satisfactorily by the principles I had discovered. But I must also allow that the power of Nature is so ample and extensive, and these principles so simple and general, that I have observed scarcely any effect which I did not straightway recognise to be deducible from them in several ways, and my greatest difficulty is usually to find out in which of these ways it is that the effect depends on them. In such circumstance, I know of no other plan than to devise afresh experiments of such a nature that their result is not the same if it has to be

[1] We review natural phenomena " not indeed so as to use them as grounds for proving anything, for we want to deduce the explanations of effects from their causes, and not those of causes from their effects, but simply so that out of the countless effects we judge possible of production from those causes, we may limit our minds to the contemplation of some rather than others."—*Prins.*, III, iv (AT, VIII, 82).

[2] Cf. " Now the principles which I have already discovered are so wide and fruitful that very many more things follow from them than we can see to be contained in this visible world, and many more even than our mind could ever survey in thought."—*Prins.*, III, iv (AT, VIII, 81).

explained in one of these ways as it would be if explained in another " (AT, VI, 64-5 ; HR, I, 121).[1]

So if we ought "to put small faith in observations not accompanied by true reasoning," Descartes emphasises quite as much the necessity of experiments " in order to support and justify reasoning." Thus the principal functions of experience and experiment, those for which no amount of deduction can be a substitute, are (i) to furnish occasions (by acquainting us with what is concrete and particular) on which we may conceive and formulate problems for solution ; and (ii) to furnish grounds for denying rival hypotheses, each of which is a possibly true explanation of its phenomenon, since it follows from some set of ultimate, demonstrated principles. In this way experience discloses particular facts of different orders for analysis : the existence of light, its reflexion and refraction ; the phenomena of sound, heat, weight ; the properties of metals, glass ; the behaviour of tides, meteorological data such as rain, snow, lightning, thunder, rainbows ; the phenomena of plants and animals—their germination and growth. The principles demonstrated *a priori* are the key to explaining all such particular, concrete objects of nature, their states, and changes disclosed to us in experience.

II

Let us now turn to Descartes's theory of the constitution of the existent natural world. We have seen that he defines Substance in two ways. Whatever depends for its nature and existence on no other existent is absolute substance, and nothing but God has such existential independence. Besides God, there are matter and a plurality of selves. These are described as " secondary substances," for the nature of a self and of the whole natural world is each defined by a single, qualitatively independent attribute. And there is a further difference between absolute and secondary substances. The nature of

---

[1] The procedure Descartes indicates here recalls Bacon's ' crucial experiment ' (cf. *Nov. Org.*, III, 36), though where Bacon's problem was to disengage the cause from a complexity of interconnected conditions, Descartes is concerned with deciding between two equi-possible explanations of an effect when we know that only one really does explain it, but are ignorant of which it is.

THE NATURAL WORLD

the former is exclusively composed of attributes that are never determined as "modes," though they are intrinsically of a determinable character, while the history or behaviour of each kind of secondary substance, though essentially definable by an exclusive attribute, are continually being manifested by some or other modes of its own determinable attribute. This fundamental difference between absolute and secondary substances is summed up in Cartesian language by saying that the nature of absolute substance never changes and that it is "perfect" or complete, while the nature of either of the kinds of secondary substances, though eternally determinable, is from moment to moment being differently determined, and so 'changing.' The determinations or "modes" of an attribute, then, articulate the *history* and *behaviour* of a secondary substance, the attribute itself expressing its ultimate nature, while an exhaustive enumeration of attributes would express the "perfect" or complete nature of absolute substance. So to say that God is "immutable" and "eternal," that God does not 'behave' or 'have a history,' is therefore to say that the determinable attributes of God are never determined into modes. These distinctions between substances, attributes and modes are, we shall see, of capital importance for Descartes's Natural Philosophy, and determine the ultimate structure of his whole Metaphysic.

Duration, we have already noticed, is a simple nature, therefore a real characteristic of substances. But time (an arbitrary though convenient and constant measure used to define particular durations) characterises not the enduring thing, as its duration does, but our percept or idea of the enduring thing. Time is a relation between any two durations, and, in a sense Descartes does not state very clearly, depends on the mind that compares them. He sees that something arbitrary has to be introduced before such a comparison can be made. The duration selected as a unit or standard of measurement (*e.g.* that of the earth's rotation about its axis), though convenient in practice, is rationally arbitrary, extraneous to that which is submitted to measurement (*e.g.* the duration that has elapsed while writing this page). And, like time, he holds that number and all universals that are not simple natures are "only modes under which we consider things"

(*Prins.*, I, lv-lix)—what we may call 'categorial ideas,' under which we think of certain particulars as resembling each other.

Descartes has been at pains throughout the Metaphysics and the Natural Philosophy to establish various distinctions. Now besides the things distinguished, the distinctions themselves call to be distinguished. He recognises three 'kinds of distinction' which he calls "real," "modal" and "rational" (*Prins.*, I, lx-lxii). Substances are *really* distinct, for any one can be conceived without the logical necessity of conceiving any other. Thus, one self is *really* distinct from any other self. And a self is really distinct from its natural body, although empirically they are always found in intimate connexion. Of "modal distinctions" there are two kinds, that between a mode and its substance (*e.g.* our earth's revolutionary motion and matter), and that between two modes of the same attribute of the same substance (*e.g.* the revolutionary motion and the spherical shape of our earth). Of two forms also are "distinctions of reason," namely, the distinction between a substance and its attribute, and that between two essential qualities of that substance (*e.g.* its duration and its extension). To express what is distinguishable in thought though not separated in existence is to draw a "distinction of reason." To recognise such distinctions as being of the kind they are is the more important, for frequently, failing to do so, we pass from permissibly characterising a thing by one quality without characterising it by another to falsely asserting it to possess the one but not the other. So Descartes distinguishes three ways of 'being different,' and thereby at least three 'modes of being.'

The Natural Philosophy, lifted out of its justificatory setting in the Metaphysics, constitutes a universal physics that is kinematical, geometrical and rigidly deterministic. This "concrete geometry" is a long demonstration, progressively more detailed, of consequences following from one ultimate and fruitful postulate, namely, that every natural event and property which is not a simple nature is completely explicable by two sets of laws, those of movement and those of extension. The logically primitive principles of geometry and mechanics are to account, without remainder, for the variable characteristics of natural bodies and for relations between them.

We may conveniently begin our survey of the Natural

THE NATURAL WORLD

Philosophy by drawing what Descartes would call a "modal distinction" between the qualitative character of natural bodies and the change and movement they exhibit, and discussing each separately. Since the former refers to the constitutive characters of *all* material bodies, it may suitably be called an account of the nature of matter, as distinct from the latter—a theory of the nature of movement. The characteristically Cartesian argument to prove that determinable extension is the one attribute necessary and sufficient to define the essence of matter proceeds by elimination of alternative possibilities. Uncritical common sense infers from unclear sense perception that the 'materiality' of what is material consists in precisely those characteristics through awareness of which a body becomes known to us as 'present.' We perceive a material body to possess a certain size and shape as well as some colour, weight, and perhaps smell or taste. But, if we perceive a change, intensive or extensive, in one of these qualities, we do not infer that the body now present is no longer the same as the one present a moment ago. Hence the essential nature of that body must consist in an attribute that it *continues* to possess throughout all its changes of state, and, therefore, in no quality that only momentarily or temporarily characterises it. And Descartes thinks he has produced conclusive grounds to show that matter can only possess determinable spatial quality along with the capacity to be moved. Other qualities than these matter *appears* to possess, or possesses conditionally (*i.e.* when it is suitably related to a nervous system), but extension in three dimensions it possesses really or unconditionally. It is quite conceivable that bodies should not really be coloured and only appear so to observers, but it is *in*conceivable that bodies should really be without any size or any shape whatever at every moment of their existence. They *need* not have qualities of the former sort (now usually called "secondary" qualities), but they *must* have some of the latter kind in order to *be* 'bodies.' Descartes is, in fact, prepared to go further. Since we cannot conceive "secondary" qualities clearly and distinctly,[1] nor understand how they

---

[1] Consider, for instance, hardness—a quality popularly believed to belong to natural objects. Descartes points out that we know nothing clear and distinct about it. If we analyse what we mean by "the hardness" of a body, we shall find, he thinks, that we analyse it away into something quite different,

'belong' to their objects[1]—as we can conceive clearly how "primary" qualities determine their objects—it follows not merely that secondary qualities *need not*, but that they *do not*, really characterise their objects. Appearance is a contingent relation, but only natures related by a necessary relation are possible objects of certain knowledge. The fact that natural bodies can and do *appear* to certain animate bodies is an important one, since it enables animate bodies to acquire the capacity of behaving fittingly towards them. The main value of appearance is utilitarian or biological. Matter depends in no way upon our minds, only knowledge of it does. Matter exists and possesses its nature independently of any perceptive or intellectual activity on our part.

Now by studying geometry we reach a number of clear, distinct and fruitful conceptions about the nature of the space with which Descartes identifies this single, determinable attribute that defines matter. We conceive clearly and distinctly that it is susceptible of partition in three dimensions, and from this property of it we can find meanings for such terms as length, breadth and depth. With these, and such simple natures as 'point,' 'straight,' 'curved,' clear meanings may be supplied for speaking of 'a surface' or of 'a solid,' of the former as circular or square, of the latter as spherical or cubical, of two surfaces or solids as being 'at a distance from' each other, or of one being 'above' or 'below' or 'behind' the other, and so on. Thus, given a homogeneous three-dimensional space of indefinite extension, and the right to conceive it as 'partitioned,' the possibility of a world of figured parts having all conceivable sizes and shapes is demonstrated. Now extendedness

substituting for it in the end the clear notion of *movement*. " Hard " bodies are those that resist the motion of other bodies that are also " hard," though less so. If, for instance, *every* body receded whenever our own body moved into contact with it, as in fact happens only to *some* bodies (*e.g.* water, air), we should never have come by the confused idea of hardness. But this would be no ground for inferring that physical bodies did not exist. Hence hardness is not an essential quality of matter.

[1] Different secondary qualities seem to stand in different relations, and not all in one and the same relation, to the body that is commonly said to " possess " them. The scent of a rose does not seem to stand to the rose in the same relation as, say, its redness. " Confusedness " in " secondary " qualities seems susceptible of degrees. It is exceedingly difficult to discover what sort of relation it is that relates the colour quality and the natural object, as is abundantly shown by the meticulous analyses of Professor G. E. Moore and others in recent years.

THE NATURAL WORLD

does not intrinsically entail a limit, so we can say of the natural world, that particular substance it characterises, is likewise unlimited in extent. It is, however, internally diversified, partitioned into homogeneous parts, and our own stellar system is simply one portion among others of this totality which is Nature.

But what justification have we for speaking of space as "partitioned," or—since matter is only another name for space—for speaking of material bodies in the plural, rather than of a single, undivided whole of matter ? And, again, even though the real nature of matter can be exhaustively described by its extension in length, breadth and depth, and the most determinate characteristic of any natural body defined in terms of a space of this kind, the *behaviour* of a body having such a nature still requires explanation. For the natural world does not consist of bodies that are endlessly at rest, but of bodies that are continually moving and changing. Movement and change, however, though they presuppose spatial extension, are not deducible from it. Descartes is therefore required to account for both the partitioning of a single, homogeneous, existent space, and for the fact of movement and change in respect of its parts, partitioned items or particular 'bodies.' And it is one of the most characteristic features of his Physics that he accounts for all three—the plurality and individuality of figures or 'things,' their change of place and their change of state—in terms of one and the same 'nature,' viz. motion. This is the source of the multiplicity of natural bodies as well as of their diversity.[1] And all diversity is purely formal, none

[1] Adamson refers in his *Development of Modern Philosophy*, p. 28, to Descartes's " remarkable mode of finding a means of introducing multiplicity, variety and concreteness into the abstract representation of extended body." The introduction of " multiplicity " movement is certainly claimed to effect, also, in an exceedingly limited degree, that of " variety " (viz. purely formal variety). " Concreteness," however, it certainly does *not* claim to introduce, nor does Descartes seek to introduce it by any other means, but purposely excludes it. The natural world is not intended by Descartes to be conceived as " concrete "—there is no plurality of *concrete* or material bodies, analogous to the plurality of " concrete," conscious selves. While, according to Descartes, Smith, Brown and Robinson *really* are, and can be understood clearly to be, three separate conscious substances, a chair, a table and a stone are *not* really, hence cannot be clearly understood to be, three separate extended substances. They can only be, as indeed they usually are, confusedly *mis*conceived as being three separate, " concrete " things. They *really* are divisions within a single homogeneous substance which is existent space. Descartes's Philosophy of Nature is rigorously monistic, his Philosophy of Mind alone is pluralistic (cf. *Principles*, I, 51–3).

is qualitative. There is no ultimate difference of quality between chalk and cheese, each is simply some aggregate of particles making up a quantum of three-dimensional space.[1] Numerical and structural differences of natural objects are therefore extraneous to the nature of the world, and so must, in some sense, be " imparted " to it by, or " imported " into it from, some external source. Here, then, we come upon a necessary connexion between Natural Philosophy and Metaphysics. To deny that motion is deducible from extension is not, for Descartes, to deny that it is deducible, but to imply that it is deducible from something else. Logically, there are two courses open to him. He might try to derive it, as he derived time, from the conscious activity of existent selves, so that movement would be simply an apparent characteristic of natural bodies, and not a manifestation of their actual behaviour. Or, he might try to derive it from the only other sort of existent remaining—absolute substance or God. Descartes does not appear to consider the former alternative (which Kant adopted later), and would probably have argued that we had a clear and distinct idea of the movement of bodies and a genuinely ' natural ' inclination to believe in the reality of motion, so this belief would only be erroneous were God deceptive. The alternative he does select is the latter—not, however, because it is the only one left, but because God's nature is such as will allow him to deduce, besides the reality of motion, its laws as well.

Movement, the only nature suitable for determining or partitioning into modes the single, homogeneous, determinable space, must be conceived as ultimate, incapable of analysis or definition. If we try to define it as, say, ' a sort of action by which a body changes its place,' we shall be assuming (i) that " action " has an appropriate meaning and is definable independently of movement, and (ii) that " place " has significance, prior to movement. But, on the first head, it must be objected that we may only speak of " action " here by analogy with

[1] To the charge that such extension is simply a mathematical abstraction that has no existence apart from minds, Descartes ironically answers : " A pretty objection indeed ! . . . that all things that we can understand and conceive are, considered in themselves, nothing but imaginations and fictions of our mind . . . from which it follows that there is nothing except that which cannot be understood or conceived or imagined which should be received as true."

our own volitional effort or conscious activity. Such " activities," however, are purely mental in quality, therefore cannot be invoked to modify a nature that is exclusively material. Secondly, by speaking of " its place " we shall be assuming that there is one place which is " the " place occupied by a given body and which remains ' fixed ' and capable of being occupied by another body when vacated by the former. Descartes, however, holds a relational view of space. The " place " of a thing is determined by its relation to other things which, for purposes of definition, we agree to consider immovable. So we cannot say of any one body, without reference to any further body, that it is moving or that it is at rest. To say that a certain body moves or has moved is to say that it is no longer related by the same relations of distance to the same other bodies as it was at a prior time, but that it is now related either to the same bodies by different relations of distance, or that it is related to other bodies by either the same or other relations of distance. A body moves only relatively to some other body to which it approaches or from which it recedes. Of two bodies X and Y, between which the distance varies, it is indifferent whether we say that X ' moves ' and Y is ' at rest,' or that X is ' at rest ' and Y ' moves.' There are, then, no points in the world that are really fixed ; " nothing has a permanent place except in so far as it is fixed by our thought." And nothing is really at rest. We may, for convenience, agree to speak of a thing being at rest, in the sense that a man seated on board a ship is ' at rest ' relatively to the ship's deck, but ' moving ' relatively to the shore. Movement is real—it is indeed an ultimate or simple nature—but place is a " distinction of reason."

Though this identification of matter with space strikes us as odd, it does so, Descartes thinks, only because of two widely held but erroneous beliefs concerning (i) rarefaction and condensation, and (ii) the existence of empty space (*Prins.*, II, v-vii ; xvi-xix).

(i) It is popularly supposed that a body can vary in volume under certain circumstances, that it is bigger when expanded than when condensed. The truth is that under no circumstance can it do so. A useful meaning can doubtless be found for speaking of the ' expansion ' of a body, and of its ' contraction,' but they will signify a "distinction of reason" and not a "distinction of reality." A given quantum of extension which is 'the' volume of a certain solid cannot be increased or diminished in any dimension. To speak of something (*e.g.* a gas or a sponge) as being 'expanded' presupposes that not one body but many are in question. The particles of the body that 'undergo expansion' have been separated by a greater distance than that which separated them before. Consequently the interstices between the particles have been filled by *other* matter. In all this there is no alteration in the initial, total extension of the 'expanded' body, only a displacement of its component parts. So what we commonly call 'the expanded body' refers really, not to the object explicitly mentioned *alone*, but to that object along with all the particles of matter occupying the interstices between its parts. The sponge never comes to possess a volume it did not always possess; its extension is the same when it is 'filled' with water as when it is 'empty.' The difference is one of the disposition of its parts, and nothing else.

(ii) Closely connected with this is the common belief in the possibility of regions of unfilled space. That there cannot be a vacuum is evident directly we identify matter with space, for wherever there is space there is extension. All that it is permissible to mean by 'empty' space, then, is a region of space not filled with its previous or with expected content. It is not, for Descartes, trifling to say that an 'empty' vessel is not empty but full of air. Were it literally empty it would not be a vessel, for were there no distance whatever between its walls, they would coincide. Space, then, is essentially continuous, for it has no interstices or 'gaps' unoccupied. And from this it follows that there can be no atoms (*Prins.*, II, xx), for space is infinitely divisible, but an atom, though imperceptibly small, would have some extension, therefore its existence would constitute a limit to the divisibility of space.

Such is Descartes's account of the constitution of natural bodies, and of the conditions under which they come to exhibit their purely formal diversity and their internal changes of state. It remains to consider the change, not of state, but of place, that they manifest. Local movement is to be accounted for in terms of the properties of motion. Motion is manifested geometrically through variations of position, and, we saw, needs no reference to "action." Here Descartes recognises the possibility of a plurality of independent though correlated movements, and so renders possible the elaboration of a strictly rational kinematics. The general *character* of motion examined, he turns next to investigate its *causation* (*Prins.*, II, xxxvi).

We must distinguish between the cause of motion (its " first cause "), which explains how there should be movement in the world at all, and the cause of a particular movement (" secondary cause "), that on account of which a body acquires movement of specific velocity and direction which it had not before, and which it can " communicate " to another body. The former or " first cause " is God, and the quantity of motion " imparted " and preserved in Nature is constant (*Prins.*, II, xxxvi). For motion cannot be 'imparted' by space itself, since no property of space entails movement ; nor by selves, since motion presupposes spatiality, but no self is extended. Hence motion must be imparted by the only other kind of substance remaining, namely, God. And God, being omnipotent, does have sufficient power to impart motion to extension, and being unchanging, the quantity imparted and conserved must be invariable. So by two arguments—one from exclusion of possible alternatives, the other from the perfection of his formal reality—God is shown to be the ultimate source of all the motion in Nature. From this general conclusion Descartes proceeds to deduce a set of five " rules " or natural laws, adequate to explain the cause of this or that *particular instance* of movement manifested by some or other particular extended thing.

The first, an immediate consequence of the quantity of movement being invariable, is the law of inertia. " Every particular body, so far as in it lies, continues always in the same state, and a body that is once moved continues always to move."[1] No body changes spontaneously from its state of

---

[1] *Prins.*, II, xxxvii (AT, VIII, 62). The dual character of the formula is brought out more clearly in the French version of the *Principles* (AT, IX, 88), and in the *Monde*, ch. vii (AT, XI, 38) : " Each particular part of matter continues to be in one and the same state while the juxtaposition of other parts does not constrain it to change . . . if it has a certain volume, it will never become smaller unless others divide it, if round or square, it will never alter that shape except by external constraint, if it stops at a certain place, it will never move on unless another drive it, and if it has once begun to move, it will always continue moving with a certain force until others stop or retard its movement."

rest or of motion. The first half of the law asserts that some cause is always necessary to initiate movement, and this had long been recognised. But the second half (that a moving body unimpeded by another would continue indefinitely in motion) was quite an innovation.[1] The common supposition that a moving body slackens down and stops of itself is a prejudice formed in infancy from uncritical judgment based on sense-experience. Descartes's second law, that a moving body tends to continue its movement in a straight line, recognises that curvilinear motion requires the intervention of other factors than that which initiates its motion. These two laws are, together, substantially the same as Newton's famous " first " law, formulated some forty years later in his *Principia*. When, however, Descartes comes to consider velocity, difficulties of his " purely geometrical mechanics " come to a head. Velocity is not a geometrical property, not an extensive but an intensive one, to account for which he falls back on mass,[2] their product defining ' quantity of movement.' Having identified matter with space, he is able to define mass as volume, but, as Leibniz showed later, this device does not free him, for it is impossible to explain retardation of movement by volume or space alone. What is wanting is a property of *dynamical*, not geometrical,

---

[1] Descartes is, of course, fully aware of this. In the *Monde*, ch. vii (AT, XI, 41), he says: "We are exempt from the difficulty the learned encounter when trying to explain why a stone continues to move a while after it has left the hand that cast it. For what we should really ask ourselves is, why does it not always continue in motion ? The answer is easy to return : for who can deny that the air through which it moves offers some resistance to it ? We can hear the air whistle when the stone divides it, and if it be stirred by a fan or any object at once light and expansive, we may even feel it hinder the hand's movement. . . ." More than one of Galileo's published writings contained this ' law of inertia ' implicitly. Descartes may have discovered it independently, or he may only have made more plain and precise what was obscurely seen by Galileo. Descartes's letter to Mersenne (AT, I, 303) seems rather to indicate the former. Whichever it be, he was the first to have formulated, completely and logically, the conception of conservation of velocity in a straight line, and to have made clear its importance for a general kinematics. See further, P. Tannery, " Galilée et les principes de la dynamique," *Revue générale des sciences*, xiii, 33.

[2] James Ward's objection (*Psychological Principles*, p. 9) that " Dynamical concepts, such as those of mass and force, which only experience could warrant, were smuggled without clear definition or derivation into a physics that professed to be ' nothing but geometry ' " seems mistaken. True, such concepts can be derived only experientially, but I have tried to show that Descartes *can* so derive them, and such derivation does not destroy the geometrical character of his physics. The dynamical property in question is to be understood not as derivative from space, but as an ultimate, unanalysable property of the *movement* that is ' imported ' into space.

character, and Descartes seems to have seen this, but refused to introduce what probably he considered " occult," and what would have been inconsistent with the strictly geometrical character of his whole Physics.[1] The third law, that of impact, includes the other two, and sums up the conditions under which any particular movement occurs. " If a moving body that impinges on another has less force to continue moving in a straight line than the other has to resist it, it loses nothing of its movement, though it changes its direction ; whilst, if it has greater force, it moves the other body with it, losing so much of its movement as it imparts to that other "[2] (*Prins.*, II, xl). From these most general laws Descartes deduces seven special laws, applicable to typically different cases of impact[3] (*e.g.* as between two isolated bodies, between ' perfectly hard ' bodies, etc.). Liquids are distinguished from ' hard ' bodies in being constituted of small particles that tend to move equally in all directions, while the particles of a ' hard ' body, though touching one another, do not tend to move apart.

The more detailed and particular information this general geometrical physics can afford about the constitution, and even the origin, of such single, ' concrete ' bodies as the sun and this earth, is worked out in the third and fourth parts of the *Principles*. The results of Descartes's investigation of ' departmental ' problems, recorded in the *Dioptric* and the *Monde*,[4] supplement and complete the Natural Philosophy, when shown explicable by the primary principles of geometry and mechanics, and their connexion with the Metaphysics eventually established. Throughout Descartes's investigations, the formal unity presupposed in his views about both the character and the method of strict knowledge controls his

[1] Cf. Ch. XI, sect. III.
[2] Rather than clear and distinct ideas, " capacity to move " and " communication of movement " seem to be what Meyerson would call " irrationals." Cf. Ch. XII ; also E. Meyerson, *Identity and Reality*, ch. ix (Eng. trans., London, 1930).
[3] For a convenient summary see Bordas-Desmoulin, *Le Cartésianisme*, pp. 314–5. Paris. 1874.
[4] For a very full account and expert estimate of Descartes's contributions on these matters, and to geometry, see G. Milhaud, *Descartes Savant*, Paris, 1921. Valuable material is also contained in Millet, *Histoire de Descartes avant 1637*, Paris, 1867 (especially chs. v and x), and Bordas-Desmoulin, *Le Cartésianisme* (especially part ii). The main contributions to optics have been summarised very briefly by F. Wootton, " The Physical Work of Descartes," *Science Progress*, Vol. XXI, No. 83.

choice of problems, the order of their treatment and the use he intends making of their solutions. The *Monde*, a celestial and terrestrial physics, forms a systematic unity of doctrine concerning specific bodies whose nature is known by deduction, but whose existence can be known only by experience. His several conclusions about the distinctive behaviour of astronomical bodies and the conditions of its occurrence constitute, collectively, an elaborate and unified account of the natural world—an account which he believes can be made exhaustive and detailed without introducing any further explanatory principles except such as may be deduced from the principles of geometry and kinematics. The most general problem selected for analysis in the *Monde* is the nature and behaviour of light. For the purposes of this research, light constitutes an " absolute " term or nature, and its exhaustive, general analysis is shown to depend upon the solution of a number of subordinate problems. Descartes is enabled, by each successive explanation, to account at once for further peculiarities of light, and for its relations to a series of " relative " natures. Thus he is compelled to investigate in turn the sun and fixed stars, since it is from them that light mainly proceeds ; the heavens, as the transmitter of light ; the comets and our earth, as its reflectors ; then different types of body on this earth, for, if opaque, they reflect it, if transparent, they transmit it ; and lastly, that special type of body or " machine " that is so constituted as to perceive it. This last, an extensive and complicated problem, raises a number of additional questions which have no direct connexion with the physics of light, and is therefore treated in a separate work, the *Traité de l'Homme.* It is to the solutions of those questions which relate more closely to the rest of his Metaphysics that we shall pass in the next chapter.

VI

BODY AND MIND

" La philosophie médiévale distinguait le corps et l'âme moins réellement que Descartes . . . mais, par un renversement curieux des positions, à partir du moment où Descartes se décide à unir l'âme et le corps, il devient beaucoup moins capable que la philosophie médiévale de les distinguer. Ne pouvant les penser que comme deux, il ne peut les sentir que comme un, si bien que le protagoniste du spiritualisme pur en vient nécessairement à dire que l'on ne peut concevoir l'âme comme unie au corps sans la concevoir comme matérielle."—GILSON.

DESCARTES'S Natural Philosophy is a serious attempt to prove in detail two theses—that the character of all material bodies is to be adequately explained by the geometrical properties of an existent, homogeneous space, and that the behaviour, however varying, of those bodies, animate and inanimate, is ultimately reducible to instances of impact between them or their particles. And the ulterior aim of his metaphysics, we saw, is to demonstrate two things—that material bodies do exist and that they are in nature really and completely different from minds. Now it is precisely these four dominant theses which lend unusual significance in his philosophy to the problem of how mind and body are connected, and make its solution so desperately difficult for him. The defining attributes of body and of mind being wholly different, direct causal interaction between them is, he maintains, necessarily impossible. Its possibility is further precluded by the deduction that the quantity of motion imparted to, and conserved in, the world, is necessarily constant. For the self to initiate, by volition or any act, a movement in its body, would be for it to create and communicate an additional quantum of motion to that which has already been imparted to the world, from which it would follow that the total quantity is not constant but increased by increments whenever a voluntarily initiated movement occurred. Change or activity, then, consists in the occurrence of events in either of two mutually exclusive orders. Movements in space we call 'physical' events, changes of state in a self we call 'mental' events. Causes of physical events are always physical, never mental, and causes of mental events are always mental, never physical. All this is not, however, a *consequence* of the " real distinction " between attributes, but simply what it *means* to say in Cartesian language that " thought " and " extension " *are* " really distinct attributes." So it would appear from the outset that the question ' How are mind and body connected ? ' must be answered by a flat denial that they are connected. But Descartes cannot bring himself to maintain this. For we can be as certain that the natural body we call ' ours ' exists as we can be that any other natural body does. If experience warrants me in believing the sun and the stars to exist and to be material, with equal certainty does it warrant me asserting my own body to exist and to be material. Of the *existence* of this particular body I am assured by experience, and of its essential *nature* I can be assured, Descartes thinks, by observing its behaviour and explaining it in the light of his natural philosophy. But of the *connexion* between my self on the one side, and the body I suppose to ' belong ' to it, on the other, experience offers only a confused idea. Can ' understanding ' reach a clear and distinct one that can replace it ? Is their ' union ' deducible from any principle or set of principles established in the Metaphysics or the Physics ? The conviction with which we ordinarily believe that mind interacts with body, and body with mind, is of the strongest : it is presupposed in all our daily behaviour, both reflective and involuntary. What Descartes denies, however, is not the strength but the truth of this conviction. Even though the interaction were only apparent—a confused idea and one of the many ' prejudices ' unconsciously formed during childhood —still, how are we to explain such clear differences in outward conduct as are normally explained by assuming interaction ? If my body stumbles and falls I feel pain, if a stone falls I do not. But why do I feel pain in the one case and not in the other, if I am no more intimately connected with ' my ' body than I am with the stone ? Again, when I will that my body should move, my legs move, when I will that Jones's legs should move they do not. Why should these two bodies behave differently, if my mind is in no more intimate connexion with the one than with the other ? If such differences in outward behaviour of bodies do not prove interaction, but are simply a sample of the kind of observed fact from which I have falsely inferred it, how is the difference in relationship between my self and ' my ' body and my self and a stone to be explained ? Though we are not clear what sort of connexion it is that subsists between a self and the body it embodies, we *are* quite clear that it is a different relation from any that connects the physical body that is mine, and any physical body that is not mine. Can nothing more be said than that it is a " different " relation ?

It is one thing to adduce grounds to show that the connexion between the order of physical processes and the order of mental processes is not one of efficient causation—that only events of one and the same kind can be *causally* connected—and quite another thing to show that there is literally no connexion whatever between the two series. The latter view Descartes certainly never proposes. All the same, what he does adduce about their connexion does not constitute a definite or acceptable solution to the problem. Even though causal interaction be only apparent and affirmed through erroneous inference, *some* sort of connexion there certainly is, Descartes admits, between body and mind. Thus two questions arise for him to answer : (i) How do we come to *know* that there is a connexion ? and (ii) How is the connexion so known to be described ? (They should be distinguished, for it is quite possible that we should know the fact *that* mind and body are connected, and yet not be able to discover in *what* sort of connexion they stand.) Descartes's answer to the former, epistemological question, is that " the union of soul with body " is intuitively disclosed—that it is a fact having its place among the simple natures.[1] In reply to the second question, as to what is the

---

[1] Cf. his letter to the Princess Elisabeth, 1643 (AT, III, 664–5) " First, I hold that there are in us certain primitive notions. . . . Besides the most general, such as existence, number and duration, which are ingredient in whatever we can conceive, there are, for particular bodies, (the notion of) extension . . . for the soul, that of thinking . . . and lastly, for the union of soul and body together, we have only the idea of this union, on which depends our idea of the soul's power (*force*) to move the body, and the body's power to act on the soul by causing feelings and emotions."

The extreme unsatisfactoriness of this answer is too evident to call for long comment. All simple natures that are not relata but relations are " necessary," none are contingent. But that extended substance and thinking substance are *not* related by a necessary relation (it being possible to conceive

kind of connexion, all Descartes can say positively is, that mind and body are so related that whenever they appear to interact, the state of mind then existing is " the occasion " of the ensuing physical change that occurs in the body, or, that the state of the body then existing is " the occasion " on which the ensuing mental operation occurs in mind.[1] The grounds for this, which he considers " stronger than any met with formerly," come forward in his psycho-physics, so we must wait awhile for Descartes's final word. The highly general principles of kinematics outlined in the last chapter, being applicable to all natural bodies, inorganic and organic indifferently, are too general to account for the specific detail which differentiates animate from inanimate bodies, so further and more specific principles have to be introduced.

The anatomy and physiology of Descartes's natural philosophy is all in line with his celestial and terrestrial mechanics. The animated body or " machine " is differentiated from inanimate matter in no essential respect, but simply in exhibiting greater complexity in the disposition and function of its parts and greater heterogeneity among its constituent corpuscles. This Descartes sums up by saying that " the body of man is

of either without having to conceive the other) is one of the two most important conclusions reached in the Metaphysics !

Further, it is made quite clear in the *Regulæ* that the outstanding characteristic of simple natures (now rather confusingly called " primitive *notions*") is their perfect clearness and distinctness. But the ' notion ' of " union," disclosed on direct inspection of the terms related, seems, beyond question, a most confused one. The union is certainly not deducible *a priori*, yet it cannot be established by experience as certain, *i.e.* as clear and distinct.

[1] There are several places at the beginning of the *Traité de l'Homme* where Descartes speaks of the self thinking such and such a thought *on the occasion* of what is occurring in the body, and in the *Dioptric* he refers to certain movements being *the occasion* of certain thoughts. Again (letter to Arnauld, 1648), describing the physiological mechanism of memory, he refers to the flow of animal spirits in the brain as being *the occasion* of revival and thence of recognition. The term " occasion," of course, explains nothing. It covers more than contemporaneity, yet what ' more ' Descartes does not say. The difficulties of his qualitative dualism are more noticeable here than elsewhere. Arnauld saw these difficulties fully, and in the *Quatrièmes Objections* (AT, IX, 158) asks Descartes if he has not proved " too much." Had he not so separated body and mind that he cannot connect them again into a " substantial unity " ? Regius, too, saw Descartes's embarrassment, and to meet it took a step he would not take. With greater consistency, Regius deduces the consequence that the connexion is only a *contingent* one ; man is an *ens per accidens*, not a *verum ens per se*. Had Descartes accepted this (but he emphatically rejects it—cf. his letter to Regius, 1641, AT, III, 459–64) he *could* then consistently have explained our knowledge of the connexion by confused perception.

nothing but a statue or machine made of earth,"[1] a view later endorsed by Leibniz in the declaration, " all that takes place in the body of a man or any animal is as mechanical as that which takes place in a watch."[2] There is no difference of principle in the explanation of organic and of inorganic matter. The datum to be explained in both cases is a mode of " matter." Positively, the explanation will be mechanistic : negatively, it will omit all reference to " substantial forms." As we have seen, not only are all ' secondary ' qualities to be extruded from scientific explications, but the " occult " qualities which mediaeval physics ascribed to natural bodies—the " natural levitation of air," the " natural gravitation of earth," " nature's abhorrence of a vacuum "—are to be set aside, and accounts exclusively in terms of motion and determinable space are to be substituted. Thus, writing to Mersenne in 1631, he says : " I shall attempt to explain what weight is, what lightness is, what hardness is, etc.," and besides such " general qualities of bodies " as these, he tries to explain their " substantial forms " as well. For instance, the " form of heaviness " in this or that body, after being reduced to " weight," is accounted for in terms of movements of particles. The notion of " the heaviness of bodies " is scientifically otiose and unintelligible. Aristotelian physics, so far as applied to particular natural objects, was essentially an ' explanation ' of that type, and physics remained ' explanatory ' only in this sense until the advent of Galileo and Descartes. It was a study of Nature in the sense of a study of natural as distinct from artificial " forms." The physicist was occupied with discovering and classifying the substantial forms or generative principles which account for the origination of natural objects, their change and the succession of concrete characters they temporally assume. The ' matter ' of these objects was ' an irrational,' indispensable but unintelligible. All that was thought to be understandable was " the forms " that informed such irrational matter so as to render it the actual concrete individual substance known to us. Thus, for instance, a cold body was said to possess coldness " in act " and warmness " in potentiality." Given a

[1] *Traité de l'Homme* (AT, XI, 120).
[2] The simile of a watch became a stock illustration at this period. Before Leibniz, Descartes and Geulincx had both made use of it.

K

suitable cause (*e.g.* fire), that body becomes hot " in act," and therefore said to possess " the form of fire," and so to be endowed with " the faculty of burning."[1] Descartes seeks to make a clean sweep of all such " forms," and denies any explanatory value to such " faculties." And he is, he thinks, by this means, enabled to reduce biology in its entirety to a mechanistic physics. Aristotle had tried to connect biology with psychology so as to form one composite science, Descartes tries to separate them completely.

Organic bodies capable of movement as wholes (*i.e.* other than vegetable organisms) are of two kinds—those which are, and those which are not, so connected with a self as to form a substantial unity. The former, ordinarily called ' animals ' are machines or automata pure and simple. Instinct, usually regarded as the most characteristic peculiarity of animal activity, is reducible to automatic movements essentially like those performed by any machine artificially constructed. The actions and reactions possible of performance by the " *bête-machine* " are more varied and complicated, but they presuppose for their explanation no more than " some or other particular disposition of their organs."[2] The spider, for example, is simply a weaving machine, naturally, not artificially, constructed ; the mole, an automatic digging and boring

---

[1] The practice of making explanatory use of " occult " qualities dominated natural philosophy in varying degrees from Milesian times down to Descartes. In its extremest form it is responsible for the view that " the world is animated by, and is full of, ' gods.' " Thus Thales attributes a " living soul " not only to plants, but to amber and magnets, to account for their characteristic behaviour. Cf. Tannery, *Pour l'histoire de la science hellène*, 2nd edn, p. 77, Paris, 1930. For full example of the use of substantial forms in the physics of Descartes's youth, cf. Gilson, *Index Scolastico-cartésien*, pp. 126 *et seq.* Paris, 1913.

[2] Descartes, who stoutly advanced and defended Harvey's theory of the circulation of the blood, had apparently reached an essentially similar result before reading Harvey. Afterwards he finally rejected a large part of the Scholastic view and the " faculties " it had assumed to explain action of the heart. Unfortunately, however, Descartes did not also reject the Scholastic notion of " animal spirits," and seems still to have regarded them as semi-mental and semi-material, and hence suitable ' material ' for receiving impressions, or " direction," from an active spiritual substance (the self). Yet he had no right so to regard " animal spirits," which are, as Dr. Broad puts it, " just as material as methylated spirits ! " Until this time the Aristotelian conception of the soul as the animating and informing principle of the body had met with general acceptance. Now it is replaced, and the body regarded as a ' going concern ' on its own account—a conception highly favourable to a thinker who, above all, wants to maintain an ultimate disparity between ' mental ' and ' material.'

apparatus. And, so far as purely physiological activities are concerned, the human body, Descartes could have agreed with Samuel Butler, is " but a pair of pincers set over a bellow and a stewpan, and the whole fixed upon stilts." The characteristic activities of all animate bodies are to be fully accounted for through behaviourist concepts, in terms of mechanistic actions, reactions and " conditioning " processes. Nature exhibits no purposive action, this is possible only to organisms that exist in some real union with a rational and volitional self. The functions of a human body, then, are simply those of an exceedingly complicated piece of mechanism, but human conduct in its widest sense, including cognitive and volitional operations, cannot be exhaustively explained in terms of matter and movements alone, but require resort to the other determinable attribute—mentality—and its derivative characteristics.

The explanatory principle Descartes substitutes for interaction and attempts to carry right through his psycho-physics is a form of parallelism. The apparent interaction of mind and body is wholly though falsely inferred from sensory, affective and emotional experience. From sense-experience we infer the independent existence of material bodies, and are enabled, with the aid of memory, to imagine a world of such bodies which we never directly experience. Descartes does distinguish between sensing activity and sensum or item sensed. Sensing, imagining and remembering are mental acts requiring suitable physical situations as the " occasion " of the occurrence. The items sensed or imagined, however, are not, like sensing and imagining, shown to be modes of consciousness or modes of matter. On the vexed problem of the status of sensa and their relation to physical objects, Descartes offers no positive information, and, indeed, the problem remains unsolved to this day. A sensum specifically characterised cannot be accounted for mechanistically, and is, in fact, an ' irrational,' for no quantity of information about the physical conditions under which, say, vision occurs, can make intelligible the relation between light rays of certain amplitude on the one hand, and the determinate hue of the visual datum on the other. The problem, a large and most difficult one, cannot even be stated in a manner that is at once brief, accurate and non-technical. Of the main embarrassment, which consists in

the complete unintelligibility of the *de facto* connexion between
qualitative and quantitative determinateness, Descartes is
well aware, and this it is that leads him to call sensa of all
kinds " confused ideas," in contrast with simple natures which
are completely understandable. Sensa are occurrent items,
but the latter are not; further, they are complex, whilst the
natures are not, so he reasonably feels that the former demand
explanation, while the latter, being ' ultimates,' do not. That
sensa are " confused ideas " Descartes seems to hold for these
reasons : (i) Their nature is so peculiar that it cannot be deduced
from any set of simple natures belonging to any of the three
classes recognised, namely, ' mental,' ' physical,' and ' common.'
Being in fact other than complexes of simple natures, it follows
that they cannot be analysed into them by thought. Nor (ii)
are they themselves simple natures (though many are characterised by a simple *quality*), for relations between simple
natures can always be discovered, and once found, are seen
clearly and distinctly to be ' necessary,' whereas the relation
between a confused idea of sense and every simple nature is
peculiarly unclear. It certainly cannot be *seen* to be necessary,
and this Descartes takes as equivalent to saying that it is seen
not to be necessary. His assertions about the status of sensa
are not, however, always consistent, as we shall see in the next
chapter. He is definite on the point that sensa are ' epiphenomena,' and they are illusory if interpreted as belonging to
matter, since bodies, animate and inanimate, whose changes
are " occasions " or part-causes of the occurrence of sensible
appearances, are not characterised by the qualities that inhere
in sensa. In a word, ' things ' are not really characterised as
they certainly *appear* to us to be. All the same, the appearance of sensa to us is of the greatest usefulness. Their function
is to serve as ' signs ' signifying the existence of bodies whose
local presence to our own body may be harmful or advantageous
to it. Sensible signs, however, do not resemble the things they
signify, any more than the set of letters composing a name
resembles the thing that it names (cf. the *Monde*, ch. i; AT,
XI, 4). The body presented for perception consists in fact of
a unity of particles in varying relations from moment to
moment, but we perceive that body, not as a unity of moving
particles, but as a stationary, ' inert ' thing, having certain

shape, size, colour, weight and similar qualities. How far can Descartes carry his mechanical explanation of this paradoxical state of affairs ?

There are evidently two general problems here that he is required to solve, one the inverse of the other. How is a material object able so to affect a human body that its self can come to experience that object ? How does it come about that when a self wills to move its body, or a part of it, the body or part does move ? Or, briefly, how are we to explain apparent action of matter on mind, or of mind on matter ? Let us consider the former case first, taking sensory experience as a fair sample of specific problems of its type.

Descartes's account of sense-perception divides into three consecutive stages : (i) that series of causally connected events comprising both those occurrent in the ' exciting ' body and those stimulating the nerve-endings or sense-organs of the percipient's own body ; (ii) a continuation of the series of movements propagated from the affected sense-organ, along the nerves[1] and terminating in the pineal gland located in the centre of the brain, on which gland (iii) an impression is produced (conceived quite ' mechanically ' as an impression by a seal upon wax), on the occasion of which physical impress a conscious act (awareness) occurs. Such are the ' bare facts ' Descartes proposes in explanation of sensory stimulation and the perception it occasions. The last stage it is that prevents him from finally dismissing the ' mind and body ' problem. How is he to explain, compatibly with his metaphysical certainties, transition from a physical impression on a physical organ (the pineal gland) to the self's purely mental operation of perceiving ? All events leading up to this last " impress " form a purely physical series causally connected, but at this point the continuity is broken ; the relation between the glandular impression and the ensuing act of awareness cannot,

[1] Descartes conceives each nerve as a cord surrounded by a sheath, the animal spirits flowing between them. The *modus operandi* of, *e.g.* the optic nerve, is as follows. The retinal change occurrent when an object approaches the eye agitates the cord in the optic nerve, this in turn agitating a certain part of the brain. The last movement forces a quantity of animal spirits back along the tube of the nerve, thus increasing its pressure and so moving the eye-muscles. For the connexion between Descartes's " animal spirits " and the πνεῦμα of Greek physiology see the interesting remarks in A. E. Taylor, *A Commentary on Plato's Timæus*, p. 545. Oxford, 1928.

for Descartes, be a causal one. Yet it is not simply a relation of temporal succession. Moving particles can initiate motion in other particles suitably situated, but in no possible situation can a moving particle initiate motion in that which, *ex hypothesi*, is immovable and unextended, and therefore without spatial situation. The transition from quantitative to qualitative determination can be effected by interpolation neither of physical intermediaries nor of mental ones, however numerous. But though the theory fails to render the connexion between stimulation and perception intelligible, it has the lesser merit of simplifying the theory of visual perception current in Descartes's own day, according to which the direct ' object of vision ' was a " picture " resembling the natural object, deposited in the brain. For similarity of " image " and object, Descartes substitutes an irreducible *dis*similarity, the function of the image being, not to copy, but to signify.

But he does not always consistently observe this qualitative dualism among events. When outlining the mechanism of memory, for instance, he permits himself to speak of traces in the brain predisposing it to " move the soul " in the same way it had moved the soul formerly, " just as creases in a sheet of paper or linen make it more susceptible of being folded afresh in the way it was folded before, than it would be had it never been so folded." The factor in memory that consists simply of revival is quite mechanical, but not so the more characteristic factor of recognition. This last is a specifically mental act that occurs on the occasion that the physical image is reproduced.

The same hiatus yawns in Descartes's account of our feelings and emotional experiences which he calls collectively " passions." He first uses this term very widely to refer to any state whatever that occurs to the self on the occasion of some change in its body, therefore as *any* mental counterpart of certain kinds of physiological occurrence. And he speaks of " passions " in a narrower and more convenient sense to denote " those perceptions, feelings and emotions of the soul . . . which are caused, maintained and strengthened by some movement of the animal spirits " (*Passions of the Soul*, I, xxvii). This is approximately the use of the term in present psychology, and covers all affective states, including organic sensations with their

BODY AND MIND

accompaniments of pleasure and displeasure, and such emotions as anger, fear, joy, etc. Thus, in the wide sense, there are three kinds of "passion," distinguished by their origin, namely, those referred to some external, physical object as their ultimate source of stimulation (*e.g.* experiences of sound, colour, etc.), those referred to parts of the percipient's own body for their source (*e.g.* temperature, organic and kinæsthetic experiences), and those referred to the experiencing self for their origin (*e.g.* emotions of fear, joy, etc.). All such "passions" are confused; they partake both of the nature of awareness (hence are referred to as "perceptions") and of the character of feeling, the self being 'passive' when modified by them (hence are called "passions"), while the acutest of them may fairly be called "emotions," since they 'disturb' or 'agitate' the soul in a more lively way than do clear and distinct ideas.

Now any set of movements which constitutes the physiological counterpart of a sensation or an emotion gives rise to "reactions," in the sense that it continues into, or incites, a further set of movements within, and sometimes also without, the stimulated body. In this way the mechanism of emotion is able to effect all that volition can secure, or is in the habit of securing. This natural tendency of 'afferent' motions to be continued and so stimulate 'efferent' motor nerves and end-organs, taken with what we have been told about the mechanism of habit, shows how emotions may "incline the will" or influence it to act, without such action involving 'expenditure of energy' on its part.

But on some occasions the will is not so "inclined." Rather than endorsing the inclination lent by present emotion, it turns *volte face* in opposition to it, and '*counter*-acts' present feeling. Here, then, is a particular example of the second form of the 'mind and body' problem (raised on p. 149), in which the terms are related in inverse order. And when we consider what Descartes has to say about apparent exercise of will on body, essentially the same difficulty as before arises, though accent now falls on the mental rather than on the physical term in the relationship. The self is "free." But this, for Descartes, is merely an analytical proposition, an assertion that the self is active in its activity, and passive in its passivity or endurance of "passion."[1] Being free, its actions cannot be constrained by any physical cause. Free action of the self, then, or its volition, can counteract a "passion"; not immediately, however, by checking the emotive process during its course in the nervous system, but only mediately, by "directing" the flow of animal spirits[2] so as to repress or inhibit efferent movements occurrent in the peripheral nerve-endings or organs. Facility to arrest such efferent movements from taking external effect is gained by practice and is explained by habit, or, as we should now say, by the 'law of exercise.' Thus, to illustrate, the self cannot directly enlarge or contract the muscles of the eye, but it may do either indirectly, namely, by voluntarily causing the object of vision to approach or recede from the eye. Thus by will it is possible to train the body to perform certain actions and refrain from performing others, and with application, we are told, "even the feeblest souls can acquire quite complete dominion over all their passions." So it would presumably be more appropriate to speak of training the body than of training the will in connexion with the moral regulation of conduct.

Do these solutions Descartes offers to the several restricted problems, each a special case of the general problem of what sort of connexion it is uniting body and mind, make the 'substantial union' intelligible? Surely it is evident they do not. Sensory perception, memory, emotional experience, willing, and formation of habit—in each of these interaction is virtually assumed, though it is expressly denied in accordance with the

[1] "Of the two sorts of thoughts distinguished in the soul (of which the first is its actions, *i.e.* its volitions, the others its passions . . . which comprise all kinds of perceptions), the former are absolutely in its power and can be changed only indirectly by the body, while the latter, on the contrary, depend absolutely on the actions which produce them, and they can be changed only indirectly by the soul. . . . The whole action of the soul consists in this alone, that, in willing something, it causes the little gland to which it is intimately united to move in the way required to produce the effect relating to this volition" (*Passions of the Soul*, xli ; AT, XI, 361–2).

[2] This does seem to presuppose a direct action of mind on matter, though not an intervention that involves increasing the total quantity of motion in the universe. Cf. Hans Driesch: "The Non-mechanical might *turn* portions of matter with all their inherent forces, and so change the direction of given forces. This would not alter the principle of the conservation of energy in its most general form—though it would, if this principle were enunciated for any of the three dimensions of space separately . . ." (*The Problem of Individuality*, Eng. trans., p. 37. London, 1914). But is not an alteration, even in the *direction* of the flow of animal spirits, a case of one-sided interaction?

terms of explanation Descartes has allowed himself. It is true that, as a result of these several investigations, we may now substitute for the general query : ' How can a conscious substance form a compound unity with a mode of matter ? ' the seemingly preciser one : ' How can a conscious substance be constantly " present to " the pineal gland ? ' But of what avail is this re-formulation ? *Is not the " presence " in question as unintelligible as the " union " ?* Descartes seems to suppose that he has dissipated confusion and obscurity by (1) selecting the pineal gland as the single, ultimate and central recipient to which all afferent movements in the human body converge, and from which all efferent ones depart ; (2) identifying that gland with " the seat of the soul " ; and (3) distinguishing purely mechanical movements (which explain physical change) from the flow of animal spirits (which explains physiological change). But is it not plain, with regard to (2), that, since the self is neither extended nor spatially situated, to speak of the pineal gland as " the seat of the soul," or of the soul being " present " to it, is to speak not merely in metaphor but in misleading metaphor, since its meaning rests upon a *spatial* analogy ? And is not Descartes further mistaken in supposing that because the animal spirits are rarefied, active and almost gaseous, they are therefore less ' material,' and hence of a nature more fitted for interaction with a spiritual substance or self ? Nerves, which are physical objects, are the media of animal spirits no less than of movements. The interpolation of intermediaries to make physical functions seem more mental than they are, and mental functions seem more physical than they are, is simply procrastination. Granted the conclusions of the Metaphysics and the Natural Philosophy, there is no logical way of avoiding collapse. Descartes fails to show how the self can move the pineal gland when it cannot move an arm or a leg, or how the self can act counter to physical changes in the muscles of peripheral organs, when it cannot act directly upon external matter at hand. Matter may be never so rarefied but it still has extensity and is still movable, therefore, on Cartesian principles, is, first and last, thoroughly ' material.'

VII

KNOWING, KNOWLEDGE AND THE SELF

" Du connaître à l'existence la conséquence est bonne."—DESCARTES.

" To proceed in an orderly manner," Descartes writes in the *Third Meditation*, " I must first arrange all my mental operations into certain classes, and ask in which of these, it may strictly be said, truth and error are to be found. Of these mental states, some are, so to say, images (*imagines*) of things, and such alone are properly named ' ideas.' Examples are, my thought of a man, of a chimera, of heaven, of an angel, of God. Other states have certain other forms as well ; for instance, in willing, feeling, affirming, denying—though I always apprehend a certain thing as being the object of my mental operation, that operation nevertheless contains something more than the idea (*similitudinem*) of that thing ; and states of this kind are called, some volitions or affections, others judgments " (AT, VII, 36–7).

Thus there are three ultimately distinct kinds of mental states occurrent in a self: (i) those which Descartes calls collectively " ideas " (*ideæ*) in a wide sense, *e.g.* awareness of sensa, images, concepts ; (ii) those he calls collectively " judgments " (*judicia*) ; and (iii) those which may, in a wide sense, be called collectively " affections " (*voluntas sive affectus*); ranging from elementary ' likes ' and ' dislikes ' to the emotions (*passions*) of joy and sadness, and states of desiring and willing. In accordance with this division, Descartes conceives the unique defining attribute of the self (*cogitatio*, i.e. ' consciousness,' not ' thought ') as a determinable quality that is being continuously manifested in three ultimately distinct modes that are related thus : volitions and judgments, though each possesses its differentiating character, are both based upon modes of the first kind, called compendiously " ideas."[1] In the fourth

[1] Descartes seems to have been the first to perceive that " ideas " and judgments were radically distinct. Brentano makes some valuable observations on the point in his *Origin of our Knowledge of Right and Wrong*, Eng.

KNOWING, KNOWLEDGE AND THE SELF

Meditation, where emphasis falls on the epistemic rather than the psychological character of cognition, and again the *Principles* and the *Notes*, Descartes refers collectively to the two classes of judgments and volitions as " voluntary determinations " (*determinationes voluntatis* and *operationes voluntatis*), to distinguish them from mere awareness or contemplation of " ideas," which he calls " act of understanding " or " intellectual activity " (*operationes intellectus*). The factor that is present in both " judgment " and " volition " but absent from " ideas " is a conative one ; there is an active, ' assertive ' element present in judgment as in desiring, and absent from mere contemplation or ' acquaintance.' Descartes's analysis of mental modes is careful enough to place beyond doubt that he is conscious of the equivocacy of the word judgment, according as we intend ' proposition,' whose import is simply contemplated or whose truth is no more than entertained in mind, or as we intend that act of assertion or denial by which, in W. E. Johnson's convenient phrase, we " pass judgment *upon* " that which is so entertained or contemplated. Thus there are several distinctions important for epistemology to be noticed. Though judgment presupposes acquaintance with some or other items sensed, imagined or conceived, it is not simply a conjunction of those items. On the other hand, what is contemplated is an object towards which attitudes of affirmation or denial may be significantly adopted, therefore acts of affirming and denying are other than that towards which they are adopted. So we may describe judgment as an intermediate mode of mental process. It resembles ' *ideæ* ' in the wide sense, since, like sensa, images and concepts, it is an object of acquaintance ; it resembles ' *affectiones*,' since, like desiring,

trans., pp. 13-14. London, 1902. The view that ideas and judgments are fundamentally indistinguishable, he says, " regarded judgment as consisting essentially in a combination or relation of ideas to one another. This was a gross misconception of its nature. We may combine or relate ideas as we please, as in speaking of a golden mountain, the father of a hundred children . . but as long as nothing further takes place there can be no judgment. Equally true is it that an idea always forms the basis of a judgment, as also of a desire ; but it is not true that in a judgment there are always several ideas related to one another as subject and predicate. . . . Whoever says ' God,' gives expression to the idea of God ; whoever says ' There is a God,' gives expression to a belief in Him."—Brentano suggests that sufficient attention has not been paid to Descartes's observations : " they were soon quite forgotten, until in recent times, and independently of him, they were again discovered. Nowadays they may lay claim to sufficient verification."

choice and decision, it includes a volitional factor. And both these characteristics—'contemplative' and 'volitional'—that characterise judgments, are *sui generis*, therefore indefinable.[1]

It will be our business in this chapter to consider what Descartes has to say concerning (1) the various cognitive activities of the self, and certain important epistemological problems connected with them; (2) the affective and volitional states of the self; and to see what more determinate knowledge of the self is possible in consequence.

The relations and distinctions of the three fundamental classes of mental facts which we have just considered are of high importance for Descartes's theory of the self and still higher for his theory of knowledge. He readily sees that the crucial problem of epistemology is to explain, not the possibility of knowledge, but the possibility of error. And what he sees so clearly is not merely that no theory of truth which fails to provide a satisfactory theory of error is acceptable, but the further fact, that by examining the constitution of erroneous belief we shall be laying bare at the same time the constitution of knowledge.

The truth of what is clearly and distinctly perceived is, we saw, ultimately guaranteed by a veracious and omnipotent God. In that case, how does it come about that we ever fall into error? Descartes's explanation is an ingenious attempt to do justice to this undeniable fact in terms that are at once compatible with his analysis of cognition (in *Meditation III*) and with his ascription of veracity and omnipotence to God. He first fixes upon a peculiarity of volition, not found in understanding. In respect of any proposition we can contemplate, it is possible for us to affirm or deny it. No doubt in actual practice we intend to affirm only what we believe true, and to deny only what we believe false. But it is certain that we often affirm and deny propositions of whose meanings we are but vaguely aware, or of whose import we do not fully seize. And though it is not our practice to affirm and deny capri-

[1] Descartes, it is true, expresses this difference between the 'contemplative' character of acquaintance and the active character of *affectus sive voluntas* rather awkwardly and probably inaccurately when he says that the former (understanding) is "passive," but the latter (will) is "active." If the antithesis, however, is taken as relative (as, *e.g.* Leibniz takes 'rest,' namely, as a small degree of motion and not complete absence of it), then probably none would disagree, and such a sense is all Descartes seems to require.

ciously, it is none the less quite within our power to do so—to assert that which we know to be false and to deny that which we know to be true. So far as 'power' to affirm is concerned, then, what we actually do does not coincide with what it is possible for us to do. There is, in fact, no proposition we can contemplate that we cannot affirm or deny or both affirm and deny if we choose. There is no limit assignable to the range of possible affirmations and denials. This fact Descartes expresses by saying that our volition is "perfect," "infinite," *i.e.* unlimited or 'complete.' But, when we turn from assertions and denials to the contemplation or understanding of the propositions affirmed or denied, we do not find that our understanding is "perfect" in an analogous respect. Some propositions are such that when we perceive them, we perceive them clearly and distinctly, therefore adequately; others are such that when we contemplate them we have only a 'more or less' clear insight into their import. In such cases, it seems that the propositions contemplated vary one from another in clearness and distinctness, and that these variations are quite independent of our volition. Even though we will to understand clearly that which we perceive unclearly, we very often fail to do so. So while our will is capable of affirming or denying every proposition capriciously, it is not capable of causing every proposition or sense-idea to be clear. This we may sum up *more Cartesio* by saying that while our will is perfect, our understanding is imperfect. In a different respect, however, Descartes maintains that our understanding is no less perfect than our will. True, there are many things we cannot understand, yet what we do understand clearly *is*, exactly as we perceive it. Though the limitations of our understanding are many, in no instance is understanding inherently "deceptive" or positively misleading in its disclosures. Therefore God is not to be blamed as a deceiver, for instances of 'imperfect understanding' are instances in which something is lacking in what we perceive, not instances in which something positive and deceptive is superadded to what is genuine in the disclosure.

So, Descartes decides, both will and understanding are "perfect" each in its own different way. If so, how does error arise? Not from either in itself, but precisely from their combination, answers Descartes. The combination of a restricted, limited understanding with an unlimited free will explains the occurrence of error. So long as we confined ourselves simply to contemplating our thoughts as they arise, never affirming or denying, we could never fall into error. But neither should we ever become possessed of any knowledge, for 'contemplation' or passive understanding is simply historical occurrence. Truth and falsity can relate only to propositions *about* what exists or occurs, not to occurrences. But the more eager we are to reach knowledge, and the less experienced or habituated we are in withholding assent from propositions proposed to our minds, the more readily do we give assent where we are not fully clear about what it is we are asserting. So erroneous judgment occurs when we use our perfect freedom imperfectly, asserting or denying what we do not clearly understand. We use this freedom rightly when we affirm only what is quite clear and distinct and refrain from assenting to what is unclear. For we are not compelled or 'determined' in the use we make of our will; it is as possible to suspend judgment as to give assent. And there are two sorts of occasion when we ought to abstain from affirming, namely, when we are not fully and clearly aware of the import of our proposition, and when, though fully aware of 'what is meant,' we are nevertheless ignorant of whether 'what is meant' is true or false, since we do not see that it is, or that it is not, implied by relevant knowledge. So it is never understanding but always precipitate assertion that leads us astray. And this freedom we exercise in yielding or withholding assent is the single characteristic we possess to " perfection " or without limitation, therefore the single respect in which our nature resembles God's nature. The freedom exercised by God and man is " infinite."[1] Now since in erroneous judgment we assert as true that which is false, it follows that if what we so

---

[1] Descartes is at pains to insist (*Prins.*, I, xxvi–xxvii) that to be infinite is not the same as to be indefinite. For what is infinite is clearly conceived to have no limits, whilst that which is perceived as indefinite is seen as having limits. Nor are they contradictories: the contradictory of infinite is finite, not indefinite, and the contradictory of indefinite is definite or distinct, not infinite. Infinity is an objective characteristic of a thing or quality; indefiniteness a character appertaining to our cognition and not to its object. Thus Descartes will say that God is known to be infinite, but space and duration are only seen to be indefinite. What, however, appears as indefinite must really be finite or infinite, and we can only *know* which it is by acquiring a clear and distinct idea of it.

assert happens to be that a certain sort of action or line of social conduct is right, and if we then adjust our behaviour in accordance with that erroneous judgment, the conduct resulting will be 'vicious' or morally wrong. Right and wrong actions are the counterparts in behaviour of true and false judgments, and Descartes, in company with Socrates, explains the occurrence of vicious conduct as a consequence of falsely asserting ourselves to have *knowledge* respecting possible alternatives of action. Our wills are free, and we choose and act on the wrong alternative because of erroneous judgment: *omnis peccans est ignorans*.

It is plainly of the greatest moment, then, that we should identify these characters of clearness and distinctness whose absence from cognition is followed by such serious consequences for knowledge and for conduct. Unfortunately Descartes's own statements about them are not themselves as clear and distinct as we could wish, though he frequently renews effort to make them so. He certainly does not use the adjectives synonymously: " The perception into which certain and indubitable judgment can enter must be not only clear but also distinct. I call that ' clear ' which is present and manifest to an attentive mind, and that ' distinct ' which is so precise and different from all other ideas as to contain only what is clear " (*Prins.*, I, xlv ; AT, VIII, 22). Further point is given to the distinction by an example (*Prins.*, I, xlvi), which shows that whatever is distinct must be clear, though what is clear need not be distinct. He says, " When one feels acute pain, the perception of the pain is exceedingly clear, but it is not always distinct, for we usually confound it with the obscure judgment that we form about its nature, thinking that there is in the suffering part itself something similar to the sensation of pain, whereas the pain alone is clearly perceived " (AT, VIII, 22). So there can be clear but indistinct perceptions, but no distinct perception that is unclear. And Descartes gives a second and very different account of what it is ' to perceive clearly ' (*Prins.*, I, xi) : " We know a thing or substance more clearly in proportion as we discover in it a greater *number* of qualities." The two statements do not, however, betray inconsistency, for what is being perceived clearly and distinctly in the two cases is very different. In the former it is a single, homogeneous quality or state; in the latter it is a complex of qualities related to an existent as its nature. But even so, in what exactly clearness and distinctness consist is not so distinct as to set aside all possibility of erroneous judgment respecting their presence or absence on particular occasions, even when due care has been exercised. A great deal turns on their precise meaning and difference, however, for the proofs that (i) material bodies exist independently of our 'ideas,' and (ii) that the nature of those bodies is composed of wholly formal properties, both depend on certain ideas being not only clear, but also distinct. And the conclusion that no material body really possesses a sensible quality depends on certain ideas being clear, but not on their also being distinct.

Now the difficulty we frequently encounter in identifying these characters of clearness and distinctness in particular contexts diminishes considerably their utility as criteria for giving or withholding assent. Much of the merit of a criterion perforce lies in it being final and unhesitant in its pronouncement as well as in being easy of application. Descartes does not overlook these desiderata. And if in the end he does not furnish us with a test that is absolute and easy, it is probably because no 'rule of thumb' exists. He therefore does the next best thing: he sets us on our guard against the kind of occasions on which we are especially liable to mistake for clearness and distinctness something very like them, but which is often deceptive and never trustworthy, namely, 'familiarity.' Many beliefs are persistently held, not because they are seen with clearness and distinctness to be true, but because, in common with our fellows, we feel an overwhelmingly strong inclination to affirm them, and that there should be the slightest need to examine them has never occurred to us. Further, among such beliefs, some that are not axioms nevertheless seem to possess one of their peculiar characteristics and are consequently frequently confused with them. Like genuine axioms, these " natural beliefs " seem clear to cursory inspection, and since they are not denied or questioned by ordinary people, we feel no need to try and justify them. But the familiarity of that which is " taught us by nature " must not be confounded with self-evidence: " When I say I am so taught by nature I mean that I am led to believe things by a certain spontaneous impulse . . . and not that their truth is manifest to me by a natural light. Now these two are vastly different, for what my natural light shows to be true cannot be in any degree dubious . . . (since there is no other faculty equally reliable that can teach me that what appears true to the natural light is not true). But of natural impulses, I have noticed in the past when choosing between right and wrong, that my natural impulses have often led me to declare for the worse part. Why, then, should I trust them more in other matters ? " (AT, VII, 38). Though what we sometimes accept *is* what " nature teaches," never may we accept it *because* nature teaches it. And that whatever is distinct constrains a percipient to assert it, does not imply that whatever a percipient is constrained to assert is distinct.

A careful reader of Descartes's discussions on these points will have noticed that he has more than once shifted his ground. He has quietly made a transition from speaking of " clear and distinct *judgments* " to speaking of " clear and distinct *perception* " and of " clear and distinct *ideas*." Now neither of the latter two ever constitute knowledge. To understand how the three are connected, and to facilitate consideration of the two principal epistemological doctrines that remain (concerning the representative and innate characteristics of knowledge), it will be useful to draw up a conspectus exhibiting the main differences and dependencies among those factors of cognitive situations that Descartes compendiously calls " ideas." ' To have an idea ' seems to indicate such different situations as these :—

(1) *Apprehension of Propositions :* i.e. awareness of what is present to mind in " judgments " (*judicia*) and capable of being asserted or denied, but excepting the assertive act itself. Propositions, we saw, may be unclear, or clear but indistinct, or clear and distinct. The last alone, after being asserted, can constitute ' knowledge ' for their assertor.[1] And such know-

[1] Borrowing W. E. Johnson's terminology (*Logic*, I, ch. iv) we may conveniently define Descartes's view of knowledge (*i.e.* ' what is known ' as distinct from ' knowing ') as : the class of those tertiary propositions whose primaries are characterised by ' distinctness,' and these secondaries by ' being certified intuitively or demonstratively.' Thus there is a certain uniformity of logical structure in whatever is ' knowledge,' the second and tertiary characters composing a constant factor, the primary proposition the variable one, in each instance.

ledge divides into primitive propositions established by a single intuition and derivative propositions established by a sequence of intuitions.

(2) *Apprehension of Concepts* : *i.e.* awareness of the immediate objects of conceptual or " pure " thought activity. These objects are " ideas " of either some discrete simple nature or a complex of simple natures, and therefore of a differentiating attribute, or some mode of it, or some particular determination of some mode, or a simple nature of the ' common ' class (*notiones communes*).

(3) *Awareness of Sensible Appearances.* These are (*a*) complexes of sense-ideas, analysable into simpler ideas or sensa (but never into simple natures, for these are purely conceptual and non-sensory), or (*b*) complex images, ' revivals ' or new combinations of ideas previously sensed.

Now every piece of knowledge is wholly explicable in terms of (1) and (2), and every occurrence experienced by sense in terms of (3). The mental operations concerned in (1) and (2) —*intellectus* or " pure thought "—are exclusively modes of the self's activity, whilst the sensory operations that are factors in producing (3) are wholly activities of our physiological organisms, and therefore modes of matter. The brain is always active in sensing and remembering, but never in thinking.

This epistemological dualism of knowledge and experience is a necessary counterpart of the original ontological dualism between materiality and mentality. Knowledge, being a function of the self's nature, is logically independent of the knower's body and its activities. By pure thought alone we know the nature and existence of a material world. And by pure thought we know it to be independent of our minds for its existence and nature, which independence is a prominent feature in all realist theories of knowledge. We never *perceive* the natural world or parts of it : we perceive only that which represents, and, indeed, mainly *mis*represents that world in sensory media. But though the materials of sense are logically independent of the materials of knowledge, since they contribute nothing that is even partly *constitutive* of knowledge, they are not psychologically independent of it (cf. pp. 127, 171). Descartes conceives the dualism between knowledge and experience to be so rádical and complete that he does not hesitate

KNOWING, KNOWLEDGE AND THE SELF 163

to say that if our self had existed apart from our body, and therefore apart from any sensory experience, we could still quite well come to a knowledge of the universe by the self's unaided operations. The fact remains, however, that the self we each know is not a disembodied one, and Descartes is well aware of the psychological dependence of the self's activity on that of its body. Thus sensory experience, a product of wholly physiological causes, serves as the occasion on which the self that is aware of the product as " confused idea," initiates its characteristic activity in respect of that obscure content seeking to replace it by a distinct idea on which judgments that are certain may be based and knowledge so attained.

Sense experience, then, has no direct epistemological value. Its value is, in a wide sense, utilitarian and biological. First, as we have just seen, it is instrumental in supplying the occasion on which intellect becomes actively enlisted in, say, formulating some hypothesis or solving some problem. And here its rôle is analogous to that of particular diagrams in solving a geometrical rider, namely, to aid memory or facilitate concentration of attention on relevant concepts. Secondly, sense experience is instrumental in a definitely biological sense. In fact, its primitive and principal function, like that of instinct, is not knowledge but adaptation. It enables animals, human and non-human, to control their body or animate machine, and hence their behaviour. Given, besides present perception, memory of similar situations experienced in the past and of successful responses then made, the body can now initiate movements that are again likely to prove successful in attaining a desired end, or that will so adapt it to present circumstances as to secure its preservation. Such ' correct ' responses as are made to satisfy bodily wants or to avoid harmful contacts with other bodies, plainly presuppose some form of prior ' stimulus ' or ' experience ' (cf. *Prins.*, II, iii). And the range of this primitive biological adjustment that is possible to animals may be extended on the part of humans by employing instrumentally conclusions reached through purely intellectual operations, deductive and inductive. The ' working success ' of these conclusions, however, does not establish their truth but simply their usefulness. There can be no compromise between the useful and the true. Though sense experience is sometimes instrumentally useful in the acquiring of knowledge, it more often is not ; and never is it, even partly, constitutive of that knowledge. Science is developed always from clear conceptions, never from unclear appearances. Indeed, these more often conceal than help to reveal the genuine character of things. Our awareness is thus on some occasions representative, on others misrepresentative, according as its objects genuinely represent things as they really are, or positively represent them as they are not. But even in such misrepresentations there are certain *de facto* connexions, empirical uniformities of co-existence and succession, and these we can observe and use as principles to predict the probable occurrence of appearances in the future, and so direct our behaviour along lines that have proved profitable.

The second epistemological problem raised by Descartes's account of cognition concerns not its worth but its causation, and the causation not of its " objective reality " but its " formal reality." In *Meditation III*, when examining " ideas " with a view to discovering which, if any, can vouch for the existence of something that is other than ' idea,' he divides all ideas into three classes. There are those we deliberately construct for ourselves (*e.g.* ideas of sirens and satyrs), those that seem to be caused by objects external to our minds (*i.e.* sense appearances), and those caused neither by our wills nor by external particulars (*e.g.* the primary axioms of logic and mathematics, ideas of existence, substance, duration, etc.). Now the occurrence of ideas of the first kind offers no special difficulty. Granting there are relatively simple ideas, and that our mental activity is on occasions ' constructive ' or combinative, the possibility of forming complex ideas is explicable. And the possibility of ideas of the second class occurring is provisionally met by his hypothesis of sensory mechanism outlined in the last chapter. But the possibility of our having ideas of the third sort (which he calls " innate ") has not yet been considered. Now the existence of simple natures shows how many (though not all) " innate ideas " should be *thinkable*. If asked ' How should existence or duration circularity or straightness, be *possible* objects of thought ? ' Descartes's answer would plainly be, ' Because the universe actually contains formal realities which are the objective causes of those conceptions, and for which reason those conceptions *are* conceptions *of* those realities.' But if it should be asked—not how such thoughts are thinkable—but how it comes about that we *do actually think* them, the reply must consist in assigning causes, not for the " objective reality " of those ideas, but for their " formal reality," as actually occurrent modes of mental activity. To state the issue otherwise, since strict knowledge consists in assertions respecting ideas of the third class alone, the question Descartes is raising is virtually the one which occupied Kant a century and a half later, namely : ' What explains the fact that we do actually possess knowledge, having due regard to the structure which that knowledge exhibits ? ' It could be no reply to point to simple natures, for their existence can do no more than explain how knowledge, constituted as ours is, should be possible ; it could not explain how that which is thus possible is further actual or occurrent. The doctrine of innateness, then, claims to account, not for the character of ideas of the third class, but for the fact that we *think* them—that we can and do think ideas of just those kinds. Our immediate question is then, briefly, ' What causes us to have such mental states as we do have when we are thinking clear and distinct ideas ? '

Now ideas of simple natures have two peculiarities which enable us to infer that their occurrence is not due to any constructive activity of our minds, nor to any causal action by external things. These ideas are ' ultimate ' in the sense of being irreducible or unanalysable into simpler ideas. And from the very fact that they resist resolution by analytic thinking on the one hand, and that they cannot have been constructed by combinative thinking on the other, it follows that they are so far ' imposed ' on our minds, and, being ultimate ideas, that they are ' imposed ' as *ultimate modes* of our thinking. The ideas thought, being ' necessary ' or invariable (since our minds can do no other than accept them), determine that our knowledge shall assume the form of an *a priori* and certain system, and that our thinking shall be ' objective,' ' constrained ' or ' necessary.' Nor can our minds be caused to think such ideas by the action of material bodies. Such causal action could be nothing other than movement. Now if any particular movement could cause a mind to think clearly and distinctly about anything at all, it could cause it to think only about itself ; the movement being particular, the thought would be *of* a particular. But ideas of the third class are—some axioms, others 'common notions'—ideas neither of particulars nor of movements. Hence material bodies and their changes could not be the cause of our thinking ideas of the third class. Nor could they for a further reason. Our assumption that a particular movement could cause a mind to think even that particular thought is inadmissible, for modes of matter can cause nothing but other modes of matter. Material bodies and their actions cannot possibly cause thoughts of clear and distinct ideas to occur, for physical actions and thoughts are modes of two mutually exclusive attributes. An event or state (mode) of one order, we have already seen, cannot cause an event or state in the other order. And if natural bodies cannot cause us to think clear and distinct ideas, no more can unclear appearances of sense. That ideas of universals are not derived by abstraction from sense appearances with which we are acquainted, Descartes maintains very definitely[1] and in opposition to Thomist teaching. It is notorious that no sensible appearances literally exemplify the initial concepts of geometry. Nothing that is strictly a point, that is perfectly straight or circular, as Euclid defines them, has ever been seen or felt. How, then, could we abstract in mind that which is in no sense 'contained' in the idea present to it ? And the radical incapacity of sensible appearances to cause clear and distinct ideas is still easier to see where the thought in question is one of God. This idea we certainly do think at times, and there is a sense in which we may be said to 'possess' that idea at times when we are not actually thinking it. But we could come neither to think nor 'possess' that idea as a result of abstraction from sensible appearances with which we have been acquainted, nor through combination of any sense given materials. For though in this case the idea is a complex one, it is not a complex of characteristics with which we can be separately acquainted in sense, as we are with the several characteristics of a 'composite' image, like that of a winged horse or a mermaid. And though it is true that the defining

---

[1] Cf. "But as to the essences which are clearly and distinctly conceived, such as triangularity or that of any geometrical figure, I shall easily compel you to acknowledge that the ideas existing in us of those things are not derived from particulars . . ." (*Reply to the Fifth Objections*, AT, VII, 380-1 ; HR, II, 226-7).

qualities of God's nature do happen to be possessed in limited degrees or " imperfectly " by particular persons, we could never have attained a clear conception of those qualities as existing completely or " perfectly " in God by simply removing in thought the limitations that restrict them in instances where they characterise particular individuals. Our conceptions of the various " perfections " that make up God's nature could not therefore have been reached through mental abstraction and elimination.[1] So it seems that no ultimate conception which enters into the clear and distinct ideas we think is reached abstractively from sensible appearances we are aware of, nor are we caused to think them by changes in material bodies, however related to our organism.[2] These results, then, give us the principal part of the negative meaning of Descartes's assertion that all such thoughts are " innate." But what more positive meaning does it convey?

Unfortunately his theory of innateness is not worked out so fully and clearly as we could wish. He appears not to have been interested in the matter on its own account, as a ' mixed ' problem in psychology and genetic epistemology, but to have pursued it only so far as it seemed to him necessary for explain-

[1] Descartes sums up all this by saying that our conception of God's nature is a positive and not a negative idea. It is impossible to explain the fact that we can think of a being who is completely good, truthful, etc., by the hypothesis that we recognise Smith, Jones and Brown to be good and truthful people, and then proceed to eliminate from our thought the limits to which these qualities are manifested by them, and so reach the idea of '*perfect*' goodness, " infinite " or " perfect " veracity—which *would* be to show that our ideas of those perfections are negative ideas. It seems plain that much criticism of Descartes along the lines indicated just misses his point. For he would ask, ' But how is it that we can think those peculiar qualities at all, even in the limited degrees they characterise Smith, Jones and Brown? ' Surely not by abstraction from sensible appearances of their bodies? The very fact that we do recognise these qualities, even imperfectly, to belong to them, itself presupposes that we can already think those qualities without having to refer to any specific limit or restriction. The hypothesis assumes something that has to be explained ; namely, our *ability to recognise* those qualities. Now the capacity to think of veracity, goodness, power, etc., as such, *i.e.* as " perfections " or completely (which does not, of course, entail that we can define or describe them), is not to be explained by a capacity to abstract them from particular instances in which they are present. For to abstract them we must first recognise them, and we could never recognise them as present in a limited degree unless we could think them unlimitedly and independently of instances. So to recognise that those qualities are 'imperfectly' present in this or that instance presupposes we can already conceive them positively and apart from any determination or limit, *i.e.* 'absolutely.' (Cf. further, pp. 241–2.)

[2] Cf. Descartes's criticisms of the ' manifesto ' of Regius at Utrecht : *Notæ in Programma quoddam* (AT, VIII, 357–9).

ing the fact that we can and do think some ideas without our will or external bodies causing us to do so.

What exactly is it that is " innate " ? Sometimes Descartes says that it is the *ideas*,[1] sometimes the *thinking* of them, at other times the *faculty*[2] of thinking them. Now although ' idea thought ' and ' act of thinking it ' (called indifferently mental " modes ") are not separate or independent existents, they certainly are diverse in character, hence distinguishable components in mental modes or occurrent states of mind. So to affirm the one to be innate is plainly different from affirming the other to be so. There seems no *a priori* reason for supposing that innateness on the part of the one should entail innateness on the part of the other. Which, then, are we to understand Descartes to declare " innate," the subjective or the objective factor in the pure thought situation ? Had the matter been set before him in these terms, it seems he would have answered that both were innate. And it is probably this two-sided innateness which he first of all had in mind as justifying his provisional division of " innate ideas " from " adventitious " and " factitious " ones, though that division, as he himself saw later, is indefensible. This two-sided innateness thus differentiates those mental modes which consist in our thinking of simple natures from the mental modes that are states of remembering or imagining. Those ideas that are thoughts of simple natures are " innate " in the sense that all minds, whatever their individual differences, agree in being constitutionally or naturally

[1] Cf. letter to Mersenne : " I hold that all those (primitive geometrical ideas) which involve no affirmation or denial are *innate* in us, for the organs of sense bring us nothing like the idea that arises in us on the occasion (of their stimulation), and so these ideas must have been in us beforehand " (AT, III, 418).

[2] " He (Regius) appears to differ from me only verbally, for when he says ' the mind has no need of innate ideas or notions or axioms,' and at the same time allows it a faculty of thinking (imputed ' natural ' or ' innate '), he is plainly asserting the same as I, and dissenting only from my verbal expression. For never have I written or affirmed that the mind needed innate ideas which were in any way different from its faculty of thinking, but when I observed certain thoughts in me that proceeded, not from external objects nor from a determination of my will, but solely from the faculty of thinking within me, then, so that I might distinguish the ideas or notions (which are the forms of these thoughts) from other thoughts, I called these *adventitious* or *factitious*, and the others, innate. In the same sense do we say that generosity is innate in some families, and that diseases like gout or gravel are innate in others, meaning not that babes in those families suffer from these diseases in their mothers' womb, but that they are born with a certain disposition or faculty to contract them " (AT, VIII, 357-8).

predisposed to produce those thoughts, and to re-think them in fresh combinations and in different contexts.

What is first postulated, then, is the existence of an innate *capacity* of a certain sort (namely, a native disposition to produce clear and distinct ideas which are all ideas of simple natures) after certain (unspecified) mental development has been completed. To be sure, it is difficult to discover what exactly we are to understand by a ' capacity.' But the difficulty is not one that Descartes alone has to face, and it is not directly due to his view that only pure thought is capable of producing those cognitive situations in which the objective constituents are ideas of simple natures or ideas deducible from them. Explanations of the phenomena of memory and imagination invariably assume some form of more or less permanent dispositions and traces, and the very conception of knowledge being ' owned ' or ' possessed ' by persons assumes it no less. At no one moment of our life do we have explicitly present to mind literally all the countless miscellaneous items composing our stock of knowledge to date, but we do not regard their absence from mind as evidence that we do *not* know them, but only as showing that we cannot think of everything at once. Thus there are two importantly different senses in which we are said to ' know ' a thing—that in which the thing in question *is*, and that in which it *is not*, being contemplated by us at the moment when we are truly said to ' know ' it. And it is in both these senses that we are rightly said to know, for instance, mathematical tables, conjugations of verbs, stanzas of poetry and learned material generally. Even though we do not have, at any given moment, those " ideas " explicitly present to mind, we do have, at that moment, the capacity to bring them to mind. And in speaking of this *capacity* as " innate," Descartes adds no new difficulty to those already attaching to the notion of ' disposition ' or ' ability ' to reproduce or combine that underlies the ordinary assumption of implicit knowledge and memory-knowledge.

The peculiar difficulty and element of novelty Descartes's theory of innateness *does* introduce arises not from postulating a ' tendency ' that is innate, but from postulating a special class of ideas (in the sense of ' *objects* of thought,' ' thinkable items ' or pure concepts) which it is the proper business of this capacity to originate and reinstate in mind from time to time. We should indeed be quite clear that to originate just those pure concepts which are ideas of simple natures and ideas deducible from them is precisely *the* peculiar property which differentiates Cartesian intuition from other mental dispositions that are likewise innate. The mnemic dispositions and retentive capacities ordinarily postulated in psychology do not claim to be *originative* of something never before experienced, but simply to explain the *revival* of that which *has* been experienced. But the innate disposition of pure thought which Descartes introduces is to explain the *origination*, as well as the reinstatement, in mind, of ideas that have never been given in sense-experience and which cannot be extracted from it—namely, ideas of simple natures. The capacity of pure thought is innate, then, not only in the sense that any other radical mental function is, but in the further sense that when certain stages of mental development have been passed through, it produces of itself the ideas directly contemplated throughout the passage of judgment and inference. Now such an originative, creative disposition cannot be wholly structureless or indeterminate. The clear and distinct ideas that it produces, however general, are always determinate, hence the capacity (or set of capacities) to produce them must be determinate too. It is a capacity which presents to, and so proposes for, contemplation, a pure concept (*i.e.* the idea of some simple nature) or an " eternal truth " (*i.e.* a primitive principle or axiom) that is " necessary " and so not certifiable by sense alone. The active search for, and discovery of, new truths is a progressive operation of pure thought, an activity of the self alone, and its method of procedure (since the knowledge it is to attain is of natures and principles whose interconnexions are necessary) can be none other than one of *a priori* deduction. Descartes then would deny, as against Locke, the possibility of an *a posteriori* derivation of knowledge from contingent, experiential data ; what is admittedly sensory and contingent cannot impart to its percipient what it does not contain, namely, conceptual precision and necessity of connexion, and whatever lacks precision in its definition and necessity in its certification cannot be " knowledge " for Descartes. So underlying his conception of such an innate psychical disposition is the hypothesis that selves or minds have in common a certain definite constitution, and that, since they are essentially active, this constitution determines the character of the objective content or idea contemplated, so far as that content is made up of ideas of simple natures. Thus innateness ascribed to pure concepts (as distinct from its ascription to the capacity) has two important significations. Negatively, it indicates that the direct object of contemplation is not reached abstractively from sense-experience, but is generated or supplied by pure thought itself. Positively, it indicates that the direct object of contemplation so generated discloses representatively to the self, in its contemplative activity and knowledge, something of the real character and structure of the universe transcending it. In this way do our minds transcend themselves in knowing. They can do so because the pure thoughts they generate (categorial concepts, limiting concepts, primary principles) accurately reflect characterisations and relationships obtaining in reality. Thus a completed knowledge completely unified would be a complete reflexion of all reality.

The relation of the empirical to the *a priori* is not, at least, in the large, difficult to seize. The office of experience and education is to furnish occasions suitable for stimulating our innate capacity to evoke pure concepts. Experience, that is to say, is a necessary (though an insufficient) condition both of our mental development and of the stimulation of our innate powers, but in neither case does experience furnish anything that enters constitutively into ' that which is known ' in consequence of intuitive or deductive operations. But in view of Descartes's epistemological dualism, his insistence that our minds are never directly cognisant of physical bodies or events, but only of ideas that represent them, it follows that innateness must be ascribed not simply to those pure concepts and primitive principles he first of all divided off from other ideas and called " innate," but equally to the ideas from which they are divided, namely, those he called " adventitious " and " factitious." In view of what " innateness " has turned out to mean, *every* idea—" confused " no less than " distinct," " sensible " no less than " pure," " illusory " no less than " genuine "—must be innate, and the provisional tripartite classification of ideas (*Meditation III*) is superseded. That classification is in fact the result of an analysis which stopped short at a level no profounder than that of common-sense supposition. But these hasty and superficial speculations, resting upon mistaken assumptions about the causation of our mental modifications, cannot withstand criticism and must yield to a more coherent theory concerning the constitution of our minds. This Descartes thinks he supplies in terms of native dispositions and their correlative concepts and principles, which done, the antithesis is seen properly to be *not between the innateness and non-innateness of activities, but between the confusedness and distinctness of the items directly apprehended.* In other words, the *fundamenta divisionis* of a serviceable classification of ideas will be characteristics of the contents apprehended, not characteristics (causal or other) of the apprehensive activity. This seems to be the nature of the ' correction ' which Descartes's theory of innateness introduces into the naïve account of cognition.

VIII

THE SELF AND ITS FREEDOM—"*OMNIS PECCANS EST IGNORANS*"

"If, in point of fact, the surest knowledge is that of the self, the reason lies, not in the necessity of the case and not in the nature of knowledge, but in the superior interest of the psychical and the greater preoccupation with it."—J. LAIRD.

FROM considering the cognitive characteristics of the self's states and dispositions, we now turn to their affective and conative peculiarities, and notice in conclusion what are Descartes's final words on the self as a persistent substance.

All mental states are modes of some one or other self's existence. Of those states, some occur to the self only provided certain physical changes have taken place in its body, others occur independently of bodily changes and follow directly on some previous mental modification. Thus there are two sorts of occasion—bodily and mental—on which affections and conations may occur. States presupposing bodily changes of any sort for their occurrence Descartes calls " passions " of the self [1] and " actions " of its body; [2] those requiring certain mental changes, but depending on no sort of physical change for their occurrence, he calls " actions of the self." Accordingly, all awarenesses (contemplations but not affirmations) of clear and distinct concepts or of self-evident principles are " passions " or passive states in a self's history, no less than sensations, unclear perceptions, feelings and emotions. A self is active or

[1] Pascal follows Descartes in regarding as "passions" all states that a self directly experiences but does not initiate by its will: cf. *Discours sur les passions de l'amour*. Such states are " thoughts that belong purely to the mind though they are occasioned by the body."

[2] Cf. *Passions*, xvi : " How all the members (of the body) may be moved by objects of sense and by the (animal) spirits, *without the soul's assistance*. . . . All the movements we make without our will conducing to them (as in breathing, walking, eating, and, in short, in all the actions we perform in common with the brutes) depend on naught besides the natural disposition of our members and the course that the spirits . . . pursue naturally in the brain, nerves and muscles—in the same way that the movements of a watch are produced by nothing else than the strength of its spring and the shape of its wheels " (AT, XI, 341)—my italics.

assertive in discriminating, judging and willing; passive in sensing and feeling. Volitional acts, which, in strictness, are initiated by the self alone, divide into two kinds, according as their end or fulfilment lies in some further state of the self that wills (*e.g.* desire for greater knowledge), or as it lies in some state of that self's body (*e.g.* desire for more physical strength). Our cognitions likewise fall into two classes : those that are perceptions of our own mental modifications, hence self-awareness in all forms (such cognitions being " actions " of the self), and those that are perceptions of physical objects and changes as they are present to us in idea, all such being " passions " of the self. The latter, too, are susceptible of innumerable degrees of confusedness and indefiniteness : the less confused are cognised as sensible appearances of physical bodies (*e.g.* a visual appearance of my own body to myself), the more confused as either organic, kinæsthetic sensations[1] more or less vaguely localised in the body, or as emotions (*e.g.* joy, love, sadness) which, though often intenser, are still less distinct and unlocalisable. In this way Descartes comes to define quite generally the self's passions or affective states as " the perceptions, feelings or emotions of the soul . . . which are caused, sustained and strengthened by some motion of the animal spirits " (*Passions*, xxvii). For passions may be fairly called " perceptions," since, though unclear, they are more like clear perceptions than they are like volitions ; " feelings," since the self's attitude on their occurrence is rather one of reception than of assertion ; and " emotions," because no other state disturbs the self in such a lively or even vigorous degree.

It is significant and characteristic that Descartes's general definition of passion should be a psycho-physical one. The inmost quality of feeling of pleasure or displeasure, or of the primary emotions, is, in each case, indefinable, not only because it is simple, but because the state itself is confused. Affective states are, indeed, examples *par excellence* of what is confused. They cannot, therefore, be direct objects of distinct and certain

[1] Descartes distinguishes sharply between the sensational and the volitional factors in ' wants ' and appetites. Cf. " The natural appetites, such as hunger, thirst, etc., are likewise sensations excited in the mind by means of the nerves of the stomach, fauces, etc., and are entirely different from the will which we have to eat, drink, etc., and to do all that we think proper for the conservation of the body ; but because this will or appetition nearly always accompanies them, they are called appetites " (*Prins.*, cxc ; AT, VIII, 317–8 ; HR, I, 291).

THE SELF AND ITS FREEDOM

knowledge, but only of immediate, intermittent and momentary *experience*. We can experience them, remember experiencing them, record the fact, and no more. Affective states, then, can be objects only of indirect knowledge. That is to say, they can be known only descriptively, as being those directly experienced states that are the confused, unanalysable epiphenomena of certain analysable physical changes collaterally occurrent in the experient's body. So Descartes's psychology of affection must, from beginning to end, be a physiological psychology. For the only explanations we can hope to reach that are precise and certain will be statements directly about certain bodily movements that are correlated with affective states, since it is only of physical properties that distinct ideas, hence strict knowledge, can even theoretically be attained. So Descartes establishes one of the most important general results in his theory of the passions (cf. *Passions*, xxvii–ix), namely, that that character of mental states he calls their " confusedness " is— in all the innumerable degrees of its manifestation—directly, a function of the state's intensity ; indirectly, a function of certain characteristics of its correlated bodily state (viz., of the quantity, direction and location of movements in the experient's body). The degree of confusedness in appetitive or affective or emotional experiences (*e.g.* feelings of hunger or cold, of pleasure, of anger or fear) vary concomitantly and directly with the intensity and other characteristics of the physical disturbances occurring in the nervous system and connected parts of the individual's organism.

All emotions, then, have essentially the same cause—a physiological change of determinate character and location. So this change plainly cannot serve to explain the phenomenal differences among emotions revealed in immediate personal experience. Hence, since emotions can be classified only on the basis of characters that differentiate them, Descartes must now consider, not the mechanism of their initiation, but their relations to those apprehensible objects that are invariably co-present and are popularly and loosely said to cause them. Now objects that excite emotional reactions are capable of doing so, not because of any peculiarities their appearances present to the observer, but because of their efficacy in affecting his body helpfully or harmfully. Thus the sorts of object, the awareness of which is emotionally significant for him, are those which he apprehends, by instinct or past experience, as being instrumentally and biologically useful.

Accordingly after explaining the physiological mechanism underlying emotional reaction, Descartes turns to the properly psychological business of disengaging the irreducible kinds of emotion discoverable on retrospection. These primary kinds, once elicited, are to be described in terms, not of their phenomenal but of their functional characters, not of their inner experiential peculiarities but of their potentialities for affecting our bodily behaviour, and consequently social conduct. In which and how many ways can external bodies facilitate or obstruct the desired and desirable behaviour of our own bodies? To answer this question seems to be the purpose of Descartes's analysis of affective and conative experience.[1] Now one and the same object can at the same time affect different men in different ways, and within limits affect the same man differently at different times. That which paralyses one man with fear excites courage or temerity in another.[2] The exciting object is the same, hence the differences in its emotional effects, and the dissimilarity in outward behaviour expressive of their different emotions, must be due to differences inherent in the

[1] Descartes is evidently working out the psychological prolegomena to any system of ethics that could fairly be called 'Cartesian,' and what would have doubtless served as a basis for his own ethics, had he constructed one. No ethical theory at all systematic or comparable in detail with his physical theory was ever supplied. Even the *Passions de l'Ame*, in which he is to investigate only *en physicien* and not *en orateur ou en philosophe moral*, was composed (he declares in a letter to Picot, 1648 : AT, XI, 324) " to be read by none but a Princess, and one of such uncommon powers that she understands without effort things which present the greatest difficulty to our doctors." (The " Princess " is, of course, Elisabeth.) His reason for refusing to publish any systematic work on Ethics is apparent from a letter addressed to Chanut some two years earlier (AT, IV, 536) : " The professors are so incensed against me on account of my harmless principles of Physics, and so angered at failing to find in them a pretext on which to denounce me, that, were I after this to write on Ethics, they would leave me no peace." The completion of Descartes's philosophy in this respect falls to Geulincx.

[2] " The same impression that a terrifying object makes upon the gland, and so causes fear in some men, can awaken courage and daring in others, the reason for which is, that all brains are not disposed in the same fashion. The same movement in the gland which in some excites fear, in others causes the animal spirits to enter the crevices of the brain and so be drained off, partly into those nerves whose function it is to move the hands for defensive purposes, and partly into those which agitate and drive the blood towards the heart in the way required to produce the spirits proper for continuing this defensive action and for retaining the desire to do so" (*Passions of the Soul*, xxxix).

bodies of the men affected (*Passions*, xxxix). Relatively slight dissimilarities in organic structure and physiological function are sufficient, Descartes thinks, to explain the occurrence of extremely unlike and even opposite kinds of emotion. So though the objects capable of exciting some kind of emotional response in an organism are too numerous for enumeration, the different ways in which those objects can affect human bodies and the different sorts of emotional state they can excite in human minds, are, on the contrary, astonishingly few. For there are, according to Descartes, only six kinds of emotion that are really primitive and irreducible, namely : states of unmixed wonderment, love, hatred, joy, sadness and desire. Evidently there are very many emotions that are not purely and simply one or another of these, but all those others, Descartes maintains, are derived from these primary ones. They are ' derivative ' in two senses of the word, being either, like esteem or disdain, a " species " of some primary emotion (cp. *Passions*, cxlix), or, like pity (cp. *ibid.*, clxxxv), analysable into a species of one primary emotion blended with some other. Seldom do we experience a primary emotion in its primitive purity, but usually a secondary and complex one, generated from some sentiment or organised system of emotional tendencies centred in a specific kind of object. The combinations possible are, in fact, innumerable, so there are many ' mixed ' emotions for which we have not single names, and which must therefore be indicated by descriptions.

The first of the primary emotions is wonder, that " sudden surprise of the soul which causes it to consider attentively whatever seems rare and extraordinary," or the surprise at finding the object different from what was expected. Wonder has four peculiarities :[1] (i) it is based on an awareness of the thing that evokes it, but not, as with other emotions, because of the evil or good that thing bodes us ; (ii) its occurrence is a

[1] Cf. *Passions*, lxx : " Of Wonder, its Definition and Cause " (AT, XI, 380 ; HR, I, 362). Ribot, in his *Psychologie de l'Attention* (Eng. trans., pp. 29–30, Chicago, 1890), having described surprise or astonishment as " spontaneous attention augmented," declares that Descartes (in the above place) has specified " nearly all the elements that we have endeavoured to point out in the mechanism of spontaneous attention "—that, allowing for verbal differences, Descartes clearly enumerates " the augmentation of nervous influx in consequence of the impression, its partial conduction towards the muscles, the action of these muscles in order ' to support ' and ' to strengthen.' "

M

precondition of the occurrence of any of the other five primary emotions ; (iii) it has no contrary, for if there is nothing in the object perceived that moves us in the least—if no element of novelty is disclosed—our observation of it is passionless ; and (iv) the " shock of surprise," so intimate an ingredient, attains its full force from the very onset. And when an object is perceived to be " suitable " or beneficial, we feel a liking or love for it : when seen to be bad or hurtful, then a dislike or hatred of it. Love and hatred are therefore described as emotions which incite the self, ." to unite itself freely with," and " to will to separate itself from," objects it has judged to be favourable or harmful. So Descartes plainly sees that such states contain an intellectual as well as an affective factor—an active besides a passive one. But unlike wonder and surprise, neither love nor hate can be felt until a judgment of good or evil[1] has been passed on the object perceived ; that is, until the self has re-*acted*, by volition, to its cognition. And there is another respect in which the self is active here. For to unite itself " *freely* " (when loving) with the object perceived, or " to *will* " to separate itself (when hating) from the hated object, marks an act of consent or dissent—in either case, an act of will respecting certain incipient movements in the experient's body that are preparatory to suitable outward behaviour. The self's action in passing judgment, too, illustrates a further dependence of the self on its body. For the very possibility of it evaluating the object present presupposes past experience of that object's effects on the body to have survived, concentrated and united, in the present. But this survival, whether or not now accompanied by an act of memory, is possible only through the instrumentality of the body, and, in particular, of certain preformed traces in the brain and certain physiological changes now occurrent there.

[1] Prof. Brett comments on this : " Descartes is well aware that one of the links in this chain of causation is a judgment of value ; he accepts the fact that an emotion is caused by the relation of some external datum to the person, and that this relation only exists in and through the person's valuation of the object. To sustain his mechanical explanation Descartes is compelled to make this appreciation a brain-process capable of moving the animal spirits in a unique manner, and so changing the character of the blood. In modern terminology this might be considered as equivalent to explaining emotions by vasomotor disturbances and changes in the secretions. Descartes was inclined to accept such formulæ, but he was not ready to reduce emotions to nothing but physiological changes " (G. S. Brett, *History of Psychology*, Vol. II, p. 238).

THE SELF AND ITS FREEDOM

Descartes's analysis of the emotion of love is both curious and acute. First, we have seen, he uses the term in a very wide sense. It is defined as that emotion by which " we regard ourselves . . . as united with what we love, in such a way as to imagine a whole of which we form only one part, and the thing loved another,[1] whereas in hatred we conceive ourselves alone as being the whole concerned and as absolutely separated from the thing for which we have aversion."

Denying the common view that love has several species,[2] Descartes maintains that the difference between benevolence (well-wishing by the self for the object loved) and concupiscence (the self's desire to possess its object) is based, not on an essential difference in the love itself, but on differences among its effects. However dissimilar its objects, however various its effects, liking, or love, is essentially the same in all its manifestations, and these vary only in intensity. All the same, distinctions may be conveniently drawn on the basis of the ratio that a self's love for the loved object bears to its love for itself. Thus, if one's feelings for the object, say, an animal, is less than that felt for oneself, the degree of love is named " simple affection " ; where the liking for the object equals the esteem one feels for oneself, the degree of love is one of friendship (and this can be felt only for persons) ; and when one's esteem for the object is far greater than one's self-esteem, then there is devotion. Devotion, however, may be felt towards things other than persons—for a country, for an institution—as well as for persons.

And it is from belief in the beneficial or detrimental effects that the object contemplated can have on our nature—*i.e.*

[1] Further point is given to this definition, and the " love which is purely intellectual " is distinguished from " love which is a passion," in Descartes's illuminating letter to Chanut, dated 1. ii. 1647 (AT, IV, 600 ff.).

[2] The ways of common speech are an unsafe guide through suggesting distinctions in what is undistinguishable as well as through failing to distinguish what is distinct. It is not accurate to say the miser loves his gold, and the drunkard his wine, says Descartes. The drunkard and the miser have love solely for the *possession* of those objects ; the love is not for the objects as such, on their own account. But the lover or the father has love solely for the persons beloved themselves. He seeks their good as his own, or even before his own, since his love for them is greater than his love for himself, he therefore conceiving himself as the lesser part of the whole in which he stands related by his love to his beloved. Unlike the miser, the father loves not the *possession* of his child, but—his child, directly and absolutely : unlike the father, the miser does not, in strictness, *love* money, but *desires* money ; what he loves—the direct object of his emotion—is the *possession* of money.

from an intellectual evaluation of the object in relation to our own well-being—that all other passions, as well as love and hatred, arise. In this way, for instance, joy results from the self's present possession of some good. And besides joy, the self " receives no other fruit from all the goods it possesses, so that when it finds no joy in them it may be said not to enjoy them more than if it did not possess them at all." Now this joy or pleasurable emotion, occasioned by bodily change, is to be discriminated from " the joy that is purely intellectual," initiated by the self's proper activity alone. This " intellectual joy," immanently caused, in which the self is conscious of itself as actively enjoying, is not a pure and unmixed experience, but is accompanied by, or fused with, the other kind of joy (gladness)—that passive condition in which the experient feels his general sensibility heightened. In those common situations, where a sort of undercurrent, pleasurably toned, forms a setting to the self's assertive attitude in *active* enjoyment, both factors are wholly mental, the latter being an action of that self, the former, a passion co-existing with certain actions in its body.[1] " Intellectual joy " and " intellectual sadness " proceed from a knowledge or belief that what we are possessing has some degree of goodness or of badness. In either case the evaluation is not a cold and colourless judgment of good or bad, but an assertion affectively qualified. Sometimes, however, we feel joy or sadness without fixing on any particular thing as its object, and therefore without performing an intellectual act of evaluation. On these occasions the self is so far passive in its experience. Consider, for example, the gladness we feel when our health is good and the weather bright : this gaiety is due to no operation of our intellect, but is an agreeable affection (*passio*) of the self following on some heightened or regular behaviour of its organism. And so constantly is one kind of physiological activity connected with joy and another

---

[1] Joy is intrinsically good, and sadness bad, hence, so far as the self alone is concerned, there could not be too much of the one nor too little of the other : " If we had no body . . . we could not too completely abandon ourselves to joy and love, nor too completely avoid hatred and sadness " (*Passions*, cxli). But since the self is related to a body, excess is only too liable to occur, for the corporeal accompaniments of unrestrained abandonment may, if very violent, be detrimental to bodily health, though if only moderate, be highly favourable to it. To speak of ' excess ' of an emotion has meaning then only in reference to a human body indirectly related to the emotion.

kind with pain that we normally fail to discriminate in the whole situation that which is a physiological condition of the body from that which is an emotional state of the self. In this way, the epithets ' pleasurable ' and ' painful,' properly applicable to states of the affected self, become silently transferred to co-existing conditions of its body.

Likewise emotional love (*amour sensuelle ou sensitive*) must be distinguished from " intellectual love " (*amour intellectuelle ou raisonnable*) to which it is related as a means.[1] The former confused state disposes the self to pass judgment on the object, and it is this active state (*pensée claire*)—an affirmation by the self—that constitutes, with its characteristic hedonic quality, *l'amour raisonnable*. Descartes is careful to emphasise that there are three factors discriminable in the situation: (i) certain physiological actions occurrent in the experient's body; (ii) their sensory counterpart, consisting of organic or kinæsthetic sensations, pleasantly or unpleasantly toned (the whole being *pensée confuse*); (iii) that immanently initiated state of the self (*pensée claire*) by which the self becomes " united with its object "—an act that is at once volitional and intellectual. That the third factor really *is* distinct from the second is evident, Descartes maintains, from the fact that in some situations, *e.g.* those of love, a self may experience the second (here, " sensual love ") without experiencing the third at all, as when the self fails to meet with an object that is for it lovable and therefore fails to become united by " intellectual love." Or again, a self may encounter an object with which it would willingly unite itself by intellectual love, but yet fails to experience any sensual passion respecting it, because its body is not suitably disposed towards it.

Love is " extremely good," for, " uniting us with what is truly good, it so far increases our own excellence." It can never be too great, for " even the most excessive love can but so completely unite us with this good that the love we have for ourselves is indistinguishable from this love." Nor does it

[1] And similarly, for each of the primary emotions, there are two forms, one due to the self's immanent activity, another due to its body's transeunt activity, both being, however, states of the self and not of its body: *e.g.* states of ' intellectual ' love, joy, sadness, and desire; and states of ' physical ' love, joy, sadness, and desire (passions). The former, Descartes points out, could quite well occur were the self unconnected with a body (Letter to Chanut, 1647; AT, IV, 602).

ever fail to produce joy, for " it represents to us the object of our love as a good that appertains to us " (cf. *Passions*, cxxxix).[1]

What is loved or hated is something existing in the present or the past, *i.e.* existing along with, or earlier than, the emotion itself. But states of desiring usually refer to future time. Not only do we desire to acquire in the future a good we do not at present possess, or to avoid an evil that may befall us in time to come, but in wishing for the continuance of a good now enjoyed, or the removal of an evil now suffered, our desire relates to a state of something at a date yet future. And desire stands among the primitive emotions in a special position, for each other one tends to facilitate its intervention. There is a natural order among emotions both in their evocation and in their connexions. Presentation of an object awakens surprise at it, and this, the onset of spontaneous attention, is accompanied by wonder which disposes us to acquire fuller knowledge of the object, and in particular of its goodness or badness for our physical well-being. On account of this cognition there arises a liking or disliking of the object, a love or hate of it in respect of its causal characteristics, this attitude making possible an ' enjoyment ' that is predominantly pleasurable or painful, *i.e.* the state we designate briefly as one of ' joy ' or ' sadness.' Lastly, the love and its consequent joy, or the hate and its consequent displeasure, move us to desire the continuance and

---

[1] Descartes's distinction between love which is a *passion* and that which is not is made to depend solely on an intellectual evaluation of the object in relation to the self. This can be justifiable if, and only if, our love for persons in *all* instances is caused by appreciation of qualities they possess or are judged to possess. Where there is love for a person there may also be appreciation of that person's qualities, but it does not follow that the love is felt *on account of* the qualities appreciated. See, on this point, J. McT. E. McTaggart, *The Nature of Existence*, Vol. II, p. 151, Cambridge, 1927 : " While the love may be *because* of those qualities, it is not in *respect* of them." McTaggart, who distinguishes love as a species of liking felt only for persons, would presumably endorse Descartes's view of love *of persons* as consisting in a union of a unique kind : cf. " when B loves C, he feels that he is connected with him by a bond of peculiar strength and intimacy—a bond stronger and more intimate than any other by which two selves can be joined . . . there are times when the intimacy of the relation in love is felt to be scarcely less than the intimacy of a man's relation with his own self. And this seems to me to be the essence of love. Love is an emotion which springs from a sense of union with another self. The sense of union is essential—whenever there is a sense of a sufficiently close union, then there is love, whatever may be the qualities of lover and beloved, and whatever may be the other relations between them " (McTaggart, *op. cit.*, pp. 150–1).

THE SELF AND ITS FREEDOM

well-being of the object loved, or the cessation or annihilation of the object hated. In this way, one emotion tends to introduce another, and all to culminate in a desire. All the primary emotions, except surprise and wonder (which is a surprise of longer duration, centred in the same thing), are thus founded on their objects' helpfulness or harmfulness to our organism, or else on an assertion of value, true or false, respecting the objects' effects, directly on our organism and indirectly on our self. So a desire directed to conserving or realising some state of affairs will be ' good,' if and because that state of affairs is *truly* judged beneficial, a desire will be ' bad ' if and because the end to which it is directed has been *erroneously* judged beneficial. Bad desires, then, are not in essence different from good ones, their difference derives from the truth or falsity of the judgment on which they are founded. Hence the importance for conduct of a *knowledge* of the truth : *omnis peccans est ignorans*. Aversion is not an opposite of desire, for desire has no opposite. Objects desired *are* very various, and may conveniently be classed as positive and negative,[1] but there is no difference in the desire itself. A desire not to have X differs from a desire to have X only as ' not having X ' (or, ' the absence of X ') differs from ' the possession of X.' But this difference is not a difference in the desiring (for this is " always one and the same movement," a pursuit of what is believed better), but a difference in what is desired.

To sum up, that our emotions are in general beneficial may easily be realised by supposing an experient to lack them entirely and be capable of only cognitive and volitional action. His only way of discovering in particular cases whether he should, *e.g.* will his body to remain in, or to move from, the vicinity of some present object, would then be by *deducing*, from his present stock of clear and distinct ideas about both that object and his body, the physical results which should ensue from their spatial proximity, and thence infer whether those results would be conducive to, or obstructive of, the preservation and good functioning of that body he calls his

---

[1] McTaggart, who discusses positive and negative desires ' with extreme lucidity, reaches substantially the same result as Descartes : " desires are neither positive or negative . . . all desires accept something, though that which they accept is often itself of a negative nature " (Cf. *op. cit.*, Vol. II, section 449).

own. But in countless instances, it is plain, where the physical results are destined to be 'obstructive,' the obstruction—or destruction—would have occurred before the deduction had been completed! Self-preservation, then, requires a readier means to adaptation than that which could be supplied under the conditions of strict knowledge. That our emotions are beneficial may be further seen by noticing three distinct respects in which they benefit us, namely (i) some, in being inherently and wholly good, in and for themselves—good in being just the experiences they are, hence in being occurrences whose recurrence is desirable and desired; (ii) in being *psychologically* useful, by helping to perpetuate and maintain the vivacity of those thoughts which, though advantageous to us, would speedily be effaced without enforcement by some emotion; (iii) in being *biologically* useful, for, since all passions relate to our body, and in fact occur only because our mind is so intimately united with it, their " natural use " is to incite the self " to consent to, and promote, those actions that may serve to maintain the body or to improve it " (*Passions*, cxxxvii; AT, XI, 430). But, with regard to (ii), though an emotion can be mnemically useful, it can also be detrimental, if its intensity is such as causes the thoughts it perpetuates to outlast the period of their usefulness in application to behaviour. For instance, wonder heightens our present perception, so aiding us to retain in memory that of which we were previously ignorant. So much a perception of novelty alone, unstrengthened by feeling, would not secure. And to be born with an inclination to wonder is good, because it disposes the mind to the acquirement of knowledge. But it may also be detrimental, if we permit it to control us. For excess of wonder, besides preventing or perverting the proper function of reason, may easily dispose us to form the habit of dwelling on each novel thing simply to marvel at it, of seeking out only the rare and curious, not for the sake of attaining more knowledge but for the idle amusement of a blind curiosity. And, with regard to (iii), this utility is normally secured by a fairly uniform precedence in the order of occurrence. Thus, biologically, 'sadness' and 'joy' are really primary. The presence to a human body of something hurtful has, for an immediate mental counterpart to the physical lesion, a painful sensation, which is imperiously

THE SELF AND ITS FREEDOM 185

signified to the self by imparting to it a characteristic sadness or displeasure. This displeasure is followed by a feeling of hate for the object indirectly causing the pain, and on this hatred there follows in turn a desire to rid the body of contact with that object. Sadness is, indeed, to be ranked above joy, and hatred above love, *in biological utility*, for it is more important to repel things that can injure or destroy the body, than to acquire those which, though they improve it, are not essential to its preservation.

Emotions, then, are always indirectly, never directly, initiated. When *externally* excited, the direct effect of the body's contact with, say, a harmful object is a physical injury to that body. The sensation of pain, with its pervading tone of ' sadness,' and the intervening hatred of the object are both indirect and correlative consequences co-present in mind. So, too, when the emotion is *subjectively* (*i.e.* voluntarily) excited or repressed. Its instatement in mind is never a direct, but always an indirect consequence of the act of will. For on such occasions we must first of all image or recall the things that are usually associated with the emotion we want to experience, or the things that have been found incapable of co-existing with the emotion we want to expel.[1]

Eliminating in thought all mental modifications concomitant with bodily activity—passions which the self ' lives through ' or ' enjoys ' rather than experiences as objects—we are left with only those mental occurrences that are volitions, occurrences which the self recognises as being caused by its proper activity alone, and as incontrovertibly manifesting its own existence. Now we have already noticed certain general facts about human volition: we saw, for instance, that though no man ever wills to err, yet it is only by his will that he does err; we saw that our will is far more ' perfect ' than any other mode of our activity, for the range of its possible affirmations is unlimited, and we saw that the bodily changes which serve as a physiological basis for sensations and passions incline the self to will one or another kind of

---

[1] Thus, to summon up courage and banish fear, it is insufficient merely to *want* to feel courageous and unafraid. We must first of all " consider such reasons, objects or examples as will persuade us that the peril is not great," and then imaginatively anticipate the emotion we shall experience if we triumph, and the very different emotion that would accompany our defeat.

action.[1] It remains to notice what further characterisations Descartes makes when examining volitional activity expressly on its own account.

The self may not only be modified or even dominated by its passions, but is also competent to resist and act counter to their inclinations. Now the set of bodily changes that form the occasion on which these inclining passions occur, are all strictly determined in accordance with the laws of physics and bio-chemistry. But the volitional acts by which the self gives or withholds assent, when 'inclined' by its emotion, are not determined according to any physical laws. And this is the negative sense in which its acts of will are " free." Freedom of will, for Descartes, amounts to our capacity to assent to, or to reject, what is proposed to the self for cognitive determination. But let us first be clear about the opposition Descartes indicates between what is 'determined' and what is 'free' when he says " the will is by its nature so entirely free that never can it be constrained " (*Passions*, xli). " Free " and " determined " are contradictory, not mere contrary, predicates, and actions of both kinds are actually found. It is evident from his natural philosophy and from his epistemology that he recognises at least two kinds of 'determinism,' intimately connected yet ultimately distinct : (i) *physical* determinism—the highly general fact about the natural world that any change of state or local movement on the part of a natural body is completely explicable by the principles of rational mechanics ; (ii) *logical* determinism—the highly general fact about a body of strict knowledge that any proposition in it (except a primary and axiomatic one) follows with necessity from some certain other, so that the whole collection of constituent propositions forms a deductive system. Now among realities there are some falling wholly outside the field of what is either physically or epistemically determined, and so are, in that sense, contingent. Among these are the self-initiated volitions of every human being, acts which manifest not only

---

[1] Cf. " The principal effect of all passions in men is that they incite and dispose their soul to will those things for which they have prepared their bodies " (*Passions*, xl.). It is just because the physiological mechanism of emotional excitement issues in consequences that are naturally and normally secured by volition that it is *able* to incline the will to yield assent to actions it is on the point of inaugurating.

his existence but his freedom too. This freedom cannot, however, be in every sense unconditional, for such a ' liberty of indifference ' would imply a radical irrationality, and so much (or so little) Descartes denies can be the *sine qua non* of the self's essential activity.[1] What he has to show then is, in what sense will can be conditioned without being determined.

Although, in order to act rightly, it is indispensable that the action contemplated should be seen clearly to be good, this does not entail that a wrong action must issue from a clear perception that the act contemplated is bad. Were it seen distinctly to be bad its occurrence would never be willed, at least, at no time *that* it was perceived to be so. (What is perceived, clearly or unclearly, as being bad, on one occasion, may, of course, be perceived unclearly or clearly as being good on another.) In order for wrong conduct to ensue, it is sufficient and necessary that the self should will what it perceives confusedly (and so misperceives) as being good, or else, what it believes it *remembers* having formerly judged to be good without now attending to the reasons which it supposes would prove it so.

Has Descartes then overlooked or denied the possibility of a psychological determinism ? It is true he makes no allusion to what is usually regarded as a clear and typical instance of it—the association of ideas. He does not appear to recognise even the limited forms of association that Aristotle had admitted—those ' by resemblance ' and ' by contrast.' But even though, unlike his great contemporaries Hobbes and Malebranche, Descartes makes no use of principles of association, it is clear that had he done so he would have considered them particular cases of habitual action, and therefore purely

---

[1] Cf. the important letter to Mesland (1644?) : " I did not say that man is indifferent only where he lacks knowledge, but that he is the more indifferent in proportion as he has fewer reasons that incline him to choose one alternative rather than another " (AT, IV, 115) ; and later, in the same letter, he concludes that liberty consists not in indifference but in " a real and positive power of self-determination " (AT, IV, 116). Cf. also the passage in *Med.* IV : " . . . that indifference I experience when I am not inclined towards one alternative rather than another by the weight of any reason is the lowest degree of liberty and testifies rather to a defect of knowledge than to a perfection of will, for if I always knew what is true and what is good, I should never encounter any difficulty in deciding what judgment or what choice I ought to make, and thus *I should be wholly free without ever being indifferent"* (AT, VII, 58 ; HR, I, 175) —my italics.

physical principles.[1] Hence we should have had only a further example of physical determinism before us. This instance, it is true, would have implied, derivatively, a *psychological* determinism, namely, among the mental states collaterally occurrent with those associated physiological actions, but since these states are "passions" and not "actions" of the self, that psychological determinism would have been quite compatible with the absence of *any* kind of determinism among the self's actions. Volition, that is to say, would remain so far unaffected and "free," for it is only the actions of the self that Descartes maintains to be undetermined in *every* sense.

How then, to repeat, is Descartes to conceive volitional action as conditioned and yet undetermined ? For liberty, quite generally, consists in the self's power to act or not to act in the way to which it is inclined by present emotion or desire. Its decisions, Descartes fully sees, are none the less conditioned. For, confronted with clear and distinct evidence that the action to which it is inclined is good, that perception alone is sufficient to secure consent to, and actual initiation of, the action itself. Confronted by a clear and distinct cognition we cannot withhold assent.[2] So far, then, what conditions the self to act is its clear and distinct cognition. But, it may be asked, is it not plain from this that the self, far from being *un*determined in its decisions, is, on the contrary, quite evidently determined ? For what can such ' conditioning ' be but psychological deter-

---

[1] Cf. *Passions*, xli–xlii. Consider, for example, the communication of thought by speech. What we *think* of is not the movements required to be made by the tongue and lips, but the sense to be expressed. By means of purely physiological habits previously formed, when a self thinks certain thoughts and wills to communicate them, its vocal organs can produce the whole series of movements without the intervention of a separate volition for each movement being necessary. Such habits or purely mechanical laws (connexions established between particular kinds of movements in our vocal organs and particular physical, vocal sounds) are not imposed on our mind at all, but on its body. The various kinds of habitual action are wholly mechanistic and automatic—all the self does is to ' start ' the machine by a suitable volition.

[2] Cf. " It is certain that *ex magna luce in intellectu sequitur magna propensio in voluntate* ; so that when we see quite clearly that a thing is appropriate (to our need) it is exceedingly hard, indeed I think impossible while we are of the same mind about it, to stay the current of our desire. But since the mind is naturally prone to rest only momentarily on one and the same thing, so soon as our attention turns from the reasons for which we knew the thing to be appropriate, retaining only the recollection that it appeared desirable, we can represent in mind some other reason which makes us doubt of the former, and thus we suspend our judgment and perhaps even form a contrary one" (Letter to Mesland, 1644 ? ; AT, IV, 116).

mination? Has not Descartes muddled the matter? Is he not denying psychological determinism for no better reason than that it is not physical determinism? Has he not virtually admitted that will *is* determined, namely, by clear cognition?

Descartes would answer, and rightly, that he is not guilty of this confusion, and the supposition that he is comes from overlooking one essential factor in volitional process, the invariable presence of which exhibits precisely how the self is free. For, he would ask, by what means does this clear and distinct cognition occur? Is the occurrence of clear perceptions, and the failure to supplant unclear by clear ones, always a matter of pure hazard and wholly independent of our will? And, after having considered the reasons for and against a contemplated action, is not our *recognition* that the idea eventually accepted *is* clear itself largely due to the thoroughness and sincerity of our examination, and to having restrained ourselves from judging precipitately? The perception *that* a cognition is clear is not something straightway vouchsafed on a first casual inspection of the reasons, but rather a result of unremitting care and continued concentration of attention. And to persist in such close attention and to insist on complete clarity of insight before ' making up ' our mind, when it is so much easier to decide precipitately and despatch the matter, is not only meritorious (*une bonne action*), but also a *free* action on the part of a self that is also free to act otherwise if it chooses. Descartes therefore concludes that our freedom is evident from the fact that we *can*, that we sometimes actually *do*, and sometimes actually *do not* (i) voluntarily postpone deciding until clarity of insight is attained ; (ii) examine scrupulously and ' weigh up ' the reasons *pro et contra*, thus refusing to allow our attention to be diverted. Now what (i) and (ii) describe are plainly *acts of will* occurrent at a *pre*-final stage in a deliberative process. Further, the stage in question is one at which the self is acting *freely*, for, *ex hypothesi*, it has not yet been conditioned by a clear perception of the alternative it is eventually to adopt. This perception occurs *afterwards*, forming the final stage of the deliberation, and is, as it were, a recompense to the self for its earlier effort (*i.e.* volitions) to reach a clear understanding of the alternatives open to it. And though the final and clear cognition is, in respect of its specific content, quite independent of our free action, the fact that we *should finally attain* clarity in our perception of this content (when we could so easily have failed to do so) is *not* independent of our will, but is emphatically due to it. Such meritorious and free action on our part presupposes that we have previously accepted the injunction never to assert an idea that is not perfectly clear. And when the idea happens to be one concerning right conduct, this amounts to saying that we have previously accepted the injunction not to consent to a proposed course of conduct until we have clearly perceived that it is good. But, even though acceptance of this principle and application of it to particular cases argues that in moral action we are conditioned by a rational principle, such ' determination ' of the will, it must be noticed, is a determination of it by nothing other than our very own self. This ' determination ' may therefore, with greater propriety and less ambiguity, be called our freedom. For the determination in question is neither a physical nor a psychological one, and surely it is pointless to say that an act of will is not undetermined because it is determined by the self that wills ? For what else does this mean than that acts of will are freely initiated by the self ?

This argument, however, if sound, shows no more than that the self's freedom is logically possible ; it does not establish that such freedom is an actual fact. So to complete the matter, Descartes produces empirical grounds. That we *are* free in willing, he maintains, is straightway disclosed to us on self-inspection. For when we invoke the most rigorous form of doubt conceivable, supposing unlimited risk of deception, we then experience, with unusual clearness, a freedom in ourselves. That we *are* free to refrain from asserting what is unclear is immediately disclosed to us, and is not known discursively. Whatever we are unable to doubt on such occasions (*inter alia*, this very freedom) is as certain as anything we can ever know (cf. *Prins.*, I, xxxix). Our freedom, therefore, is known " without proofs, and simply by the experience we have of it." The conception of the self as free in willing is a primitive notion, one that cannot be deduced from another more primitive, hence an idea that is innate in us (cf. letter to Mersenne ; AT, III, 259).

One consequence that seemingly follows from Descartes's

THE SELF AND ITS FREEDOM

physiological psychology is that so long as we confine our interest to particular happenings in human minds or bodies, we *can* discover which specific mental states are correlated with which bodily ones, as well as much about the detailed nature of those bodily correlates. And we may reasonably expect to discover a great deal more on such matters than we can ever hope to know about the relation between the self and its body. For it is just a ' brute ' fact that the self is embodied. The bare fact and no more can be known by the self : it directly *experiences* " the union," but certainly does not *understand* it. The self is powerless to make any determinate statements about it. The connexion, it is true, cannot be seen to be either a ' necessary ' or a causal one, but nothing positive can be said of it beyond, perhaps, that it is the sort of connexion that has been described as ' the mechanical union of a corpse and a ghost.' Descartes's study of mental and physiological processes does not result, then, in making intelligible the union of the self with its body, but simply in insisting on their essential opposition and connexion. The fact of their connexion is an ultimate ' irrational ' for his metaphysics : a datum that *must* be accepted but *cannot* be understood.

Nor does this physiological psychology throw direct light on the self's intimate nature as a persistent substance. Yet Descartes has further information to offer on this highly important point. The substantival view of the self[1] is, of course, a refinement of the common-sense notion of a particular continuant capable of acting and suffering and therefore of having

---

[1] The formal elaboration of this conception of substance and of the thesis that the self is one, is the work not only of Descartes, but of Hobbes, Locke, Leibniz, Berkeley, Wolff, and—in our own times—of McTaggart. The view is no longer accepted by most thinkers ; McTaggart is the most eminent exception to this generalisation. In this, as in many respects, he is " impenitently pre-Critical." He agrees with Descartes *that* the self is known directly—by acquaintance—but disagrees that it *is* so known is ' obvious.' McTaggart attempts to *prove* that " if ' I ' can be known at all, it must be known by awareness," and, if it is *not* so known, " we are not justified in asserting any proposition in which the term ' I ' occurs." But Descartes does not feel the need of proving either of these things. McTaggart also differs from Descartes in holding that " the ' I ' is much more elusive than those other existent realities of which we are aware by perception." Cf. his extremely important discussion in *The Nature of Existence*, Vol. II, Bk. V, ch. xxxvi, especially sections 381-94, also his article ' Personality ' in *Hastings' Encyclopædia of Religion and Ethics*, Vol. IX, pp. 773-81. The view that the self is known by direct perception seems to me true, and McTaggart's demonstration that it *is* so known, quite conclusive.

DESCARTES

a history. Now, so far as the self alone is concerned, the *cogito* situation discloses, according to Descartes, (i) the existence o some or other determinate conscious state ("mode"); (ii) the existence of something indicated by "I"; (iii) the fact of that state being a state *of* this "I"; and (iv) that the "I" in question is a substance (*me esse rem quamdam sive substantiam*), *i.e.* the subject in which particular conscious states directly inhere, and which, through those states, manifests its own existence and its passive and active nature (AT, VIII, 161 ; VII, 174, 176 ; V, 156). Now these mental states empirically disclosed in self-inspection are momentary and intermittent in their existence. Despite this, Descartes maintains that the self is *always* conscious (*l'âme pense toujours*). So we may ask with Gassendi (cf. *Fifth Objections*) what reasons Descartes has to advance for this view. For, whether or not it can be *dis*proved empirically, it does not seem capable of being established empirically, even if true.

But how far *can* experience take us towards its confirmation ? First of all, the self has many states, active and passive, which show indubitably that it is conscious in waking life. But what evidence is there that the self is conscious during profound and dreamless sleep, or while it is in an 'unconscious condition,' or, as Gassendi asks, "while it is in the womb"? Does it not seem more plausible to suppose that whether or not there was a 'first' conscious state for each of us, at least there are considerable periods during which consciousness is 'suspended'? Yet this plausible *primâ facie* objection is itself exposed to objection. For though in waking life we often remember tha we were conscious in a previous dream-state, on the other hand often we do not remember our dreams at all, and sometime. only conclude that we were dreaming by inference from certair bodily movements (cries, talking) we are reported to have performed, and which we take to be outward expressions of imagings and emotions privately experienced during sleep. So we are probably conscious more often than we recollect having been. Again, that the self is, in *some* sense, conscious during sleep seems probable from the fact that, having 'willed' ourselves to awaken at a certain hour fixed in advance, we actually do then awaken. Further, if in an hypnotic condition we "accept" a suggestion to act in a certain manner at a future time, we do so act when the time arrives, whether or not we are then aware *that* we are so acting or *why* we are doing so. Such phenomena do seem to lend some plausibility to the view that we are conscious in *some* sense during so-called suspension of consciousness, though they do not show that the sense in which we are then conscious is necessarily the same as that in which we are conscious in normal waking life or in self-awareness. And though it may seem that to assert that I am ' *un*-conscious ' denies that I am conscious in any sense at all, yet, on ' recovering ' consciousness, do I not assert that I am the self-same, the identical ' I ' that previously ' lapsed from ' consciousness ? And it seems difficult to believe that I am mistaken in this judgment—(*i.e.* to believe that what really is in question here is two *numerically* different selves, one of which supposes itself to be—not the self it is, but the other self !)—as it is to believe that what persisted in the meantime was a numerically single self lacking any nature whatever—a mere ' de-natured ' existent. Lastly, if it is difficult to believe that a conscious self existed before our body's birth, is it any less difficult to believe that at some particular moment in time there occurred a mental state of a self that simultaneously came into existence, and a state which was the ' first ' of the series composing that self's mental history ? As Descartes points out, the fact that we do not now recall earlier mental states during our existence in the womb or in infancy should not surprise us, for very many mental states, experienced in maturity and when the physiological mechanism of memory has attained its full development, cannot be recalled. Can we now recall what we were doing at this very hour on this very day seven years ago ? But if failure to recall in the latter cases does not prove that we *had* no states *to* recall, why then should it be held to prove this in the former ? " Is it remarkable if the brain of an infant, or our own in a stupor, is unfit to receive residual impressions ? "

What is the net result of this empirical survey ? It seems to show that if such empirical facts do not conclusively establish that we are conscious at literally *every* moment of our existence, no more do they conclusively disprove it. It does not follow that a conscious state *must* be accompanied by the self's perception *that* it is at that moment having the state. It may well be (in dreaming and hypnotic conditions) that we often have mental states that are unaccompanied by self-awareness. But this would not establish cessation of our consciousness. Nor, on the other hand, does it establish that we are always conscious, but it does show, not only that we can be conscious without knowing that we are, but that we are conscious more often than we ordinarily suppose.

Although Descartes shows that he is aware of the strength and the weakness of this sort of evidence, it is not along these lines that he replies to Gassendi's " difficulty " about whether the soul " always thinks." Descartes blandly replies : " But why should it *not* always think, when it is a thinking substance ? " The naïveté of this answer suggests that he regards the assertion " The soul always thinks " as simply an analytical proposition. He does, in fact, regard it an *a priori* statement that neither needs, nor is susceptible of, *a posteriori* proof. The essential nature of selfhood—that attribute without which a self would not *be* a self—is ' to be conscious ' in some determinate mode, just as the essential nature of matter is to be extended and to manifest this, its determinable nature, in various determinate modes at different dates. But it is quite clear that Descartes saw that the truth of the assertion " *l'âme pense toujours* " is not settled by definition. It is one thing so to define ' the soul,' quite another to show there exists something to which that definition applies. He maintains that we are empirically assured that the definition does in fact have application, and so defines something really existing. We are assured of the existence of *une substance pensante*, for, in perceiving our self to exist we at the same time perceive it to be conscious in some determinate manner—to be hoping, believing, doubting, joyful, or sad, etc. And in thus perceiving some or other mode *to be* " our " present mode of existence, we *eo ipso* perceive that mode to be a specific determination of the determinable attribute ' consciousness.' Just as we know what it is ' to be coloured ' in and by knowing what it is ' to be red,' ' to be blue,' etc., so we know what it is ' to be conscious ' in and by knowing what it is ' to be doubting,' ' to be willing,' etc. So, by way of illustration, supposing Descartes right that the necessary and sufficient condition of anything ' being material ' is, that it should possess determinable extendedness, then, given that we know of an existent *that* it occupies some determinate region of space through some duration, we are thereby assured that the existent is a material one. And in order to *know* that it does satisfy this necessary and sufficient condition it is not required that we should have perceived it throughout its whole history and have observed that it never failed to manifest some shape and some dimension. Were assurance of materiality possible only *a posteriori*, we should never attain it. We can, however, know an existent to be material by analysing what is disclosed to attentive inspection of it, for in and by perceiving it to have some determinate extension we also perceive it to be the sort of thing whose existence is *essentially* spatial. By this means we know intuitively and not discursively that whether or not it will always occupy the region of space it now occupies, it will, so long as it exists, occupy at all times *one or another* region of space. Now the case is precisely similar, *mutatis mutandis*, when the existent is *une substance pensante*. Analysis of what is disclosed in self-inspection shows that in perceiving some determinate state to be " ours " at a given moment, we *eo ipso* perceive that state to be a determinate mode of consciousness : *i.e.* we perceive this transitory state to be a particular determinate *of* that determinable quality which is our self's defining attribute. Hence, to deny that the self " always thinks " would be to deny the self to *be* a self, and this would be self-contradictory. So in maintaining that the self " always thinks " Descartes is not asserting a proposition that is *directly* about the whole collection of determinate states composing the self's history, nor a proposition merely about the self as disclosed *at particular moments* of its existence. The proposition is *directly* about the self's ultimate nature, and it asserts of that nature that it is a unique, determinable quality, the possession of which by any substance confers on it once for all, apart from all reference to temporal dates, the inalienable character of selfhood.

Thus a self's consciousness is typically exemplified in and by any single, determinate state that it has, but it is not ' exhausted ' in that state. Is a self's consciousness, however, ' exhausted ' in and by *all* its states collectively ? Clearly it could be only provided there were a certain state which was 'its last,' after the cessation of which that self ceased to exist. So the question of cessation or 'complete suspension' refers properly, not to the self's defining *attribute*, but to the self's existence *as a substance*. For to ask whether a self can continue to exist after an absolute discontinuance of its consciousness in every sense is an absurd question, since it is asking whether a substance with a given essential nature could exist while not having that nature. Therefore the question should be restated in the form: 'Can *a substance* (and, in particular, one that is conscious) cease to exist?' Now to ask this is not at all absurd, and the problem raised, when the substance is a self, is that of its mortality or immortality, for the 'cessation' questioned is that of an existent substance, not that of a quality.

If a substance can cease to exist, the cause must be a transeunt one of some kind, and not an immanent one. So much Descartes apparently takes as self-evident. He then proposes that, in view of what has already been established, there are only two such causes possible. Hence to prove that *in fact* the soul is not mortal requires a disproof of either possible cause being operative. The first, and that usually suggested by those maintaining the self's mortality, is the death of its body. But, says Descartes, the death of a human body could not possibly *cause* the non-existence of the self it embodies, since that self is qualitatively and existentially independent of it. Nor could the self cease to exist 'on its own account,' as the body does, for dissolution of the body occurs through partition, but the self has no parts into which it could be resolved. Bodies, human and non-human, are susceptible of decay or partition precisely because they are *not* substances: selves are incapable of it, precisely because they *are*.[1] (While there is a plurality of substantival selves, there is no corresponding plurality of substantival bodies, but only one substance, which is all matter

---

[1] Scholasticism regarded self and body as incomplete and dependent on one another. "The complete substantiality of the soul having been established for the first time by the *Meditations*," writes M. Gilson, "Descartes could not have done other than think his philosophy the first to permit legitimately the assertion of our immortality" (*Discours de la Méthode, Texte et Commentaire*, p. 437). At this point, then, Descartes's reform consists, negatively, in expelling 'substantial forms' and the 'vegetative soul' from the philosophy of mind, positively, in showing that immortality of the self is simply a corollary of the indestructibility of substance, and of the complete disparity of mind and matter.

THE SELF AND ITS FREEDOM

and of which particular bodies are *modes*.)[1] The other possible cause of the self's cessation is that formal reality on which it depends for its existence—God. And here the case is different. God, argues Descartes, being the cause *eminenter* of the self's existence, could equally well be the cause of its annihilation. So whether the self *in fact* eternally survives the death of its body can be answered only if we have a knowledge of God's future decisions. But this we do not and cannot have: hence, *ignoramus et ignorabimus* is the sole answer we can return on the question of *fact*.[2] But on the *possibility* of the self's immortality we may say that if God does not will its annihilation then nothing else could possibly cause it, and the self will continue to exist despite and after the death of its body.

[1] Clearly there are relations between two bodies which connect them into a compound body (*e.g.* a nut and its shell), but there are no analogous relations between two selves so connecting them as to form a compound self. The nut and the shell are thus 'parts' of all matter in a sense in which Smith and Jones are not 'parts' of any third self.

[2] *Reply to Second Objections* (AT, IX, 119-20; HR, II, 47).

PART III

IX

THE CARTESIAN SCHOOL

"Parmi tant et de si grandes vérités que l'école cartésienne a mises au jour . . . elle a seulement failli dans les substances, n'ayant pas su en pénétrer la constitution."—BORDAS-DESMOULIN.

LET us now turn to consider the influence Descartes exercised on the thought of his contemporaries and immediate successors. What was the precise character of that influence, what were the developments of Cartesian doctrine proper, what the extensions beyond it and the departures from it? These may best be grasped by eliciting how the principal findings of the Cartesian School were designed, some to complement, others to correct, certain deficiencies and errors in Descartes's own metaphysics. From its earliest and most Cartesian phase that prolongation issues finally in a doctrine of complete Occasionalism. Then the introduction of certain new, non-Cartesian conceptions divides the main stream, on the one side towards Pantheism, and on the other towards a form of spiritual pluralism. In its course, the chief moments of the whole movement are marked by the transitions from Régis to Malebranche, thence to Spinoza in the one direction and to Leibniz in the other. Although the problems under examination in the latter half of the seventeenth century vary materially (being successively in the main ontological, ethical, and epistemological), they are nevertheless all more or less directly connected with one fundamental definition of Descartes—that of Substance. The difficulties to which this definition gave rise cannot be resolved, we shall see, without passing beyond the limits imposed by his own final word.

Descartes's metaphysics culminates in the view (cf. p. 117) that the universe is existentially pluralistic and qualitatively dualistic. Thus the word 'universe' refers, not to a unique *substance* (as for Spinoza later) but to a *collection*, viz. one comprising the substance which is God, the substance which is all matter, and the class of substances each of which is a self.

Now 'substance' Descartes defined as that which depends on nothing for its existence or for its nature : that which is independent in every sense—*subsistens per se*. Answering to this definition there is only one existent, the one, namely, that is further characterised by the eternal and immutable possession of all positive qualities that are ultimately distinct, each in its fullest degree, *i.e.* completely or 'perfectly.' And such an existent is God. All that exists and is other than God depends for its existence upon God. Dependence, however, is a matter of degree. Of those existents that are the *least* dependent (all matter and each self) no one depends on any other, each is so far independent. Yet each does depend on God and so far is dependent. Existents of which this is true are called 'secondary substances.' They are 'substances' in that the existence of no one entails that of any other; they are 'secondary' since none is absolutely independent or unconditionally existent, but, being dependent on God, each exemplifies dependence at its first remove. Other existents again (modes) are directly dependent on secondary substances for their existence (formal reality) and indirectly dependent on God. This Descartes sums up by speaking of God as 'uncreated' substance, and of all matter and each self as 'created' ones, so suggesting an ultimate bifurcation among the existents constituting the universe. He completely fails, however, to make intelligible the *creation* which results in the dependence of created, finite, secondary substances on the infinite, independent and creative substance that is God. He appears to suppose that 'creation' is a conception properly falling to theology for elucidation. But it is impossible to acquiesce in such an abandonment of the difficulty, for the employment he has made of the conception is unquestionably a metaphysical one, and is vital to that view of God and the world which he believes himself to have rationally demonstrated. This failure to analyse the concept and to justify its use, then, can be regarded only as betraying a want of thoroughness in Descartes. It was natural and useful, therefore, that subsequent criticism should fasten on this very neglect. The relation of an uncreated God to the world he has created is far from being clear and distinct, and it is made no whit the clearer by speaking of the continued existence of finite substances as being virtually a new creation by

God from moment to moment—the regular recurrence of a miracle.

We saw besides that Descartes inconsistently admits interaction between mind and body in assuming uncritically that mind alters the *direction* (though it does not impart the quantity) of motion present in physiological change. Even though direction by mind of motion already existing in the body is plainly a different thing from mind causing the existence of motion there, both are alike incompatible with the complete qualitative disparity of mind and matter that is essential to Cartesianism.

These are the two principal defects lying at the heart of the Cartesian position which are subjected to continual modification during the second half of the seventeenth century in France. Superficially, the effort is to explain the relationship between God and the world, not by insisting merely on the ' necessary ' character of that relationship, but by exhibiting in some detail the several conditions under which there can be an effective *commerce* between its terms. Formally, it is an attempt to work out, with the least deviation from Descartes possible, a theory of the universe which would manifest a higher unity than that of a collection, as well as greater coherence in the determination of its parts. The critical and constructive effort of the first period, to which Régis, De la Forge, Cordemoy, Geulincx and Malebranche all lent their strength, was to prove a failure too, though the reasons for that failure are instructive. A synthesis that is at once more systematic and internally less inconsistent becomes possible only after the substance of Descartes has been displaced by the Substance of Spinoza and the Individual of Leibniz. The extent to which they withdrew from Cartesian principles and introduced other and original ones results in such wide divergences from Descartes and weakens so radically their affiliations with him, that, in the end, Cartesianism can hardly be regarded as being substantially constitutive of the new philosophies, though its formative influence in their developments cannot be doubted. Thus it is only in a ' historical ' sense permissible to refer to Spinoza and Leibniz as ' Cartesians.'

I

One thing which becomes increasingly evident in the transition from Descartes to Malebranche is the inexactitude of speaking of 'action' or 'causation'—be it of mind on body, or body on mind, or even of one body on another. For the term 'action' may designate with equal propriety two quite distinct things, viz. (i) the fact of *causing the occurrence*, hence the *existence*, of a change or movement; (ii) the fact of *determining the character* a change shall assume, or the location and direction of a motion, but *not* causing its occurrence or existence. To deny direct action between mind and body should mean in strictness a denial of 'action' in *both* these senses. But Descartes, we saw, denied it in the former sense alone. He repeatedly affirmed action in the second sense, and yet maintained there is no interaction. And according to the view they take on the possibility of direct action between secondary substances, Descartes's continuators fall into two groups. There are those, like Régis and Clauberg, who follow him in allowing 'action' in the second sense while denying it in the first; and those like Cordemoy, Geulincx, and Malebranche, who deny action in both senses. And the question to which these thinkers return their various answers may be expressed in these terms: 'Under what conditions are secondary substances active or causative at all?'

Before reviewing these several answers and their grounds, however, we should notice briefly the views developed by Henry le Roy (*latinè*, Regius[1]), who was early an enthusiastic admirer and a correspondent of Descartes, and also the first of his followers to break completely with his essential doctrine. Le Roy had made extensive use of Cartesian physiology in his medical lectures at the University of Utrecht. On the whole, the worth of his zeal was perhaps dubious. His *Fundamenta Physicæ* reduced the Cartesian dualism of matter and mind to a materialism, and contained so many unproved assertions that Descartes had openly to disclaim all responsibility for it.[2] It

---

[1] Regius is not infrequently confounded with Régis, concerning whom, cf. p. 206, n. 1.
[2] "I feel myself compelled," writes Descartes, "to warn everyone who regards him (Le Roy) as a stout defender of my opinions, that there is scarcely one of these which he does not mis-state and the meaning of which he does not

would seem, however, notwithstanding Descartes's annoyance, that Le Roy is right in insisting that, on Cartesian premises, man can be only " a being *per accidens* " and not a substance. For, though Descartes had maintained the self's connexion with its body to be so intimate as to constitute them a ' substantival unity,' he is wholly unable to give this phrase a positive meaning that is at once clear and compatible with his definition of substance. Whatever Descartes may have supposed himself to have established, or desired to establish, concerning the embodied self or human being, the only account of it he is logically entitled to offer is—not that of a *substance* of any sort—but that of a unique kind of compound. It can be nothing other than a compound consisting of a substance (self) related by some unspecified relation to a series of material *modes* that are collectively to be designated ' the body of that self.' Such a compound is plainly not a Cartesian substance, primary or secondary, And the breach opened by this un-Cartesian view of Le Roy is irreparably widened by his further declaration that mind is nothing but a mode of corporeal substance—an opinion which De la Mettrie and d'Holbach were to develop more fully in the next century,[1] and that connects him with the current of modern materialism.

Louis de la Forge,[2] too, seems to depart from Descartes's position (though less radically than Le Roy) in apparently maintaining[3] that our voluntary acts, but none others, both cause the existence and determine the character of those actions of our body that are purposive. In volition we not only seem, but really are, both productive of the ensuing change and directive of it, since we determine it to be of a character suitable to achieve the end intended—an innovation obviously

pervert, in what concerns metaphysical, no less than physical matters." Cf. *Renati Descartes notæ in programma quoddam sub finem anni 1647 in Belgio editum cum hoc titulo : Explicatio mentis humanæ sive animæ rationalis, ubi explicatur quid sit et quid esse possit.* (AT, VIII, 337–69 ; HR, I, 429–50). Cf. also, AT, XI, 672–87 ; Bouillier, *Hist. de la phil. cartésienne*, I, 260–7, 273.

[1] Cf. *Histoire naturelle de l'Ame*, Paris, 1745 : and especially, *L'Homme machine*, Leyden, 1748 ; also, Baron d'Holbach, *Système de la Nature*, 1770.

[2] Cf. *Traité de l'Esprit de l'Homme*, Paris, 1666.

[3] Authorities do not seem to be agreed on the import of De la Forge's distinction between ' universal cause ' and ' particular causes.' The view outlined above is that adopted by Bouillier (*op. cit.*, I, 511–13) and Kuno Fischer (*Descartes and His School*, pp. 518–19). Bréhier (*Hist. de la phil.*, II. 120–1) interprets him as being at one with Régis and Clauberg in allowing to volition no more than directive efficacy.

incompatible with the Cartesian law that the amount of motion in nature is constant.

The rest of Descartes's immediate successors agree in not accepting this exception to the attribution of all change to God. Régis[1] reaffirms Descartes's view that God alone causes or imparts motion, and allows the self, by its volition, only the instrumental rôle of determining the course physiological excitations shall follow, and, thereby, which of our internal organs shall be stimulated into action. The experience we interpret as a direct action of our self on our body is, therefore, not wholly misinterpreted, for some bodily actions are subsequent to, and determined by, our volitions. Where we err is in attributing more than this to our will, namely, in assigning to it efficacy to originate and impart a quantity of motion to our body. The fact is, according to Régis, that divine and human volitions collaborate, the former initiating a physical change, the latter directing the change initiated. Clauberg[2] too agrees that the self can do no more than " predispose " the body for the changes ensuing on volition, and that the body can exercise no action on the self.[3] The constancy in the apparently reciprocal action between mind and body is therefore referable to God's volition. What we now call psychophysical laws, and regard as instances of transeunt causation between psychical and physiological events, are, for Clauberg, instances of divine intervention in human affairs, and, being of a constant character, laws of divine psychology. It is in terms of this conception that meaning must be found for speaking of the ' union ' of self and body. The connexion

[1] Pierre Sylvain Régis, b. near Agen, 1632 : d. 1707—not to be confused with Regius—lectured on Cartesianism, with great success, at the Universities of Montpellier and Toulouse (1665–71) and at Paris (1680). He departed from Descartes in maintaining that the evidence for the existence of bodies was as clear as that for the existence of selves, and that all ideas arise from the self's union with its body, none being independently innate to it ; cf. *Système de phil.*, 1690.
[2] John Clauberg (1622–65) of Westphalia, professor of philosophy in the University of Duisburg, worked zealously at connecting Cartesianism with the Platonic tradition, and at extending the range of Descartes's influence. His principal writings are : *De corporis et animæ in homine conjunctione ; Defensio Cartesiana*, 1652 ; *De cogitatione Dei et nostri*, 1656. (*Œuvres complètes*, one vol., Amsterdam, 1691.)
[3] Cf. " The movements of our bodies are only procatarctic causes that provide the occasion for the mind, as principal cause, to summon from itself at some particular moment this or that idea which it possesses potentially at all time."
—*De corporis et animæ in homine conjunctione*, cap. 16.

cannot be one that forms a compound *substance*, still less an *absolute* substance, but one which merely co-ordinates their actions and passions. Further, Clauberg thinks, Descartes's view that persistence and succession in the human individual's existence is the effect of a continuous creation by God, calls for correction. If we have no difficulty in conceiving that our ideas cease to exist when we no longer attend to them, why, he asks, should we find difficulty in believing that created beings would cease to exist were God to cease from creating them? Indeed, the analogy suggested here is, for Clauberg, an overstatement. For we are not the masters of our thoughts, controlling what we shall apprehend, as God is the master of His creations, determining what He shall bring into existence.

So far, then, we witness hesitant moves towards Occasionalism. These measures of De la Forge, Régis and Clauberg, however, all leave untouched the original difficulty, viz., if mind and matter are wholly disparate, how is it possible for either to determine the character of a change in the other, any more than to cause the occurrence of a change in the other? Of this question, the three thinkers of our second group—Cordemoy, Geulincx and Malebranche—take special account, and think to answer it by a doctrine of complete Occasionalism. Cordemoy[1] points out that the reason rightly given for denying that will has any efficacy to produce actions in bodies must also be a reason for its inability to direct, influence or determine the character of any action in a body. And in denying the possibility of action in either sense, as between not only minds and bodies, but also one body and another, he affirms the necessity of resorting to the only other kind of substance remaining (viz., God) for an explanation of change. Man *is* a unity of a sort, but the nature and behaviour of his body-part alone does not, any more than that of the self alone, enable us to form a clear idea of the union. Mechanics is as powerless as psychology to explain it, for neither furnishes a concept which is, on the one hand, neutral as between unified bodily mechanisms and persistent selves, and, on the other, capable of integrating both into a continuous unity. God, then, must be both productive and directive of particular changes and

[1] Géraud de Cordemoy's *Le Discernement de l'âme et du corps* appeared in 1666, the same year as De la Forge's *Traité de l'Esprit de l'Homme*.

movements of all kinds. When I will to move my arm and my arm moves, or when a moving body strikes another and that other moves, the volition in the former case, and the impact in the latter, are only the ' occasions,' not the efficient causes of the ensuing motions in my arm and in the body at rest. God, it must be allowed, is active—in a sort creative. Consequently the various questions that can arise will relate, either to the different kinds of divine action that may occur, or to the place of minds in nature, and, in particular, to the place of human volitions in a deterministic physics. All particular movements occurrent in nature conform to the laws of geometry and kinematics, therefore these it must be that exhibit the character of divine design in nature. Hence the range of miracle, if not annihilated, is certainly restricted. One miracle—if such it should be called—there must be, namely, the ultimate fact that God does intervene in the world. But each particular intervention is not one more separate, incomprehensible event. For, given a knowledge of God's settled plan of action (the laws of kinematics) and of present occurrence in some region of matter, we can foretell the kind of changes about to occur. If it is miraculous that God should intervene in nature, that His intervention should be systematised and discoverable by us effectively lifts natural knowledge out of incalculable dependence on revelation and theology. Material bodies are compounds of atoms,[1] but since they possess no dynamical but only geometrical properties, it follows that no body can move of itself, and a non-material cause must be found for the occurrence and continuance of its movements. Neither for Cordemoy nor for Descartes can a mechanistic

---

[1] Cordemoy, who was, *inter alia*, trying to define more exactly the province of physics, agreed with Descartes that the behaviour of natural bodies, organic and inorganic, is to be explained mechanistically, but did not agree that they should be defined as *modes* of a single substance which is all matter. This deviation is highly significant and far from merely a verbal matter. Descartes, we saw, denied the existence of atoms and maintained that modes of matter were infinitely divisible. But Cordemoy argues that unless something *indivisible* is posited, the unity and individuality of any complex natural body will be for ever inexplicable, since they cannot be derived from a *mode* of a determinable character. He therefore introduces into the new physics, as an indispensable, primitive concept, the idea of a spread of extended *substances*, the total collection of which is all matter. And he postulates, in addition to these indivisible, impenetrable corpuscles, the reality of an empty space in which they move, so departing from Descartes and approaching the atomism of Democritus.

physics be the last word of natural philosophy.[1] And like Clauberg, Cordemoy decides that the union of self with body is to be found only in the correspondence, divinely established, between each of the states of any one self and some change in the compound of atoms commonly designated its body. His Occasionalism is, therefore, well-nigh complete. For he denies causal efficacy to secondary substances and their modes, and allows no more than the status of ' an occasion ' to a situation in which the terms of apparent interaction are (i) both physical, or (ii) mental and physical, or (iii) physical and mental, states. But the fourth possibility—where both terms are mental states of the same self—he leaves in some obscurity. Geulincx,[2] however, examines it very fully, and the conclusions he reaches form an indispensable part of the metaphysic from which his principles of ethics are deduced.

By the practice of methodical doubt, he arrives, like Descartes, at a piece of indubitable knowledge in the immediate experience of his own existence. But unlike Descartes, whose first employment of the *cogito* was to extract a criterion of certitude from it, Geulincx's immediate concern is to draw a psychological distinction relating to the origin of the experiences which the self undergoes. The self manifests its existence in and by its *activity*, this self-activity being essentially and irreducibly conscious activity. But there are two senses in which our conscious activities are ' ours.' Some are ' ours ' because it is ourself that causes their occurrence; others are ' ours ' since they occur ' in us,' though they are not caused by us. All mental states of which we know not merely *that* they occurred, but *how* they occurred, are states we ourselves have caused. " If you do not know the means by which a thing is produced," Geulincx declares, " it is not you who produced it." And this presumably means that if you are not acquainted with the entire course of events which led up to the occurrence of the state in question, that state is caused by something other than yourself. Now the mode of production of any state not caused by our self is

[1] Cf. pp. 119–21.
[2] Arnold Geulincx of Anvers, 1625–69, six years a professor at Louvain, was a devoted admirer of Descartes, whose philosophy he sought to complete by a system of ethics. Principal works : *Metaphysica vera et ad mentem peripateticam*, 1691 ; Γνῶθι σεαυτόν, *sive ethica*, 1696 ; *Physica vera*, 1698 (Amsterdam).

o

to be conceived by analogy with a state that is so caused. Hence, those "thoughts" of which we know ourselves *not* to be the cause—*i.e.* not to have *volitionally* incited—must be states caused to occur 'in us' by some other being who *does* know and will them. And this other being can only be God. When, for example, I perceive a certain change occurring in my body, will in consequence a certain action designed to secure its continuation, alteration or cessation, and then perform the action willed, the occurrence of my perception and the occurrence of my eventual bodily behaviour are both direct effects of divine intervention. This is common ground to Geulincx and Cordemoy. But for Geulincx, my volitional act is due wholly to myself, the perception God caused in me just before being the occasion on which I myself caused the volition, this self-caused volition being in turn the occasion on which God caused my bodily behaviour. So for Geulincx there are two kinds of substance which manifest their existence in and through their proper causal activity, viz., God and finite selves. On this point, however, Malebranche differs from Geulincx,[1] and, by lodging all causal efficacy in God alone, carries the hypothesis of Occasionalism to its completion. The dogma that all existents, substantival or modal, depend continually on God and on nothing else for their existence, comes to mean that the occurrence of each successive state of a finite substance is both (*a*) an effect of divine causation, and (*b*) the occasion on which God further intervenes to cause a subsequent state in that or another substance. So, for Malebranche, *none* of a self's states are caused by that self, its volitional acts are the effects of divine causation no less than changes of state or place in bodies. "I deny," he says, "that my will produces ideas in me, for I cannot even conceive how it could produce them, since, being unable to act without knowledge, it presupposes ideas, and therefore does not cause them."[2] All causality, then, is divine causality. Of this Malebranche thinks we are doubly

---

[1] It is Cordemoy's Occasionalism, rather than Geulincx's, that Malebranche carries to its logical conclusion. He does not appear to have been conversant with the writings of Geulincx, though he was with those of Cordemoy (cf. *Recherche*, ed. F. Bouillier, I, p. 86).—Nicolas Malebranche, *b.* Paris, 1638: *d*, 1715. Principal works: *Recherche de la Vérité*, Vol. I, 1674, Vol. II and *Éclaircissements*, 1675; *Traité de Morale* and *Méditations chrétiennes*, 1683; *Entretiens sur la métaphysique et la religion*, 1688.

[2] *Recherche*; *Eclaircissement* to Book IV, part ii, ch. 3.

assured; for reason leads right up to that conclusion, and revealed religion endorses it.[1] The position of Malebranche on causality and finite substances is therefore the exact contrary of that of Leibniz. For the one, no state of a substance is immanently caused by it, all are effects of a transeunt cause; for the latter, all the states of a finite substance are immanently caused by it, none is the effect of a transeunt cause.

The incomplete forms of Occasionalism turn, we saw (p. 204) on this distinction: that while secondary substances can never cause the existence or occurrence of events, some can and do determine their character. With this distinction between two senses of action (viz., between causing the existence, and determining the character, of an effect-event), complete occasionalists like Malebranche combine another. For them 'action' or 'causality' may refer either to a power to act or to an actual instance of action or expenditure of power. Though secondary substances are popularly supposed to be causally active in both these senses, Malebranche thinks they can really be so in neither. For real, as distinct from apparent, causation requires "a cause, between which and its effect the mind perceives a necessary connexion."[2] But if we examine cases of apparent causal transaction, though constancy of connexion is found, no necessity of conjunction is discoverable. Now the perfection of God implies omnipotence, and this quality implies, by definition, a will so powerful that it can never fail to produce or effect what is willed. Omnipotence being a perfection proper to will, it follows that there cannot occur an event which is not controlled by God's will. Every event is thus an effect of divine volition, and every divine volition is efficacious. So, taking Malebranche's definition of a real cause with his assertion of God's existence and omnipotence, it follows that there is no real cause but God. God would not be omnipotent were there a real cause other than His volition, hence secondary substances are never really causative. True, we do not clearly *perceive* a necessary connexion between God's volitions and natural occur-

---

[1] Cf. "The so-called 'new' philosophy (Cartesianism) . . . agrees completely with the first principle of the Christian faith. For if Religion teaches that there is but one true God, this philosophy shows us that there is but one genuine cause."—*Recherche*, Bk. VI, part ii, ch. 3.
[2] *Ibid.*

rences in particular cases. But this should not surprise us, for to do so presupposes that we have a clear idea of God's volition, and this we have not. Indeed, for that matter, neither have we a clear conception of exactly what it is that even the words 'power,' 'efficacy,' stand for. Experience, then, is continually disclosing both the occurrence of changes and constancy in the succession of changes. But never does it disclose in an object a power to originate its own changes, hence none in it to initiate changes in another object. And since causal efficacy is not empirically certifiable, neither can its alleged necessity be. Therefore we can know this or that particular occurrence to be an effect of divine volition only because we know *a priori* that all occurrences are such.

The point is illustrated by two typical cases of apparent interaction. When I will to walk and my legs move suitably, or when one body collides with another and the second moves on, my will in the former case, and the colliding body in the latter, are both intrinsically impotent. My volition and the impact in the respective situations are doubtless *essential* part-causes; they are, in fact, 'natural' or 'occasional' or 'secondary' causes of the changes subsequent to them. But the power 'imparted' or exercised in bringing about the effects—the power *of* which the effects are manifestations—is wholly supplied by God. Thus, to the question, ' Why should this or that movement have occurred at all ? ' the answer is, ' Because God acted or willed.' But to the question, ' Why should the movement have occurred just *when* it did and not at another time, just *where* it did and not elsewhere, and be of just the character it was and not otherwise ? ' the answer must be found in the character of the ' occasional ' or ' secondary ' causal-state, and in the constitution and location of the secondary substance in which that state occurs. The activity and productivity ordinarily assigned to things is therefore wholly extrinsic to them. It is God that delegates that power to things, and they exercise it in regular ways which we formulate as the laws of moving bodies or of psycho-physics. The essential function of occasional causes, then, is to determine the ' when,' the ' where,' and the ' what ' of particular events in bodies and minds. In this way a secondary substance, on the one hand, determines the being creative of change and movement *to act*, now and there, and, on the other hand, it 'receives' and determines its own modes, though it does not produce them.[1]

II

I propose now to make a *détour* from our central subject of substance and causality, and consider briefly two connected themes. (1) Our previous concern with volition was limited to examining how apparent interaction of will and body could be explained compatibly with the qualitative disparateness and existential independence asserted of them. How voluntary actions, taken as one type of natural occurrence, are related to the moral characteristics of their effects, remains to be investigated. The development of a moral philosophy characteristically Cartesian from premises mainly Cartesian was the special contribution of Geulincx. (2) And the kinds of action so far considered are all such as alter, at least *prima facie*, the things acted on. How action which appears to involve no such alteration (viz., cognition) is related to its objects ('ideas' not being things acted on) must also come under review. Malebranche's extension of Descartes's epistemology, and Arnauld's critique of Malebranche's theory of ideas, will conclude this *détour*, and, therewith, our account of the transition period.

(1) Geulincx,[2] we noticed (p. 210) does not, like Malebranche,

[1] Finite things continue in existence so long as God creates or imparts to them new states or modes. Each mode so created also serves as the occasion for a further creative intervention on God's part. And this seems to reduce the finite existent to a mere receptive instrument of God's creative action. Yet Malebranche maintains that the finite existent, though always 'receptive,' is *not* merely instrumental. For it is active in exercising the power delegated to it, and, in providing the occasions (times and places) for God's further action, it contributes to the particular occurrences expressing that action their specificity. But whatever may be the merits of this explanation when restricted to purely physical transactions, insuperable difficulties seem to arise when it is applied to human conduct. For instance, on such an hypothesis, no man may be said to have a character *of his own*, for he has been, is and will be just what God has caused him to be, so that it seems in consequence impossible to find any meaning for 'responsibility,' and therefore futile to praise or to blame anyone. Malebranche's Occasionalism is quite inseparable from a determinism, the laws of which necessitate without exception the actual course of events, both mental and physical. There seems, to be sure, something very like a double contradiction at the heart of the Occasionalist hypothesis. For (i) secondary substances are asserted to be impotent, yet they are said to determine God to act on the occasion of their having this or that state; and (ii) God is said to be omnipotent and His actions alone efficacious, yet the evocation of such actions is due, directly and solely, to occasional causes.

[2] Descartes published no systematic ethics, though his correspondence shows that he thought much on the subject (cp. especially, letters to Chanut,

deny all causal efficacy to the self. Though its volitions cannot produce changes in external matter, or even in its own body, it can produce further mental states. No action that is unconscious and involuntary is mine,[1] but I am genuinely active on all occasions that I am introspectively aware of myself *as* acting. And since my power is limited to my will, and my will effective only in producing further mental states, it follows that the field of my proper and significant action is confined to my own inner life. Where I can do nothing, there should I will nothing.[2] This is the metaphysical ' axiom ' which determines the essential character of Geulincx's ethics. The material world, mine and other human bodies, and their behaviour during life on earth, all fall outside the self's effective control. Therefore the world cannot properly be the scene of the self's moral effort. Some volitions, to be sure, *are* directed on objects which we cannot in fact control, though we suppose ourselves able to do so. Hence one volition, which *can* be effectual, should be that of *renouncing the world*; this Geulincx thinks follows with the force of a corollary. But of all volitions that can be effective, not all are permissible. To will what is permissible or right depends on *knowing* what is such, and this in turn on discovering what is

Nov. 1, 1646, Nov. 20, 1647; and to Elisabeth, Aug. 1664). So far as he expresses his views informally, he adopts the attitude of traditionalism, expressly disclaiming responsibility for any innovation. Yet he regards moral philosophy as the supreme science and the highest kind of knowledge. Much as some thinkers to-day hold that metaphysical problems can be profitably studied only after certain conceptions of common sense and science have been submitted to analysis and criticism, so Descartes maintains that ethics can profitably be studied only after all the sciences have been solidly founded, and need of their revision no longer even possible, and, in particular, only after the general principles of metaphysics have been immovably established (cp. letter to Chanut, June 15, 1646). Prof. Thouverez (in the Introd. to his edition of the *Meditations*, sect. 186) suggests that three views about the character of ethical knowledge can be distinguished in Descartes : (i) that it is a " *hygiène mondaine*," made up of an ensemble of practical rules, (ii) that it is certified by " scientific deduction," and (iii) that it is a result of " a voluntary and free acceptance of revealed religion." To complete Descartes's unfinished task, and by a method of " strict deduction," seems to have been the principal and most fruitful undertaking of Geulincx. His motive was both to develop and to defend Cartesianism, *i.e.* to build on the bare foundation, metaphysical and psychological, which Descartes had prepared but left, and to defend his teaching against certain inferences leading to materialism, to hedonistic and utilitarian interpretations of goodness, and to the denial of the objectivity to ethical judgments, which became prevalent and found encouragement in those who adhered to Descartes's mathematics and physics, but set aside his metaphysics and all that presupposed the existence of a creative God.

[1] " *Impossible est ut is faciat qui nescit quomodo fiat.*"—*Met. vera.*, pt. i, 5.
[2] " *Ubi nihil vales, ubi nihil velis !* "—*Ibid.*

the will and thought of God. Volition that so conforms is the good will. Once we have renounced the world, we come to see clearly what is right, and we will to do what is right for no other reason than that it *is right*. Virtue in general, being the result of making our will conform with divine reason, is an expression of perfect rationality : in Geulincx's words, it is " the unique love of right reason," or in Spinoza's, " the intellectual love of God." Love of reason, however, is only one species of love ; there is also a love of self, evinced in the determination to benefit oneself, and a love of others, manifested in volitions directed towards their well-being. It is from love of self that all moral evil issues. And the love he calls " amour affectif " must be distinguished from that which is " amour effectif."[1] The former is intrinsically an agreeable *emotion* which, attracting by the satisfaction it unfailingly yields, inclines us to the performance of certain actions. The latter is the tenacious resolution to perform those actions adjudged right, and is thus subordinate to enlightenment by reason. " Amour effectif " alone constitutes action that is virtuous, " amour affectif " is not itself virtuous, though it may strengthen or facilitate the exercise of love that is active.

Virtue in the agent and goodness in his will are manifested specifically in the four cardinal virtues of diligence, obedience, justice and humility. And the greatest of these is humility.[2] This is the sum, the complete realisation and concentration of all virtues, so, if it be attained, nothing can be lacking. And it is an expression in conduct of the self's true recognition and conception of itself—an outcome of adequate self-examination. Hence the importance of the dictum : γνῶθι σεαυτόν. To know ourselves as we really are precludes the possibility of pride and self-exultation. Our worldly cares and desires, born and nourished of self-love, can, in humility, be seen for what they are, and cease to torment us. And in realising our dependence on God, we recognise that the performance of duty is required of us unconditionally, and not because it conduces to happiness or protects us from harm. To such clear vision and consequent

[1] *Ethica*, Tr. I, cap, 1, § 2. Cf. the ' *amour sensuelle* ' and ' *amour intellectuelle* ' of Descartes, p. 181.
[2] Cf. " *Humilitas est virtutum cardinalium summa. Humilitas circulum absolvit ; ultra eam virtuti nihil addi potest. Igitur filia virtutis humilitas.*"—*Ibid.*

right action, diligence is contributory. For it consists in withdrawing our love from things of sense, and, by meditation of self, in becoming *attentive* to the deliverances of reason. These inward disclosures of the rightness and wrongness of actions once given, it remains to bring our actions into conformity with them, and so express the virtue of obedience. And our actions are just in proportion to the exactness with which our volitions actually conform to the requirements of reason, for it is reason alone that sets the standard or mean. So far as our conduct fails to realise the virtue of justice, so far have we erred by excess or defect, through yielding to non-rational motives and impulses. To realise the good in our inmost life is the end of all human action.

The good, the object of our rational love as evil is of our rational aversion, is not identical with the pleasing or the useful. The latter cannot be an intrinsic, but only an instrumental, good, and the pleasing can only be an aim of self-love. But love of the good is an imperative of reason. Hence, emotions and desires, being passions and not actions of the self, cannot be morally qualified. They are neither good nor bad, but non-moral. When we commonly speak of them as good or bad, we are entitled to mean by it no more than that they are pleasing or displeasing. Their ethical significance is strictly relative and due to their instrumental connexion with the love of reason. In this way, self-knowledge naturally culminates in an act of resignation. He who is good and wise renounces the world, its pleasures, honours and riches, and submits his will to the divine ordering of his life. And so the relation between the nature of the self and its place in the world—between what Geulincx calls " autology " and ethics—becomes clear. Since we cannot produce changes in our own body any more than in the world at large, we should *desire* nothing for our body—our relation to our body being one of knowledge, not one of action. Hence renunciation of the 'world and the flesh' follows; *despectio sui* is the consequence of *inspectio sui*.

(2) Turning now to those actions which have the positive character of cognitively acquainting us with that upon which our judgment may be passed, and differentiated from those last considered in that they involve no alteration or action 'upon' anything, the sources for understanding the further

THE CARTESIAN SCHOOL

modifications and extensions of Cartesianism are found in the literature of the famous polemic between Arnauld and Malebranche on "representative ideas." The controversy itself is mainly an epistemological one. It is a protracted and rather acrimonious dispute on the question of the exact sense in which knowledge is 'representative.' But though the problem is plainly one in the theory of knowledge, it arises from an ontological conclusion and has momentous consequences for theology. Its ontological source lies in Malebranche's Occasionalist view of substance and causality which denies that a substance can originate or be causative. Hence, when the substance in question is a self, it follows, since no self is causative, that no self can initiate its successive states or ' ideas.' Therefore God alone, in whom all efficient causality is immanent, initiates ideas in our minds and all changes in our bodies.[1]

Malebranche adopts Descartes's division of all existents into two exclusive orders, the mental and the physical, and agrees that neither the senses nor imagination can give us knowledge of external bodies, but only of our own mental states that occur collaterally with certain physiological changes in our brains. What we are directly aware of in perception is always 'idea,' never physical things. For our minds cannot know what is in nature fundamentally unlike them, and already we have noticed that since causal interaction between finite existents is impossible, interaction between 'external' body and apprehending mind must be impossible. Further, difference of location (distance or spatial apartness) between physical objects and minds renders direct knowledge of the former by the latter impossible, since 'to know' is "to be *intimately* connected with" what is known, and ' intimate connexion ' is impossible at a distance. The motive of Malebranche's theory of ideas is,

---

[1] In view of Malebranche's view of causality, there seems no more reason to allow that God is causative than that finite substances are. We may admit with Hume that if the efficacy of finite things is unintelligible, divine efficacy is no more intelligible. Malebranche maintains, however, that the connexion between observable changes (which are effects of the divine will) and God's volitions is a necessary one, though we cannot perceive its necessity in particular instances. So the reader must choose between the alternatives open to him, viz., either to agree with Malebranche that God's ways transcend our power of conception (in which case we shall believe *that* God's causation is necessarily related to its effects, but we shall not comprehend *how* it is so), or we shall hold that the hypothesis is unmeaning, and is due to what Kant regarded as a ' transcendent ' use of the understanding.

consequently, to show how that which is not itself mental but material can ever become known at all, since knowledge is a 'union' or kind of 'contact' between knower and what is known. Now since there *is* knowledge of 'physical objects' that are spatially distant from the percipient and even absent from his vicinity, it is necessary, Malebranche assumes, to introduce certain " representative ideas " that are existentially separate from our cognitive acts ("modifications of our minds") to do duty for—*suppléer*—those physical objects during their absence.

This, in bare outline, is the ' Theory of Ideas ' which Arnauld[1] attacks with consummate skill in his work, *Des Vraies et des fausses Idées* (1683). He starts with the proposal that it is an ultimate fact that minds are perceptive. There is no sense in asking *why* minds are perceptive, any more than in asking *why* bodies have shape, for it is just the nature of minds to perceive, and of bodies to be shaped. He next shows quite conclusively that Malebranche has used one and the same word 'idea' to denote very various things on different occasions, viz., to denote indifferently (i) perceptive acts or states of the self, (ii) that of which we are immediately aware in and by those states, and (iii) particular existents that are numerically other than either of these, and which are not particular (*e.g.* physical) things, but which are " representative " *of* them.

This preliminary analysis was, of course, of the very greatest importance for subsequent epistemology, besides focusing attention on the real matter at issue in the controversy. For, having fastened on the third sense of " idea " (which is the essential one for Malebranche's doctrine), Arnauld's critique then consists of a number of " sledge-hammer blows " (to borrow Prof. Laird's apt phrase) against the offending " otiose " entities. " Representative idea " (though not " representative perception ") is fictitious ; it is a chimera invented solely on account of the fallacious supposition that since selves are mental they cannot be related in the way of knowledge to what is

[1] Antoine Arnauld, *b.* Paris, 1612 : *d.* 1694, was the twentieth child of Antoine Arnauld (1560–1619), the famous lawyer in the Assembly of Paris, who championed the cause of the University of Paris against the Jesuits. The son— " le grand Arnauld "—was an extremely prolific writer. The forty-three volumes of his collected works published at Lausanne include writings on logic, philosophy and literature, though by far the greater part are theological.

THE CARTESIAN SCHOOL 219

non-mental. Firstly, Malebranche has confounded the admittedly indispensable " objective presence " with the dispensable " physical presence " of the physical thing. To be perceptive certainly implies that there is *something* perceived : something must be present to mind if mind is to perceive. But such " objective presence " is quite other than " local presence." When, for example, I am ' thinking of ' a person, that person is thereby objectively present to my mind, even though he is physically abroad. What is objectively present, then, is often physically absent. Malebranche's error, according to Arnauld, consists in the first place in supposing that " objective presence " entails " local presence."

The second string to Malebranche's bow is that material things, even when " locally present," cannot cause our minds to know them, because perception is a mental event in a mental substance, and there is no interaction between qualitatively disparate existents. But this objection must fail, for presentation is not a causal relation. So there is no good reason to believe, Arnauld concludes, in the existence of ' ideas ' existentially separate from some or other mind. Again and again he reiterates that ' idea ' as intermediate entity intervening between the self and the thing it is said to perceive in perception is completely otiose and offends against the principle of parsimony that we should not introduce more terms than necessary to explain our problem adequately. Malebranche sees his admission that we *do* have knowledge of an external physical world obliges him to provide an explanation of that knowledge. Such knowledge is explicable, he argues, only by means of " representative ideas." Yet self-inspection, he concedes, does not disclose the existence of any " representative entities." So, taking what is presumably the only way open to him, he maintains that in believing we know particular physical objects we fall into error and illusion. What we really know is not this or that particular body, but the formal properties of all body, and these are " intelligible ideas in the mind of God." Malebranche agrees with Descartes that matter does not really have, but only appears as having sensible characteristics ; that pure thought alone, and not sense-perception, can give us knowledge of matter. But, it will be observed, the senses ' deceive ' in very different ways for these two philosophers. For both, sense-experience is representative ; in strictness it *mis*represents, but what *is* misrepresented by it is different. For Descartes it is formally characterised *particulars* ('modes of matter' in general), for Malebranche it is *universals* in a Platonic sense that are misrepresented.

It should be emphasised that what Arnauld denies is the existence of "representative *ideas*," separate from acts of cognition ; he does *not* deny that our perception is representative.[1] He denies that 'ideas' are representative in the sense in which, for instance, a photograph 'represents' the person whose likeness it is. For such 'representation' involves the existence of a separate intermediary between the mind of the percipient and the body of the person photographed, and it is precisely 'representation' of such sort, involving the existence of a separate intermediary, that Malebranche believes indispensable for knowledge and Arnauld tries to prove unfounded. Arnauld admits that *perception* is essentially 'representative,' namely, in the sense of being *presentative* of objects to selves. In his explanation of our perception of an external world, he appears to retain only selves capable of perceptive activity and physical objects. Before his controversy with Malebranche, he accepted Occasionalism, but in his *Réflections théologiques et philosophiques* (1686) he not only allows changes of state in the self independently of divine intervention, but maintains, as against Descartes, that there is no reason why the self should not initiate changes in the external physical world. Efficient causality between the mental and physical orders thus appears to be reinstated. His prevailingly empirical treatment of the whole question recalls the works of Reid and the Scottish common-sense school, rather than the procedure of the seventeenth-century Cartesians. Yet, until his later period, Arnauld

---

[1] What *more* Arnauld means by saying that perception is 'representative' than that it is 'presentative' still has to be made out. But he *does* mean more, and this has been overlooked by such commentators as Professor G. Dawes Hicks, Professor J. Laird and Professor M. Ginsberg, who find in him a forerunner of contemporary realism. This interpretation has, I consider, been shown to be untenable by Professor A. O. Lovejoy.—Cf. G. Dawes Hicks, *Arist. Soc. Proc.*, 1905–6, pp. 275–6 ; J. Laird, *A Study in Realism*, p. 7 : and *Mind*, xxxiii, pp. 176–9 ; Malebranche, *Dialogues on Metaphysics* (Eng. trans. by M. Ginsberg, Introduction) ; A. O. Lovejoy, *Mind*, xxxii and xxxiii. The fullest account of the Malebranche–Arnauld controversy in English is to be found in the excellent *Study in the Philosophy of Malebranche* by R. A. Church ; cf. especially chaps. vi-viii.

THE CARTESIAN SCHOOL

retains the most characteristic of Descartes's conclusions, though signs of a departure from them are visible in his earlier *Objections* to the *Meditations*. For he there questioned whether Descartes's argument *does* establish that we can infer with certainty from our acquaintance with the self that its essential nature is completely other than that of material bodies, and concluded that Descartes had not shown that the self cannot be corporeal as well as conscious.

III

Most historians and commentators of seventeenth-century philosophers have, until recently, agreed to regard Spinoza and Leibniz as followers of Descartes and full members of the Cartesian School. The usual view is that each developed certain central theses of Cartesianism to their logical conclusion, and that the manner in which they did so argues that their adherence to Cartesianism was profounder than their departure from it.[1] But there is much to favour the view that in many respects the divergencies of both Spinoza[2] and Leibniz are so radical, and have so plainly the character of innovation, if not of novelty, as ultimately to exclude them from membership of the Cartesian School. This estimate seems to be justifiable.[3] Even so, the systems of Spinoza and Leibniz were dominated by Cartesianism in a greater degree than any later metaphysic. So though we shall not regard them in strictness as ' Cartesians,' it is desirable to review briefly what is Cartesian in their work and what is the character of their deviations.

[1] Such is substantially the view of Caird and Adamson, of Bouillier, Janet, Fouillée, Boutroux, Saisset, A. Léon and Kuno Fischer. And Lebniz too is very emphatic on the correctness of that estimate when applied to Spinoza, thought not when applied to himself ! This is testified in his letter to the Abbé Nicaise (1697), where he declares that Spinoza " only cultivated certain seeds in the philosophy of M. Descartes," and again in the *Théodicée* (pt. iii), where Spinozism is called " an exaggerated Cartesianism." Hegel, moreover, endorses the former view.

[2] *e.g.* in the opinion of Sir Frederick Pollock (*Spinoza*, edn. 1912, p. 86), " Spinoza was never a Cartesian at all," though he admits that Spinoza derived his natural philosophy and the doctrine of conservation of motion from Descartes. This seems to me an *under*statement of Spinoza's indebtedness.

[3] But I am bound to add that in the writings of those who adopt it I have found nothing that comes within measurable distance of having justified it. By far the best-informed and most judicious statement of the view known to me is that of V. Delbos, but it is regrettably brief—suggestive but not conclusive. Cf. *Le Spinozisme*, pp. 208-14. Paris, 1916.

According to Descartes, the formal structure of the totality of the existent is that of a *group* comprising one substance that is 'absolute' or existentially independent of everything, a secondary substance (Nature), and a class of secondary substances (selves) each of which depends for its existence on absolute substance. This formula is deduced from three propositions which he takes for ultimate, viz. : (i) A determinable and essential attribute defines whatever is substance ; (ii) There are two such attributes (materiality and mentality), and they are irreducible ; (iii) The dependent existence of anything entails the independent existence of something, and there are substances whose existence is dependent. The formula provides a convenient starting-point from which to ascertain the modifications [1] introduced into it by Spinoza and Leibniz.

Spinoza accepts (i), adopts (ii) with the amendment that besides materiality and mentality there is an infinite number of 'parallel,' irreducible attributes whose determinable natures are unknown to us, and adopts (iii), maintaining with Descartes that one substance, and one only, has independent existence, but denying that any substance has dependent existence. That is to say, he retains Descartes's qualitative pluralism, but rejects his existential pluralism in favour of a substantival monism. Unconditional existence is possessed only by the whole of what exists, and this is a unity which is determined and diversified in an infinite number of modes. So, for Spinoza, the universe is not a collection, but a single, undivided substance. His identification of this substance with Nature and with God therefore results immediately in a theistic Naturalism or Pantheism. Such a specification of the formal constitution of the universe shares in the advantage promised by every monistic formula, for in reducing the diverse in all its variety to some single, all-comprehensive existent, a more systematic and ultimate type of explanation of the diverse is rendered theoretically possible, and therewith a more intellectually satisfying understanding of it. The amendment Spinoza introduces is not, however, due merely to an æsthetic desire for greater 'systematic unity,' but to a desire to correct two radical inconsistencies which develop in Cartesianism. One is that which arises directly substance is

[1] It is, of course, the *reasons* for these modifications that are the important and informative things, but these of necessity I omit.

THE CARTESIAN SCHOOL

interpreted strictly and God is taken seriously, for then no room is left for 'secondary substances,' and yet Descartes retains them. What he inconsistently retains as the substance that is all matter, Spinoza consistently exhibits as, not a substance, but one ultimate nature or quality in which substance is manifest. And what Descartes inconsistently retains as the class of substances that are selves, Spinoza conceives as a plurality of modes of the same substance that is also manifested as all matter, though characterised by a different ultimate quality. Thus the attempt is, in sum, to exhibit particular bodies, their properties and changes, and particular minds, their actions and states, as parallel but limited (hence partial) manifestations of that one and the same substance which is called indifferently 'Nature' or 'God.' For what is positive and 'real' in these partial manifestations follows necessarily from Substance, hence is deducible from Substance expressed in this or that ultimate nature. In this way Spinoza takes over from Descartes the conception of God as creating or conserving cause of finite bodies and minds, but interprets this causality as being not transeunt and efficient, but a relation of necessary entailment, as exemplified between ground and consequent. Effects follow from their causes as the various properties of a triangle follow from its definition, viz., in being 'analytically contained in' that definition. Hence, what is positive and real in an 'effect' (*i.e.* in a mode of *Natura naturata*) is adjectival to, not discrete and independent of, its ultimate 'cause' (*i.e. Natura naturans*). Such causality is not contingent but necessary, not temporal but 'logical' or timeless, not transeunt but immanent.

The second inconsistency of Descartes which Spinoza sought to remedy is one whose correction indeed necessitates this view of causality as necessary and timeless, and therewith the conclusion that the system of the universe (*Natura naturans* with *Natura naturata*) is a strictly deterministic one. We saw (Ch. VII) that for Descartes understanding is purely passive or contemplative, never active or assertive. But without assertion there can be no knowledge, hence knowing is dependent on, subordinated to, volition. And our volition is our freedom, both in power and in action, and such free volition is a property of substance and not of mode. Now this volitional perfection in

God (viz., His 'freedom') entails that His creativity is restricted by nothing. Hence, it follows, it cannot be restricted by the facts expressed in the 'eternal verities.' For this literally unconditional freedom involves that God was as free to create a universe that does *not* presuppose them, as to create the one He did, which *does*. They so far express His 'choice,' but indicate no limit to the range of His creativity. The facts expressed in necessary propositions are not conditions imposed *on* God's creativity, but expressions *of* His creativity. In a word, God could 'change' His rational nature if He so willed, and He could so will. Now a corollary of such freedom of creativity is the presence of contingency in what is created : 'must be,' 'necessarily is,' can ultimately be only relative expressions, viz., relative to the constancy of divine will. Hence, on this view, 'necessary connexions' and 'necessary truths' are misnamed. But Descartes's method depends vitally on there being necessary connexions to discover between terms ; knowledge just *is* apprehension of such necessity of connexion in particular instances. The strictly deductive character of his epistemology, however, finds not justification but contradiction in the ineradicable contingency which his doctrine of volitional freedom allows and requires. It is thus the *logical*, not the psychological, consequences of God's unconditional freedom which breaks Cartesianism asunder.

Now Spinoza would agree with Descartes that all freedom is centred in volition, and that volitional freedom is a property of substance and not of mode. But for Spinoza there is but one substance, and that is God—(finite selves are modes)—hence volitional perfection is now confined to God, and his 'freedom' must entail that His creativity is restricted by nothing. The disruption freedom brings into Cartesianism is avoided in Spinoza's metaphysics by his explicit denial of human freedom,[1] which denial is a mere consequence of substituting implication

---

[1] Cf. " In nature there is nothing contingent, but all things are determined from the necessity of the divine nature to exist and to act in a certain manner " (*Eth.*, I, xxix). " In the mind there is no absolute or free will, but the mind is determined to this or that volition by a cause, which is also determined by another cause, and this again by another, and so on *ad infinitum* " (*Eth.*, II, xlviii). " Consciousness of freedom," which Descartes alleges is thus an illusion for Spinoza ; an erroneous belief men hold because " they are conscious of their own actions and ignorant of the causes by which those actions are determined " (*Eth.*, II, xxxv, Schol.).

THE CARTESIAN SCHOOL

for efficient causation and of denying the subordination of intellect to will in man and God.[1] The God of Cartesianism is a transcendent being whose purposes remain for ever unknowable, a substance which is existentially separate from the natural world it has created, and, for all Descartes says to the contrary, presumably created out of nothing! The God of Spinozism is rationally comprehensible as are His works, and He has no purposes *to* know. Neither is God existentially separate from Nature, but is its immanent cause—" *Deus mundus implicitus, mundus Deus explicitus.*" From the definition of God and His attributes all else is deducible. What is positive and real in particular bodies (hence, all we are rationally entitled to *expect* to be explained about them) is accounted for by the help of Descartes's mechanistic physics. This is taken over *en bloc* with the amendment that where Descartes postulates communication of motion by God and its importation into Nature (cf. p. 137), Spinoza postulates (at least in the *Short Treatise*) a *dynamical* extension, endued with the power of ' motion and rest '—or, as we should now say, with potential or kinetic energy (viz., energy of motion and energy of position)—in this way moving towards the correction which Leibniz introduced quite explicitly and more thoroughly. Further, the formula Spinoza substitutes for Descartes's (viz., that the Universe is a Substance and not a group of substances) enables him to avoid Descartes's particular difficulties about the relation between a mind and its body. Spinoza can consistently argue that their ' substantial union ' and ' reciprocal influence ' are necessarily incomprehensible,[2] precisely because what is really in question is not two existents (a mode and a substance), but one and the same mode of substance manifested in two disparate media. Accordingly all discussion of ' unification ' and ' reaction ' (which presupposes duality of existents) is meaningless. Just as one and the same meaning may be translated into French and into German, the one version conveying *in propria dictione* the meaning similarly conveyed by the other version, so every

[1] Cf. *Eth.*, I, xxxii, Cor. 2.
[2] Cf. " What does he (Descartes) understand, I ask, by the union of the mind and body ? What clear and distinct conception has he of thought intimately connected with a certain small portion of matter ? . . . In his philosophy the distinction between mind and the body is so radical that he was able to assign no single cause of this union. . . ." See, *in extenso, Eth.*, V, Preface.

P

modification of Substance is 'construed' into the attributes of extension and of thought, these two 'versions' remaining, like their linguistic analogues, uncompounded and ununified, neither 'influencing' the other, but each being merely 'parallel.' The peculiar obscurities and contradiction we encountered in Ch. VI do not, therefore, arise for Spinoza, though to be sure there are other difficulties that do confront him, and they are perhaps hardly less formidable.

Leibniz, like Spinoza, retains the definition of substance as ultimate and existentially independent. But as a result of his logical studies on the one hand, and of his critique of Atomism and of Descartes's reduction of matter to extension on the other, he reaches the conception of the universe as a group comprising an infinite number of individual, causally independent substances (monads), of which God is one. Descartes's "secondary substance," which is all matter, becomes for Leibniz a *phenomenon bene fundatum*, a collective name for an order of appearances or certain confused perceptions present in the experience of every monad, except in that of God.

Leibniz and Spinoza agree that the predicates of substance are all analytically contained in it, but far-reaching consequences result from the fact that for Spinoza what all positive predicates (possible and actual) inhere 'in' is a single substance (*Deus sive Natura*), whereas for Leibniz, what all actual and positive predicates inhere 'in' is one or another of an infinite number of substances. Leibniz reaches this result by two steps, (i) through the analysis of the logical proposition, and (ii) by resort to matter of experience. (i) Every proposition, he holds, either is or is reducible to one in which the predicate is assigned to a subject-term which cannot be predicated of any other subject. All the predicates of such a subject ordered in a certain succession collectively express the 'life-history' or 'experience' of the monad indicated by such subject-term. Thus, the distinction between 'analytic' and 'synthetic' propositions is not ultimate but only provisional; if a true proposition in which the predicate is not seen to be necessarily contained in the subject were analysed far enough so as to exhibit progressively the grounds of its truth, eventually a proposition would be reached in which the predicate *is* seen to inhere necessarily in the subject—*i.e.* we should reach a statement of significant identity. All thinking directed to explicating the nature of any ultimate subject-term is necessarily deductive. This formal analysis of judgment, however, cannot alone exhibit the material truth of propositions about the actually existent, but since it expresses a truth about the formal character of whatever can possibly exist, we can have the foreknowledge that no particular truth about the *de facto* world can really be incompatible with it. Hence, (ii) to secure that our knowledge shall not be of merely abstractly possible worlds, but of this actually existing one, Leibniz has to show that some true propositions do refer to what actually exists ; *i.e.* he must show that the subjects and predicates in such propositions refer respectively to existent individuals, and to states actually belonging to them. This can be accomplished only by resorting to perception. For it is only by and in experience that we come by knowledge of what is actual, as distinct from knowledge of what is logically possible. Now Descartes had already pointed out one clear instance of a true proposition about what actually exists, and one in which the subject and predicate terms do refer to something with which we are perceptually acquainted (viz., the *cogito*)—a proposition, too, in which the subject is predicate of no further subject, and one whose predicate is seen to characterise its subject with necessity. (' I ' *have* predicates, but ' I ' *am not* a predicate of anything.) The subject of that proposition indicates, therefore, an individual substance, the predicates true of that subject indicate states belonging to that substance, and are collectively descriptive of its nature.

And, lastly, it should be noticed how the difficulties caused by the introduction of God into Leibniz's Monadology recall, curiously, parallel defects in Cartesianism. In a doctrine which maintains ' formal ' existence to be susceptible of degrees (*e.g.* that of Descartes and of Leibniz), and in which God, by definition, has all positive perfections (*i.e.* for Descartes — has ' eminent ' existence ; for Leibniz — is wholly active and contains no ' *materia prima* '), inconsistencies are inevitable. Of God and finite things, one or the other must go. If theism be retained and the system be monistic, then pantheism is the only consistent conclusion. A consistent monadism is necessarily atheistic:[1] "so it happens that Leibniz, whenever he takes God at all seriously, falls involuntarily into a Spinozistic pantheism."[2]

[1] Cf. Bertrand Russell, *A Critical Exposition of the Philosophy of Leibniz*, p. 172. Cambridge, 1900.
[2] *Ibid.*, p. 186. Cf. also G. Dawes Hicks, "The ' modes ' of Spinoza and the ' monads ' of Leibniz," *Proc. Arist. Soc.*, 1917–18.

X

SOME MERITS AND DEFECTS OF CARTESIANISM, (I)

" L'ère de la découverte, par l'effort de l'intelligence personnelle, a décidément remplacé l'ère de l'autorité. Aucun virage de pensée n'a été plus profitable à l'humanité. . . . La France a assez fait pour le monde, disait Hegel—si peu cartésien!—en lui donnant Descartes. Il passe pour la plus puissante incarnation de la raison française."—C. BOUGLÉ.

THE second part of this book was directed not only to expounding Cartesianism in a positive and non-critical way, but also to drawing attention to the dependencies of its constituent doctrines one upon another and to places in which the character of Descartes's originality may be seen most clearly. Presented in its widest compass and reinstated in its historical context, this philosophy stands not for a single revolution, but rather for several revolutions which, through their mutual influences and interconnexions, amalgamate into one of such sort as defies adequate characterisation by a single epithet or summary formula. Historically, the Cartesian revolution, the most radical and influential in the history of thought between Aristotle and Kant, stands for the substitution of free enquiry for submission to authority, for the replacement of Faith by Demonstration. It expresses the demand that complete rational satisfaction should be given by that which is rightly to be accounted knowledge. But it was neither the aim nor the effect of this revolution to destroy the beliefs and dogmas of religion. Indeed, one of its purposes was to consolidate them by establishing them on a rational foundation. It was to the promotion of this end that Descartes's proofs of God's existence and of the ultimate disparateness of mind and matter were particularly directed.

The revolution, moreover, was no less a demand for certainty than a protest against mere probability in what is to be accounted knowledge. And it was a demand that the terms chosen as ' primitive ' for use in explanation should be wholly intelligible and ultimate ones, and so far it stood for the complete expurgation of occult qualities, faculties or substantial forms. To Descartes and his school also must be traced a new conception of the radical distinctness yet equal ultimacy of the two divisions of knowledge they called ' Natural Philosophy ' and ' Metaphysics '—a conception that does not accord with our present-day distinction between ' science ' and ' philosophy.'

We have noticed further, *chemin faisant*, how, in carrying out these projects of reconstruction, to Descartes falls the merit of having either originated or signally developed such special branches as analytical geometry, mathematical physics, mechanistic biology, physiological psychology, besides being the first to have attempted to construct a rationalistic theory of knowledge by taking mathematics as the perfect type to which all that may properly be called knowledge must conform.

Believing that to mix criticism with positive exegesis is vicious in principle and objectionable in effect, since it weakens the total force and appeal of the philosophy presented, we refrained from critical comment in our second part, seeking only to express in more modern speech and through conceptions more familiar to modern minds the sense of Descartes's arguments and conclusions. Accordingly it remains to form some estimate of their worth, to elicit what merit may be found in them and wherein lie their defects. Such will be the business of the present and the final chapters. In them we shall examine the strength and weakness of (I) Descartes's methodology ; (II) the *cogito* position, the proofs of God's existence and the transition from them to the natural world ; (III) Descartes's view of its structure ; and (IV) of the self's cognitive and emotional nature, and its destiny.

I

We saw that the new method generated in turn an analytical geometry (cf. p. 22 *n*.), a celestial physics, a terrestrial physics, a mechanistic physiology and a psycho-physics. Each of these branches, regarded as no more than a systematically developed and internally coherent description or hypothetical explanation of a certain field of concrete phenomena, forms a distinct and independent ensemble. So long as the demand for ultimacy in analysis and certitude in knowledge is held in abeyance, each

SOME MERITS AND DEFECTS OF CARTESIANISM 231

ensemble may be accepted on its own merits, without reference to any metaphysics. For, by assuming the principles of mathematics, suitable units of measurement, the laws of impact and the possibility of an unlimited redistribution from time to time of matter and motion, Descartes is enabled to propose valuable working hypotheses of the rotations of celestial bodies, the refraction of light, the functions of vision and the nervous system, the circulation of the blood, the causation of emotions, and transactions between the self and its body generally. But Descartes, of course, maintained that it is the business of science to accomplish more than this, and believed that he had himself done so. It is not an ensemble of working hypotheses or hypothetical explanations that he supposed himself to offer, but nothing less than certain and ultimate knowledge of those general principles sufficient and necessary to explain various classes of phenomena that are typical of the kinds of physical change occurring throughout wide regions of nature. Whether his Natural Philosophy does consist wholly of knowledge that is absolute and final, and whether its parts do inform us of the ultimate character of the regions of nature with which they deal, we shall later find good reason to doubt. Meanwhile, it is instructive to notice that one of two consequences must follow from his view that ' probable knowledge ' should be considered no knowledge at all, that propositions whose terms are not necessarily connected cannot enter constitutively into knowledge, and that mathematics is the type of whatever is rationally acceptable. From this it will follow that either the modern scientist is completely deceived in supposing himself possessed of any knowledge at all in the attainment of his special results, or that Descartes, by ruling out at one stroke all well-attested empirical and inductively established science, is really overstating the matter, and—overlooking Aristotle's warning not to seek certainty in our results when our materials and methods provide for, and permit, no more than probability—is exacting too much. Indeed, judged by this extremely rigorous test, of the sciences as at present constituted, pure mathematics and formal logic alone could pass muster as genuine knowledge, and even these only when ' guaranteed ' by a suitable metaphysic. In the form they have more recently assumed, the problematic character of their results would prevent physics or chemistry or biology from claiming the rank of knowledge at all. His assertion that the necessity of connexion—characteristic of mathematical knowledge—is equally to be found in the truths of natural science (a corollary of his views about our cognitive operations and about the formal constitution of reality) receives no support from present-day analyses of the logical character of the empirical sciences. The consequences to which his demands lead seem therefore unplausible. Yet what seems unplausible at one date need not be erroneous, nor need what then seems plausible be true. And Descartes himself would regard modern criticism of him here as external and inadmissible, for he would deny the validity of both the starting-point and the principle of that criticism. The former would be disallowed on the ground that it does not consist of what is strictly knowledge at all, but of what is merely provisional and problematic; and the latter, on the ground that its method is largely inductive, hence not demonstrative in principle, but no more in fact than plausible guesswork.[1] He would rightly insist that the convenience and working success of hypothesis by no means certifies its truth. In laying down this extreme demand, that what is to be accounted knowledge must be completely intelligible, Descartes, it must be allowed, is expressing, if not the belief or the hope, certainly the desire of every empiricist, namely, that his science should become as deductive as possible through retaining the fewest possible inductive generalisations and deducing from them the greatest number of laws of the widest possible generality, for it is the logical ideal of all science to deduce the utmost from the least. So, though it seems that Descartes's view of the proper procedure for resolving scientific *quæstiones* is probably an over-statement, we have as yet no right to consider it vicious or absurd. On the contrary, it is a timely reminder of the end that controls the practice of the man of science, and a summary indication of the form his science would assume were it perfected and to which it approximates in proportion as it approaches formal completion. The

---

[1] An essentially similar view is maintained by Hobbes, Leibniz and Hegel, while in our own times Bertrand Russell declared (in 1907) that induction was either deduction disguised or simply a method for formulating plausible guesses (*The Principles of Mathematics*, I, p. 11). Later, however (in *Our Knowledge of the External World*, 1914, p. 53; and in *The Analysis of Matter*, 1927, pp. 7, 167, 194), he allowed that, though difficult to justify, induction is nevertheless " indispensable " for science.

SOME MERITS AND DEFECTS OF CARTESIANISM

majority of contemporary men of science would not regard it as a merit in Descartes to have insisted on the need for basing, or to have attempted to base, science in metaphysics. The history of the advance in natural science since Descartes's time shows that its fairest examples were for the most part made by men who not only totally neglected metaphysics, but did not even attempt to justify philosophically the concepts they treated as ' given ' or ' ultimate ' in formulating their problems and their solutions to them. If the claim be allowed that the proper business of science is to provide *knowledge* (and not merely comprehensive formulæ, the interpretation and ' cash-value ' of which it is no part of science to make out), and if the knowledge is to be *of* the Universe, or parts of it, as it really is constituted (and not merely of certain conceptual substitutes found convenient in scientific practice), then Descartes's insistence on justifying science by metaphysics seems correct and important in principle, and his corollary, that unless it be so justified our science is not knowledge at all, is perhaps his most important message to us to-day, precisely because the reasons for it are so generally overlooked or misunderstood. Though we shall find reasons sufficient to show that the particular metaphysic Descartes thought would ' guarantee ' natural science fails completely to do so, the principle guiding him here, issuing from his realisation of the need of *some* supporting metaphysic, seems to me wholly right, if it be agreed that the business of science is to attain knowledge.

It is regrettable that Descartes does not expound in detail the kind of deduction presupposed in his methodology; it is certainly quite different from that of the Aristotelian syllogism. He is content to contrast it in negative ways with syllogistic reasoning and leave the matter there. But it seems that the type of inference he calls deduction, the one purpose of which is to acquire new knowledge, is such as would not reduce to a formal statement, or be analysable into a set of principles, formulæ or rules. There are indeed no rules for the making of discoveries, and the successful practice of Cartesian deduction would seem to depend on long and careful training by trial and error, and on the habits of mind such a training forms. He has a rooted objection to formal methods of reasoning, declaring that any device that permits reason " to rest from work and go on holiday " is not to be trusted (AT, X, 406). And Descartes is right in his view that there is no reason to suppose and good reason for not supposing that all demonstrative reasoning must be syllogistic. He was well alive to the peculiarity of relational arguments though he did not investigate them on their own account, nor anticipate their importance for modern logic even so far as Leibniz did. But it was not on this account that he abandoned with some contempt the use of the syllogism. His reason for doing so was simply that the syllogism is valueless.[1] Nothing new ever has been or could be discovered by its means. At best it serves to present, in a form that compels ready assent from others, something already discovered and known by oneself. It is a stylistic device rather than a logical operation, useful for persuading, but useless for discovery.

This criticism of the syllogism, later repeated by Mill, has had the useful effect of compelling logicians to scrutinise more carefully the character and conditions of inference, and to distinguish it from implication. As a result, the particular objection Descartes brings is now seen to rest on a misunderstanding of the proper function of the syllogism in reasoning. It enables us, not to discover something at present unknown, but to demonstrate with certainty that if certain evidence or premises be granted, then a certain result follows necessarily. The object of logic, as De Morgan put it, is to determine " whether what are asserted to be conclusions are *conclusions.*" Now what is at issue here is clearly not mere elegance or persuasiveness in the presentation of a conclusion, but an operation indispensable for the very possibility of systematic extension in knowledge. Descartes was therefore mistaken in reproaching the syllogism for not doing what it is not its function to do, viz., for not

---

[1] Cf. "In teaching the forms of the syllogisms their terms or matter is assumed to be known. . . ."—*Reg.*, xiii (AT, X, 430). Again: "The Dialecticians cannot formulate any valid syllogism yielding a true conclusion without having first obtained its matter, that is, unless they have previously come to know the very truth that they deduce in that syllogism. Whence it is plain that they themselves learn nothing new by means of such a formula, and consequently that ordinary Dialectic is wholly useless to those desiring to investigate the truth about things. Its only possible use is in enabling us sometimes to expound more easily to others what we have already discovered, hence it should be transferred from Philosophy to Rhetoric."—*Reg.*, x (AT, X, 406). It will be observed that though this criticism (in the earlier part) does not explicitly prefer a charge of circularity against the syllogism, it contains the points on which Mill later based that charge. The only objection expressed is that no one ever discovers new knowledge by the use of the syllogism.

SOME MERITS AND DEFECTS OF CARTESIANISM 235

discovering what was previously unknown. Its purpose is not to originate or discover, but to demonstrate or certify what is claimed to *be* a discovery. When this is grasped, the particular objection Descartes alleges is seen to be beside the point, and the charge fails.

Further, Descartes's insistence on the rôle of analysis and synthesis in the extension of knowledge is significant, the more so when their relation to his doctrine about the conditions of knowledge generally is understood. Fully to appreciate the knowledge consequent on analysing a complex datum into simpler constituents, intuiting their intrinsic character and ordering relations, and thence inversely reconstructing the given complex in mind by combining those constituents in those relationships, doubtless presupposes a funded experience that comes only from constant exercise. But one particular merit of Descartes's method can be anticipated, to some extent, by considering his conception of intuition and deduction in connexion with simple natures. If mathematics is found to be at a highly advanced stage of development and psychology at a very backward one, much of the difference has accrued from the enormous success mathematicians have had in selecting suitable " absolute natures " or even in singling out " simple natures " proper to their field, and to the failure of psychologists in eliciting suitable " absolute " terms or in discovering the simple natures proper to their subject-matter. If accurate syllogising alone were enough to advance a science, there is no reason why psychology should not have reached the same degree of logical perfection as mathematics.

Descartes, then, does stress something immensely important about both the constitution and the acquirement of scientific knowledge, though we may doubt whether the positive injunctions of his method, as stated in the *Discourse*, are of great practical worth. For they are so very general that, confronted with the complex detail of empirical material, they seem powerless to suggest how we should ascertain what is the next practical step in advance. Possibility of progress—as Descartes, himself a practical investigator, is fully aware—depends very much more on sagacity and experience than on the sufficiency of any general rules.

His retention of Intuition and Deduction, moreover, is not

a haphazard effect of the weight of tradition and authority, for without both there would be no method. It necessarily presupposes deduction because the constitution of existents is not disclosed on simple inspection, but requires for its explication the intervention of an operation of decomposition and composition, *i.e.* of deduction. For the whole object of the method is to reconstruct in thought complex relationships out of relatively simple relations and relata that are intuited directly and apprehended in isolation. So, in the end, to ' explain ' a datum that is in fact complex is to intuit the way in which a certain set of simple natures are compounded so as to form the kind of unity characteristic of the datum to be explained.

These epistemological parts of Descartes's methodology direct attention naturally to the ontological theory underlying them, and in particular to his view of simple natures. Their importance seems to have been insufficiently recognised by Cartesian scholars.[1] The view consists of two assertions, viz., that we each have a clear and distinct perception of certain quite fundamental elements that can be named but not defined, and that these simple natures or elements combine to make up various realities, and *à ce titre*, enter as explanatory factors into our knowledge of those realities. Now there is much to make such a view appear probable. Firstly, there is the historical fact that the natural sciences have already explained with surprising success the constitution of many kinds of complex phenomena by means of relatively few elements and laws. Apart from this accomplishment, moreover, it seems inherently plausible to suppose that if explanation of phenomena is to be possible at all, the number of elementary factors and the number

[1] Simple natures are not ' ideas ' but essential ' ontal ' elements, constitutive and explanatory, presupposed throughout the whole of Descartes's Natural Philosophy and his Metaphysics. The theory of representative perception is, indeed, indirect evidence of this, for, eliminate simple natures, and there is nothing left to be represented in distinct idea, or misrepresented in confused ones. His expositors think it sufficient to discuss them when treating of his method, and omit all reference to them thereafter. This seems to me regrettable, even though they but follow Descartes's example. No mention is made of them in any work other than the *Regulæ*. Yet the doctrine of innate ideas and the epistemology of the *Meditations* presuppose the existence of simple natures. His failure to carry them explicitly right through his metaphysics and to work out his theory of them in sufficient fullness seems to be mainly due to his later interest being dominated by difficulties of an epistemological rather than an ontological character.

SOME MERITS AND DEFECTS OF CARTESIANISM

of laws of their combination must be limited.[1] There are, then, grounds for believing that Descartes's view is acceptable *in principle*, though it does not seem acceptable in the form in which he states it. For, it must be admitted, he seems to have taken little pains to make his list of simple natures exhaustive, or to devise a clear principle for classifying the very diverse ones he did recognise. And though the number of simple natures should be small, it seems improbable that it could be so small as he supposed, or that their modes of combination are all of the elementary type he envisaged.

On the other hand, despite these deficiencies, subsequent science and philosophy have fully vindicated Descartes's insistence on the supreme importance of analysis for explanation and knowledge. The demand that anything complex—problem or phenomenon—should be divided into parts, that the character of each part should be distinctly apprehended in isolation from its neighbours, that the connecting relations between them should likewise be clearly perceived—such clear insight into the *desiderata* of all exhaustive explanation may fairly be considered a brilliant innovation and a permanent contribution to methodology. Men of science before Descartes had, of course, proceeded along such lines. But it required a Descartes to bring to light what were the principles implicit in their procedure, and to show, further, by reference to the formal constitution of nature, why such a procedure *should* be successful.

II

The demand for certainty necessitated introducing the most stringent test conceivable—*de omnibus dubitandum* (cf. Ch. IV). In having proclaimed its adoption a first and indispensable step in all serious philosophising Descartes performed a service of the utmost usefulness; in having himself prematurely relinquished its practice he shows how even the cautious and clear-sighted can be over-hasty. There are several observations worth making on Descartes's use of this test and on the belief he thinks satisfies it. (1) We must admit that he rightly objects

[1] A striking parallel is afforded in our own times by the principle of Limited Independent Variety proposed by Mr. J. M. Keynes. Cf. his *Treatise on Probability*, pp. 256–60, or the lucid restatement of it in L. S. Stebbing's *Modern Introduction to Logic*, pp. 412–14.

to taking the appearances which, it is assumed, external objects present to percipients, as conveying trustworthy information about the nature those existents possess independently of their relationship to percipients constituted as we are, physiologically, and psychologically. Not that suspension or withdrawal of our customary confidence in sense-perception implies that confidence should be placed in an operation wholly unrelated to sensation, but that the trustworthiness of our sensory deliverances is something that requires to be established, and not something vouchsafed by the mere fact of their occurrence. There must be no 'prejudice in favour of the actual.' And (2) from the position of doubt Descartes has provisionally adopted there is nothing fanciful in his rejection of mathematical propositions. It is well that we should, at least once in our lives, consider critically the confidence we customarily place in our reasoning, no less than that which we place in our perception. The possibility of there being some form of systematic deception in either or both is *prima facie* a perfectly sensible hypothesis; its truth or falsity is not certified by our ' instinctive ' reaction to the proposal, but only by a critical examination of its consequences. It is by reasoning that the vast majority of mathematical propositions are reached, and many of them are constantly and unhesitatingly applied to what exists. Perception alone cannot justify this application. Even if those propositions be certain, they may yet have no genuine extra-mental reference, and even though they have, perception alone cannot show this. To open, then, as Descartes proposes, a thorough-going interrogation of our normal, uncriticised beliefs and confidences is to submit to a purgation in the interests of intellectual good-health. And (3) even though Descartes acquits himself too summarily and easily of this self-imposed task, that in no degree lessens the excellence of his recommendation. Steadily to continue in subjecting to doubt whatever we are inclined to assert or whatever we habitually do assert may well be a procedure that does not produce a single positive result beyond the reach of a general mood of suspicion or attitude of mistrust. But whatever may be the positive limitations of the injunction, we can be assured of its negative efficacy. For no thinker who has not deliberately and systematically set about discovering reasons for rejecting

SOME MERITS AND DEFECTS OF CARTESIANISM

what he believes ever reaches a belief secure from doubt and worthy of retention.

But how are we to estimate the particular proposition which, for Descartes, puts an end once for all to the possibility of endless doubt—the *cogito* ? Firstly, it is no small merit to have realised the need of *some* primitive proposition which, besides being incontrovertible, should also assert existence, and, further, one whose truth is intuitively and not deductively certifiable. But several of his contemporaries and most of his modern critics, though agreeing that there is some fact immediately disclosed about which he was entitled to be certain, deny that this fact is correctly formulated by him. Their various criticisms are reducible to the objection that the existence of a substantival self is not disclosed on self-inspection, and that even if the self be a substance (which some deny) its substantiality requires establishing by independent argument and is not a certainty immediately disclosed. It has been pointed out, too, that some competent thinkers have emphatically denied any such awareness of self, while others have affirmed either that there are no substances at all or that the self is not one of them. Therefore, it is argued, the substantival existence of self *could* not be a certainty, for were it so none could fail to be aware of it. So the point of their criticism is that the fact about which Descartes is entitled to be certain should have been formulated, not as ' *cogito ergo sum,*' but rather '*cogitatur, ergo aliquid est,*' where the ' something existent ' is a present state of doubt, or, in general, some or other present mental state. So much but no more is certain—so runs the argument. A clear and representative statement of the view is given by Professor John Laird.[1] Commenting on the *cogito*, he says: " What is given, after all, is just the existence of a thought. What is concluded is that this thought must belong to a thinking substance which, in fact, has other thoughts, and remains the same substance from day to day."[2] Descartes would deny, and I think rightly, that the proposition ' this present existing thought necessarily belongs to me ' is, as Professor Laird asserts, " concluded." That awareness in which I am acquainted with my present thought is an awareness

---

[1] *The Idea of the Soul*, ch. ii ; cf. also Bertrand Russell, *An Outline of Philosophy*, p. 171.
[2] Laird, *ibid.*, p. 20.

in which I am acquainted with myself as the thinker of it. What I am aware of is 'myself-now-thinking-this-thought.' There is no inference from my present thought taken as datum to the conclusion that that datum depends upon an existent which is *not* co-datum with it. What *would* be an inference (hence " concluded " and not " given ") is the *general* proposition that all thoughts necessarily belong to some or other self. But the possibility of asserting this general proposition presupposes the possibility of asserting the singular proposition 'This thought belongs to me,' whilst this in turn presupposes that I am acquainted with my self as well as with my present thought (cf. footnote to p. 191). Further knowledge than this about myself has, undoubtedly, to be "concluded," for it is not "given." Moreover, since that further knowledge is derived by inference, it is partly dependent on memory, hence requires the support of metaphysics—*i.e.* as Descartes conceives it, presupposes God's veracity. We have here, in the philosophy of mind, simply a further instance, parallel with that we noticed in the philosophy of matter (pp. 110-1), in which the 'atheist' cannot have ' knowledge.'

Here, and in general, Descartes's metaphysic depends on proving the existence of a God that is veracious and omnipotent. And in its entirety his metaphysic stands or falls with the proofs he proposes. There seems, however, little room for doubting that these proofs are inconclusive. The arguments commonly called 'anthropological' and 'ontological' both start with virtually the same datum, viz., that men can and do *think of* God ; the idea (definition) does exist in men's minds. The former proof is based on the whole of this fact, the latter one on a part of it, viz., the conception which defines the word 'God' (*i.e.* the set of qualities forming the connotation of the term), and is directly present in men's minds when they 'think of' God. The 'anthropological' argument requires us to grant five things : (i) that Descartes's definition of God is significant and that the defining qualities are really positive and not negative ones ; (ii) that every idea has 'objective' reality ; (iii) also ' formal ' reality ; (iv) that both kinds of reality are susceptible of degrees ; and (v) that both kinds have causes. The 'ontological' proof does not, however, require (iv) and (v), and is the more elegant one. We should observe that in both arguments

SOME MERITS AND DEFECTS OF CARTESIANISM 241

the inference proper (as distinct from the explanation of terms) is quite brief, and that their constituent terms call for no protracted effort to conceive. The *expression* of those terms and of the inference in language, however, is in neither case so brief that the whole falls within a single ' span ' of attention. But the process of ' coming to understand ' the meaning of the language (which process requires some time and the introduction of memory) must be distinguished from the act of intuiting the implication of one concept by another, (which does not require duration, but is ' instantaneous ' and not itself an act of memory). The distinction we are considering here is immensely important, and we shall have to return to it later (pp. 246-8). The point, then, is that in both arguments the actual step of inference, considered alone, is quite brief, though the formulation of the arguments, *i.e.* of their constituent premises, is not so. The former may be stated : ' Since something must be adequate to cause the formal reality of an idea having the very great objective reality that my idea (definition) of God has, and since no existent other than God could have so great and the same formal reality as this, it follows that a God must exist and have caused that idea.' And the latter may be stated : ' Since the most perfect being is necessarily one possessing all perfections, and since existence is one of these, it follows that the most perfect being must exist.'

Now it remains to examine the genuineness of the conceptions which these arguments employ and which their conclusions presuppose for their significance, as well as to examine the conditions the inferences themselves should satisfy. Firstly, it has been questioned whether such phrases as " perfect wisdom," " perfect goodness," etc., really signify something positive, as Descartes maintained. Do such phrases indicate anything more than some high but indesignate degree of the quality in question, a degree, say, higher than that manifested by ourself, and one which we can successfully conceive by expelling from our thought of the quality that imperfection we recognise as limiting it in ourself ? If they express no more than this, then the ideas *would* be negative. " Perfect goodness " would be the goodness that is not limited by this or that defect present in such and such good persons. Descartes stoutly denies that the concept is reached by eliminating in thought such imperfections, and that it is a negative idea. He argues that if I did not know what perfect goodness is, and if it were not a positive quality, I should be unable to judge that I myself am imperfectly good. To recognise my own imperfection in some respect presupposes that I know what it is to be perfect in that respect. Some critics of Descartes maintain that he is here asking us to grant more than is necessary, since I can quite well recognise my own imperfection in respect of some quality by comparing myself with another person in whom that quality is present in a higher, though still 'imperfect,' degree. I have only to compare my understanding with that of Descartes to know that mine is very imperfect ; I need not have a positive idea of omniscience in order to come by this piece of self-knowledge.

This criticism appears at first sight very plausible, but it misses the point. On the other hand, it must be admitted, Descartes's discussion is inadequate. The ' perfections ' in question each relate to some different quality, none of which is ' given,' as a determinable or a determinate, in sense-experience. Therefore neither goodness, nor various degrees of it, could become known by inspection of instances in which it is actually present (cf. p. 167, *n*. 1). In order to recognise its presence there, we must first know what the quality is : we must first of all know, not some limited degree of it, but the determinable yet indeterminate quality itself. So far Descartes seems right. But his procedure is highly questionable when, from this point, he goes on to identify ' indeterminate goodness ' (goodness as such) with ' *perfect* goodness,' where this is regarded as ' quantitative,' viz., as ' all the goodness there is and could be.' Descartes is right, then, as against his critics, in holding that we could not recognise limited degrees of goodness without a prior knowledge, in some sense, of goodness indeterminate, and right in maintaining that this is something positive. But he offers no justification for the further assumption, namely, that ' the goodness ' we must know in order to identify various degrees of goodness in particular instances is ' all the goodness there is and could be.' This certainly does require justification, for it is not self-evidently true.

The distinction between (ii) and (iii), in the opinion of some critics, is unfounded. But this seems mistaken, for is there not an indubitable difference between ' idea ' used to denote occur-

SOME MERITS AND DEFECTS OF CARTESIANISM

rent mental act or state, and ' idea ' used to denote that concept or connexion of concepts which is the object of such an act or state ? Proposition (iv), that there are degrees of reality, has also been rejected by some competent philosophers, though it has been accepted by several of the greatest, viz., Plato, Spinoza, Leibniz and Hegel. Here there seems no way of settling the matter finally. Whether or not there are ' degrees of reality,' whether it is true, or, on the other hand, simply meaningless to say that one existent is *more* real than another there seems no way of proving or disproving. A clear meaning for speaking of ' more ' or ' less ' of reality can be found when the reals in question are *in pari materia*, the terms of comparison being quantitatively different amounts (intensive or extensive) of some one and the same quality that is intrinsic to the existents it characterises. But when the essential, defining attributes of the two reals are ineradicably disparate, is it not meaningless to assert one to be more real than the other ? Now the objective reality of my idea of a piece of matter has, according to Descartes, some actual piece of matter as its formal cause, *i.e.* the mode of matter itself has the requisite formal reality to account for the degree of objective reality in the idea. But is there any clear and distinct meaning in saying that the reality of a mode of one attribute (materiality) is equal to, or greater than, the reality of a mode of the antithetic essence (consciousness) ? Indeed, is not the view mistaken that ' the reality ' of an existent necessarily involves reference to the amount of this or that, or of any *quality* that it possesses ? But when the reals to be explained are not *in pari materia* the parallel suggested seems extremely dubious. Even supposing a large body were more real than a small one, there seems no reason to believe that the *thought* of the large body is more real than the *thought* of the small one ! Yet Descartes's ' anthropological ' proof requires differences in degrees of reality to be applicable to those reals that are ideas, no less than to the actual things to which genuine ideas refer. His " axiom " that the cause of an effect is of a degree of reality that is never less than, but always equal to or greater than, the amount of reality in the effect, seems in many applications, far from being clear and distinct, to be either highly dubious or even non-significant. It appears (v) that his whole theory of causality is generalised from an inadequate analysis, and his statement of that theory is not always clear. The application of causality to ideas is, moreover, complicated in a curious way by the doctrine of degrees of reality. If we remember his very wide use of the term cause, we must agree that the objective reality of an idea calls for explanation no less than its formal reality. The demand in the former case is presumably met by the assignment of a sufficient reason, in the latter by that of an efficient cause. But the legitimacy of asserting that both kinds of 'cause' should be assigned to every idea is one thing, to postulate degrees of reality formal and objective and to employ as self-evident the principle of 'eminent' and 'formal' causality is quite another.

Of the five presuppositions made by the anthropological argument, only the first two are made by the ontological proof, so the risk of error is accordingly diminished. And these two presuppositions really reduce to one, for the definition of the term 'God,' from which the argument starts, is one and the same with the objective reality of the idea of God which Descartes finds in his mind. The presupposition of the argument is therefore unobjectionable. And we may further allow that the inferential step it contains is formally valid. Yet God is not thereby proved existent. Descartes maintains that the existence of God follows from the definition of God, just as the equality of its radii follows from the definition of a circle, and that, in consequence, it would be self-contradictory to deny existence to God as to deny equality to the radii. He thus takes the geometrical theorem and the ontological argument to be of one and the same type. But the theorem which concludes that the radii are equal does not assert that circles are existent things. All that is concluded, so far as existence is concerned, is that *if* anything exists having the defining qualities of a circle, then that thing will have equal radii. Descartes seems definitely mistaken in supposing he has proved God to exist. What he *does* prove is, that *if* there exists anything having the defining properties of 'God,' then its existence would be a necessary existence (necessitated by its nature), and not merely a contingent existence (*e.g.* contingent to the rest of the universe, or to any part of it). What really *has* been proved, then, is not an existential proposition at all, but a

SOME MERITS AND DEFECTS OF CARTESIANISM 245

characterising proposition—one about the *kind* of existence God must have *if God exists* at all. God cannot be a contingent being. Either God does not exist, or the God that exists does so of necessity, absolutely, unconditionally, *i.e.* is '*causa sui.*' If it be allowed that existence is a *quality*, and only on that admission (one which Kant and many modern thinkers deny) does it follow that Descartes's argument furnishes information about the kind of existence that an existent God would have. As an attempt to prove that God does, as a matter of fact, *exist*, it seems to be a failure.

It is very often maintained that, even were these proofs of God's existence impeccable and finally convincing, the use Descartes makes of his knowledge of that existence is logically circular, and that the transition from the '*cogito*' to the existence of a physical world is vitiated by this blunder. And the passage of inference by which he thought to effect that transition is held to be vitiated for the second reason that it depends on a principle supposed to be guaranteed by intuition (viz., that of 'eminent' and 'formal' causality), and this, far from being as distinct, as the '*cogito*,' is either unclear or false.

If our objections to the causal principle, apropos of its application in the 'anthropological' argument, were sound, they would be sound in any other application of it, hence in the present one, *i.e.* in the proof of the existence of a physical world. It follows, therefore, that Descartes does not succeed in proving the existence of matter, since his proof depends on that principle. But of the first charge, still very frequently preferred,[1] I think Descartes must be acquitted. The alleged circularity, repeated *ad nauseam* in various forms, may be put in this way. Descartes is enabled to establish God's existence only after accepting the criterion that whatever is clear and distinct is true. But he is not in a position to know that what is clear and distinct *is* true *until* he has proved that a veracious God exists. In other words, it is the conclusion 'God exists' along with the definition of 'God' which *permits* him to deduce that clear and distinct ideas are true. Yet until he knows that clear and distinct ideas *are* true, he is unable to prove that a

---

[1] The charge of circularity was first brought by Antoine Arnauld in his *Second Objections* to the *Meditations*, and sufficiently met by Descartes in his *Reply.* Cf. AT, VII, 214; HR, II, 92, and AT, VII, 245-6; HR, II, 114-5.

veracious God exists, or that anything else does! Therefore, it is argued, the proofs themselves and all in the metaphysics which logically depends on the existence and nature of God are vitiated by an error of reasoning that is, in fact, so patent that any attentive reader of Descartes can scarcely escape detecting it. The charge is sometimes followed up by objecting that the demand he is here making on our credulity is well-nigh ludicrous. For he is in effect asking us to admit that the conditions under which we can have complete certainty of God's existence are such as allow us no certainty whatever in respect of a single proposition of mathematics! For, *before* God's existence is proved, methodical doubt (the malignant demon) effectively prevents legitimate assent to every proposition except the '*cogito*,' and *after* God's existence is proved the range of that doubt is curtailed only so far as to let pass one further proposition, viz., '*Deus est.*'

Both these criticisms—the charge of circularity and the last—rest on a careless misinterpretation of Descartes's text. They arise, more particularly, from misapprehension of what requires guaranteeing in order validly to effect a transition from the '*cogito*' to God's existence, and, in general, to render possible any certain knowledge besides the '*cogito*,' also from misinterpreting the rôle of divine veracity in Descartes's epistemology. Firstly, he claims, we saw, that interrogation of the '*cogito*' yields a criterion of truth. The importance of the '*cogito*' for knowledge consists therefore in this: that, being itself quite certain, it enables us to see what must be the peculiarity of any other proposition that is really certain, a peculiarity that is absent from all that can, without self-contradiction, be doubted. This criterion, now seen to be certain, is the selfsame proposition which, in the Method, had only the status of a useful working hypothesis. Now what we are here calling a criterion of certitude either is or is not such. If it is not one, it is quite impossible for Descartes to advance to a knowledge of the existence of God or of anything else, and his metaphysics remains incurably solipsistic. If it is a genuine criterion (and not merely a working postulate of the method), plainly no question of 'guaranteeing' it can arise. For to admit that the criterion itself requires a guarantee would be to admit that it just is *not* a criterion. Thus, the first error

SOME MERITS AND DEFECTS OF CARTESIANISM

committed by those who accuse Descartes of circularity consists in supposing him to think that a criterion *needs*, or indeed *could admit of*, being itself guaranteed—by God or by anything else; their second error lies in supposing Descartes to have proposed God's veracity as being that guarantee.

What, then, is it that God's veracity *does* guarantee, since it cannot be the criterion; and what is the importance, for Descartes's epistemology, of that which is guaranteed? Its importance can be understood only in connexion with the function of the *malin génie*—the principle *de omnibus dubitandum*. The object of applying this extremely rigorous form of doubt is not to discover some support or reinforcement for the criterion; the veracity of God is not a guarantee to implement or supplement the guarantee already secured and later employed in demonstrating God's existence. What God's veracity guarantees is not our clear and distinct intuitions (for they need no additional guarantee), but precisely that which has not yet been guaranteed at all, but has none the less been constantly used in arguments designed to extend our knowledge. It is to guarantee that which we claim to *remember* having intuited, when the grounds for that which we now assert ourselves to remember having intuited are no longer being intuited by us, *i.e.* when they do not accompany our present memory as they accompanied our previous intuition. For in the great majority of our demonstrations, whether in mathematics or natural science or metaphysics, premises and conclusions require to be retained in thought, held over in mind from an earlier stage of the argument to that later stage at which they are combined so as to yield a further conclusion (*e.g.* all polysyllogistic reasoning). Now such 'holding over in thought' is a function of memory, not of intuition. Hence, since our final conclusions depend on what has been thus held over by memory, no less than on what is directly intuited, the former needs guaranteeing no less than the latter. And it is our memory alone that divine veracity guarantees; intuition neither needs nor is susceptible of support. The charge of circularity results, then, from a failure to have distinguished between (*a*) a proposition which we now *intuit*, and (*b*) a proposition which we now *believe* to be one which we have intuited in the past. Unlike intuition, memory *is* fallible. But memory so guaranteed leaves us free to reintroduce into arguments as premises propositions that we are not now intuiting but only now remembering *to have intuited* formerly. Without this intervention of memory there could be no advance, only a continual marking time. For we should be either continuously thinking the same thought, or else we should never perceive a connexion between our present thought and any other just past or long past, since, *ex hypothesi*, we are not now thinking it.

Thus, as M. Gilson states the matter,[1] the object of the *de omnibus dubitandum* is to throw a general suspicion " sur la valeur du souvenir de nos évidences," since memory of past intuition is not itself an intuition.[2] For, in a system in which present intuition alone is a sufficient guarantee of truth, the validity of evidence in general is not guaranteed if the existence of a veracious God be unknown.[3] This we saw (p. 111) to be the whole point and meaning of Descartes's declaration, at first sight so enigmatical, that the atheist can have no science. And just as it is the object of Descartes's methodical doubt to cast this general suspicion, so it is his principal object in emphasising the veracity of God to revoke it. But the revocation can follow only after God's existence has been proved.

There is, then, no ' circle.' But though it is memory and not intuition that Descartes sought to guarantee, his attempt seems indefensible for empirical reasons. Memory requires guaranteeing no less than perception ; error occurs in both. But though a criterion is provided for perception, none is proposed for memory. The theory makes no provision for any illusion of memory, for divine veracity presumably guarantees every memory act. But that false recollections occur, that ideas are wrongly referred to the past, cannot be doubted. For we have ' recollections ' to which no event in the past

[1] Gilson, *Études*, pp. 236–40.
[2] Cf. Gilson : " J'ai eu dans le passé une série d'intuitions évidentes et de convictions inébranlables, mais maintenant je me reporte au souvenir des mes expériences passées et j'affirme que toutes les propositions évidentes sont vraies. Qu'est-ce qui me garantit, dans le temps où je n'éprouve plus le sentiment d'aucune évidence particulière, que j'avais raison de m'y fier tandis que je l'éprouvais ? Autre chose est avoir la certitude d'une vérité, autre chose avoir la certitude de la validité de la science en général, car bien que l'actuelle évidence se passe de toute garantie, la critique reprend ses droits et le doute règne de nouveau lorsque l'évidence est passée " (*ibid.*, p. 238).
[3] Cf. *ibid.*, p. 239; also, on the 'circle,' consult the treatment of the late Professor Octave Hamelin, *Le Système de Descartes*, ch. x (Paris, 1921).

corresponds, we have 'memories' that misrepresent the character of the event they do refer to, and others that misrepresent the date of the events remembered. Again, in some erroneous inference, the assent improperly yielded *is* so yielded because we believe ourselves to be remembering having intuited a certain proposition and its grounds in the past, when in fact they had not been intuited at all. How, then, are we to distinguish fallacious from genuine memories? How, indeed, can there *be* any illusions of memory if it is divinely guaranteed? The criterion applicable to perception (clearness and distinctness) will not help us here, for memories of past intuitions are not intuitions, and some false memories seem just as clear in their reference to past events as some veracious memories. So we must conclude that although Descartes is right in fixing upon memory as something that requires guaranteeing, he plainly fails to find a suitable guarantee for it, or a criterion.

The next main transition in the metaphysics is that from God to the existence of a material world. We certainly can and do imagine a world of particular persistent bodies changing and interacting one with another, but the suggestions of imagination, we have already seen, are a very uncertain witness to the truth. But we have other 'ideas' of particular bodies than images of them. There are those ideas which are accompanied by the belief that the bodies of which they are suggestive are in fact locally and actually present. Such 'ideas' are percepts of bodies, and if we abstract from them the element of judgment or affirmation we are left with that in which two factors can be discriminated, a formal and a sensory one. The formal factors in percepts are objects of pure thought, and from them the pure or formal sciences of geometry and kinematics are deductively elaborated. The very fact that we are able to elaborate such sciences shows that the things we commonly believe to be characterised by geometrical and kinematical properties are *possible* existents. But these sciences afford no base from which we may infer that there *actually* exist bodies so characterised. So Descartes turns to examine the other, sensory, factors, which, complicated with the formal ones, render our percepts of bodies "confused." The way in which he now proceeds is analogous to that by which he sought to establish the existence of God, namely, by means of a further application of his causal principle. What, he asks in effect, has the formal reality requisite to cause in us ideas containing these sensory factors? For it is certainly in sensation that we seem to have the most direct and convincing experience of the existence of an external world. But in sensation the self is passive. It is not I who cause the sensations that successively present themselves to my awareness. Therefore there must be a power in something other than selves. There must exist something active, reciprocating to my passive sensitivity, that is capable of producing sensations for my awareness. I can, then, be quite sure that the cause sought is no active power of my own, for the only active power proper to my mind is that of willing, and, while I can will images, I certainly cannot will sensations, for these come and go uncontrolled by my mind. In the absence of anything hot from my vicinity I am powerless to feel heat, even though I am not powerless to imagine it. Whatever is causally responsible for such sensory factors in my perceptions is therefore independent of my self and involves no reference to my essential nature (consciousness) for its causation. So, since the sensory factors in our ideas of external bodies are not caused by our volition or any other mental faculty, and since the distinction between materiality and consciousness has proved to be a 'real' distinction, and not merely a 'modal' or a 'rational' one (pp. 130-1), it follows that those sensory factors *must* be caused either by matter or by God, for there is no other kind of substance in the universe. To show, then, how sensations could be caused *in* me but not *by* me would be to account for precisely the *involuntary* character of their initiation, which differentiates them from images more definitely than any other of their characters. Now, Descartes points out, we have a very strong natural propensity to believe in matter. This 'instinctive' belief or natural tendency to affirm that the active power causing sensations is connected with matter, being innate, must have been implanted in our minds by God. And since God is veracious, this natural propensity may be trusted. Hence, since sensations do occur, it must be matter that causes them directly, and God indirectly—for matter itself is existentially dependent on God.

Descartes's proof that a natural world exists therefore depends (i) on the element of confusedness in all sensations and on the non-voluntary nature of its cause ; (ii) on the fact that minds which have such involuntary, confused states are united with parts of matter (their bodies) ; and (iii) on the trustworthiness of strong *natural* propensities to believe, as distinct from strong but *acquired* convictions or prejudices. The existence of matter has to be asserted in order to account for, not only the confusedness of sensations, nor simply their occurrence, but the *involuntary* character of their occurrence.

If we are prepared to grant (*a*) Descartes's causal principle, (*b*) the ineradicable disparity between materiality and consciousness, (*c*) that one or the other is the only and essential attribute of every substance, and (*d*) the existence of a veracious God which is responsible for our native propensities, then his proof of the existence of a material world seems unobjectionable. But we have already seen there are reasons to doubt at least the first and last of these propositions, so his demonstration that matter exists is thereby gravely weakened. And it would seem, indeed, that *any* proof that matter exists could, at best, be only problematic.

XI

SOME MERITS AND DEFECTS OF CARTESIANISM, (II)

"Sur ce qu'il y a de nouveau et de strictement original dans sa pensée, aucun doute ne saurait subsister. Descartes est la revendication personnifiée du mathématisme universel. Là est sa grandeur."—GILSON

III

HAVING proved, as he thinks, by a second application of his causal principle, that there exists a natural world independently of us and our sensations, it remains to examine what Descartes says about its constitution. Nature is in every respect a mechanism. All diversity in nature is purely formal. It contains no irrational factors, hence it is through and through intelligible. Nor are there any ultimately different natural elements. What inorganic chemistry regards as an irreducible variety of chemical elements and modes of composition are, in fact, finite parts of three-dimensional space occupying determinate positions and capable of movement. Likewise there are no ultimately different kinds of organic body, or of organisms; none of the properties they possess persistently and independently of our perception are other than geometrical and kinematical. That is to say, Descartes's biology also is purely mechanistic. The differences on the basis of which common sense divides sharply between what is alive and what is not can be treated adequately and without distortion, Descartes thinks, apart from supposing any vitalistic principle ('substantial form') and simply in terms of a homogeneous space whose parts differ only in respect of position and motion, and whose motions are definable in terms of change of velocity and acceleration. The 'living' being, then, is literally a machine: an aggregate of formally differentiated and co-ordinated spatial modes, and its behaviour as an individual is explicable by different sorts of reaction and interaction occurrent in its parts.

Let us consider the more general assumptions made in this wholesale reduction, turning firstly to the identification of

SOME MERITS AND DEFECTS OF CARTESIANISM

matter and existent space. It is of the greatest importance to remember that Descartes regards this reduction of matter to space as constituting a conclusion of metaphysics, and not merely a fruitful and convenient working hypothesis. To ask whether this conclusion is true is to raise a very large and extremely difficult question. To point out then, as we may, that the identification of matter with space has led to more important results in modern science than any other proposition is very far from establishing the truth of that metaphysical conclusion,[1] or even high probability for it. It is generally held that the identification succeeds in avoiding dependence on any occult qualities or ' substantial forms,' and this may be allowed. But the value of this attainment is very severely compromised by the condition under which the avoidance is effected. The terms into which Nature is analysed, geometrical and kinematical, may well be all completely intelligible, but the diversification itself—the partitioning of a substantial, homogeneous space into an array of separate individual bodies—is surely as unintelligible as any ' substantial form.' The reduction of matter to extension inevitably involves that matter cannot be significantly described as active or as passive.[2]

[1] The ultimacy claimed for this metaphysical conclusion has, for its epistemological counterpart the view that the sciences of pure mathematics and rational mechanics are *parts of* Philosophy (cf. Ch. III, sect. 1 ; and Ch. IV). The importance of mathematics and mechanics for metaphysics is plain, for all our knowledge of the detailed constitution of natural bodies is contained in these sciences ; the laws of their dimensions and shapes collectively form the conclusions of geometry, rules for the measurement and computation of quantities of extension are found in arithmetic, while laws sufficient to explain particular movements among bodies are furnished by mechanics. The facts these laws are fitted to explain are not ' phenomenal,' but ' ontal ' ; to know these laws is thus to know the *ultimate* constitution of one part of the universe. Descartes's position is not that of an ' epistemological idealist,' for though he holds that we are never directly apprehensive of Nature (in perception or in conception), but always directly apprehensive of ' ideas,' there *is* a Nature, independent of those ideas for its character and existence, to which they refer. This single fact that there exists an independent Nature in this sense it was one of the principal aims of his metaphysics to establish.

[2] There is nothing in the formal determination of space to prevent any number of identically determinate modes from co-existing in the same space. Given, *e.g.* any determinate sphere, there could be any number of other similar spheres simultaneously coincident with it, any one of which may be as legitimately accounted a ' mode of matter ' as any other. But one ' body ' *excludes* the simultaneous presence of any other from the same place. The possibility of any number of coincident figures co-existing in the same place is presupposed in all arguments by congruence of properties in geometry, and this is enough to show that the Cartesian reduction of matter to geometrical space precludes genuine individuality on the part of modes of matter (" bodies ").

Their identification alone, then, entails neither the existence of a plurality of particular bodies nor change or movement on the part of such bodies. For while the existence of a mode entails the existence of its substance, the existence of a substance does not entail that it has any modes. The absolute substance that is God, for instance, has no modes. Again, while movement of a mode entails that the mode is extended, for a mode to be of this shape or of that size does not entail that it must move. So the motion of moving bodies does not stand to the attribute of which those bodies are modes in the same relation as their determinate shapes and sizes stand to that attribute. Hence, for Descartes, both multiplicity and change in Nature are *extraneous to it*. So the partitioning of homogeneous space into separate bodies and the occurrence of various movements between bodies and within them must be caused by something other than space, for the substance that is all extension is not ' dynamic ' and cannot therefore generate them. Until motion is ' imported ' into space, ' imparted ' by God's volition, there *is* no plurality of corporeal modes. But what is this language to mean ? To be sure, the ' importation ' cannot be imagined, and we must not attempt to imagine it. But it *must* be conceivable—clearly and distinctly so, yet in vain do we try to conceive it. The proposal first to identify ' capacity to be moved ' with ' numerical diversity,' and then to account for *both* the numerical diversity of bodies and all their changes (of state and of place) by means of one and the same principle— motion—was doubtless a stroke of constructive genius. But again, the worth of the attempt is seriously compromised when the condition under which the diversity and change are supposed possible turns out to be such as we cannot conceive. For is not the notion of God's will being operative within extension not only *not* clear and distinct but really devoid of meaning ?[1] Failing to allow for resistance or impenetrability, or for force or energy as its ground (by implying that motion occurs without expenditure of energy), Descartes makes it impossible for us to conceive in what consists the individuality of particular bodies, and therefore how a multiplicity of them could *be* separated out from an homogeneous space. And, in

---

[1] Or rather, is not such meaning as can be given condemned by its anthropomorphic origin ? Consider Spinoza's annihilating criticism in *Epistolæ*, 81, 83.

SOME MERITS AND DEFECTS OF CARTESIANISM

the last resort, is it not incredible that Nature should be pure extension with no other co-existing quality pervading or filling it ? As Leibniz indicated, Descartes's own laws of motion presuppose that that to which they are applicable possesses some other property besides merely being 'spread-out' in three dimensions. That which is so extended must also possess inertial mass, or an equivalent, in order to move in the ways generalised by those laws ; the 'conservation of motion' must be replaced by the 'conservation of energy' as the most general law of dynamics.[1]

There seem, then, to be clear reasons for doubting whether that part of Descartes's metaphysics comprising his theory of Nature is acceptable, for not only does it fail in the end to give us the intellectual satisfaction he claimed for it, but it fails to satisfy the requirements of his own philosophy. Motion alone within what is homogeneous cannot account for the kind of diversity required and admitted to exist in Nature,[2] and the possibility of persistence, hence of individuality (presupposed in the very notion of a spread of numerically diverse *bodies*),

---

[1] Modern physics, too, affirms the indestructibility of matter, and agrees with Descartes that only particular 'pieces' of it can be 'destroyed,' *i.e.* transformed or moved. It further maintains the conservation of mass and energy, but considers this to be established empirically (by induction), and not, like Descartes, to be deducible from God's perfection.

[2] If the 'imparting of a constant quantity of motion by God' be taken as expressing, in theological dress, simply that it is an ultimate fact that where space is there is motion, it must then be observed (a) that the " ultimate fact " is a 'brute' fact, since the connexion between 'motion' and 'space' is neither necessary nor intelligible ; (b) that to speak of 'imparting' a definite quantity of motion to that which is not already and intrinsically in motion is to fall back on a metaphor which is both vague and applicable significantly only to a microscopic system and not to a macroscopic one ; and (c) that such 'imparting' of a definite quantum of motion cannot explain the *partitioning* of all space into an array of spatial particulars. If, on the other hand, Descartes means the sum total 'imparted' to be, not an 'undistributed' total but a sum of *particular* movements distributed throughout all space (*i.e.* applied microscopically), then the view involves a vicious circle. For there could be no distribution of particular motions apart from the existence of particular bodies (modes of space) whose motions they are. Hence plurality of bodies would be presupposed. But it is motion that was to effect the splitting up of what is homogeneous into this spread of particular bodies. And there is no doubt that the " motion " which God is said to impart is to be understood as *actual* movement or movements, and not potential motion, ' energy,' or mere 'capacity for motion.' 'Energy,' Descartes would have rejected as an 'irrational '— an occult quality or 'substantial form.' And, in any case, he would have needed to add to such capacity a further 'occult' factor to render it actual— though the latter conception must have been familiar to him, for there were examples to hand in the 'force' or 'attraction' of Galileo, and in the 'active powers' of Kepler.

turns out to have been only postulated and not established. Yet though the reduction of matter to geometrical extension cannot be allowed the status of an established proposition of metaphysics, it is one that has had, and continues to have,[1] enormous influence as a working hypothesis in natural science. Indeed, its success here has been so continuous and over so wide a field that some men of science have falsely supposed the exclusively geometrical and mechanistic character to Nature to have been thereby definitely established for all time.

Nature, it follows for Descartes, is very different from what we ordinarily suppose; it is vastly more simple and 'tidy,' but it lacks all the richness and variety of its sensible manifestations. For our commonplace 'colourful' but unclear view of Nature, Cartesianism substitutes one of an infinitely complex mechanism. Its infinite complexity relates, however, not to the number of ultimate qualities or elements nor to the forms of structure that enter into its constitution, for these are few in number—indeed, it seems, *too* few to explain adequately the clear conceptions we have of the dissimilar characters and changes of physical things. What *is* infinite is the number of quantitatively different determinations (modes) of the single stuff that is Nature, and the number of quantitatively different movements distributed simultaneously and successively throughout it. The complexity of Nature is thus an exemplification of the inexhaustible modal diversity into which one

---

[1] Professor A. N. Whitehead, none too favourable a witness, allows (*Science and the Modern World*, p. 180) that " Descartes, in his distinction between time and duration, and in his way of grounding time upon motion, and in his close relation between matter and extension, anticipates, as far as it is possible at his epoch, modern notions suggested by the doctrine of relativity, or by some aspects of Bergson's doctrine of the generation of things." Professor A. E. Taylor (art. *Contemporary British Philosophy*, II, p. 299) offers warmer testimony to Descartes's merit here : " What gives the 'generalised theory of relativity' at once its fascination for the physicist by instinct and the repellent character it has for the average non-scientific man is precisely that it seems to eliminate the ultimate 'irrational' stuff, 'first matter,' from scientific theory. *It achieves what the greatest of all rationalists among modern philosophers, Descartes, dreamed of three hundred years ago, the identification of 'matter' with 'extension.'* To the mind bent on ' scientific explanation,' this reduction of matter to extension has all along been the conscious or unconscious aim of intellectual endeavour, because to such a mind, geometry inevitably appears as something inherently rational and self-explanatory " (my italics). Corroboration of this estimate is to be found also in the writings of M. Emile Meyerson, than whom none may speak with greater authority of erudition in the history of the sciences or with a livelier appreciation, formed by a scientific training. of recent results in chemistry and physics.

SOME MERITS AND DEFECTS OF CARTESIANISM 257

Cartesian attribute can be determined, and is wholly numerical and quantitative, not qualitative. The physical world is merely an extended *plenum* whose composing bodies communicate movements one to another by impact.

It must be agreed, further, that the reduction of matter to space *does* enable Descartes to offer an extremely simple, elegant and wholly intelligible explanation of the expansion and contraction of bodies. For he denies, correctly on his hypothesis, that there *can* be a vacuum (*i.e.* for him, an existing volume having no dimension), and he deduces quite rightly from this that the determinate volume which defines the extensity of a particular body is fixed and constant, incapable of increase or diminution. Hence the limit of 'contractibility' of a given body defines 'the' extensity of that body; the several dimensions into which it is said to 'expand' referring to its constant extensity *plus* the total amounts of magnitude of the lesser bodies which separate its parts by entering into its 'interstices.' The explanation of 'expansion' is, then, clear-cut and attractively simple on Descartes's hypothesis of the identity of matter and space. But our earlier doubt must be reaffirmed here. If Descartes has over-simplified the ultimate character of matter by the reduction, if every piece of matter possesses further characters besides spatial ones, then the impossibility of a vacuum could not be established *a priori*, and the question would be one for empirical treatment. Hence, if his reduction is an over-simplification, his view that the intrinsic volume of a body is invariable and that an 'increase' in its size, literally understood, is impossible, would not follow. But Descartes's objection that 'the' extensity of a given porous or elastic body is not to be identified with the extensity intrinsic to the body *plus* the extensity of the sum of its pores, would, it must be admitted in fairness to him, satisfy the modern physicist.

To sum up, even though explanation of Nature by the principles of mechanics *were* the only intellectually satisfying one, it would not follow from this fact that the primitive concepts to which alone they are applicable legitimately must be geometrical or rational. The primitive 'indefinables' to which they are properly applicable might well include 'irrationals' that are reached empirically. A dynamical theory like that of Newton introduces primary 'data' which are certainly not

R

geometrical, yet by means of them and the principles of mechanics, an explanation of physical changes that is rationally satisfying and which, like Descartes's, permits of their anticipation and predication, is equally possible. So we must decide that the success of the *methodological postulate* of mechanism (viz., to use exclusively the principles of mechanics to explain physical phenomena) is very far from implying the *metaphysical conclusion* that Nature is a mechanism, if this is to mean, as it does for Descartes, that Nature consists of nothing besides determinate modes of space, duration and motion.

Nature is, and must be, a ' blind concourse ' of modes, among which there is no diversity or diversification except arithmetical, geometrical and kinematical. And from this first reduction of matter to space, there follows in Descartes's Natural Philosophy, a second great reduction, viz., that identification of the variety and complexity of behaviour exhibited by animate bodies, with the integrated sets of movements occurrent in relatively permanent groupings of inanimate bodies or organs. This factual identification is, indeed, presupposed by the methodological postulate that vital phenomena are to be explained mechanistically. The bodies or ' machines ' constitutive of animate nature, then, exhibit in their behaviour or action as persistent, complex individuals, neither spontaneity nor contingency. There are no ' final causes in Nature : no purposeful processes that are inexplicable mechanically, occurrent in its constituent machines. All matter is alike indifferent to our self's existence and destiny. For a human body is simply a system of organs whose operations and co-operations are all effects of transeunt causes (viz., of operations in bodies spatially external to it), and which is by its very nature closed against any transeunt action by the self to which that body belongs. His adoption of the principle of mechanism commits Descartes to explaining in detail *all* behaviour of the animal organism—anatomical, physiological, habitual, instinctive, sensory, imaginative—in terms of reactions on the part of organs and glands of that body. Digestion, for instance, is no longer to be ' explained ' as an operation of a special digestive " faculty," but by the chemical properties of a specific case of glandular secretion. The root idea of glandular activity is that of the secretion and emission of some or other fluid. Difference of

SOME MERITS AND DEFECTS OF CARTESIANISM

behaviour that is traceable solely to differences in glandular activity presupposes difference of localisation in the glands, difference in their organisation (determining their dissimilarity of function), and differences in the chemical composition of the fluids secreted and discharged. His view of the animal-machine as equipped with tubes or pipes (' nerves ') along which animal spirits flow, his recognition of the possibility of treating characteristic glandular activity—an intaking and outgoing of animal spirits—as a special case of purely mechanical reaction, analogous to suction and discharge by a pump, and his recognition that some outward actions of the animal body, adapting it to its environment, are causally independent of volition and are uncontrolled by it, made it possible for physiologists in the two succeeding centuries to explore the possibilities of biological mechanism and develop in detail our present conception of ' reflex action.'[1] Though it would be too much to credit Descartes with having first elaborated the idea of the reflex as understood by contemporary physiologists (for he failed to take into account ' co-ordination of centres ' and ' integration,' which are essential parts of that conception), it may be allowed that his view of reaction and glandular activity was its forerunner. Indeed, it is not too much to say that Watson's behaviourist psychology, in method and result, is largely Cartesian.[2] Only when its principle of ' conditioning ' is ex-

[1] The term ' reflex ' appears to have been coined by Willis (1699), and not until 1784 was the general theory of reflexes at all fully elaborated (viz., by Prochaska), but in what consists the difference between voluntary action and unconscious reflex was first stated definitely by Marshall Hall in 1833. Descartes's biological application of mechanics was implemented and developed in the eighteenth century by Cabanis (who showed that the mechanical principles sufficient to explain reflex action were equally sufficient to explain cerebral activity), and by Bichat (whose analysis of the structure of tissues and their reduction to a few elementary types which combine to form organs and glands virtually founded the science of histology). Descartes's mechanistic treatment of animal psychology also has recently received some empirical confirmation. Dr. Bethe's experiments (1906) on bees and ants led him to corroborate Descartes's claim for the explanatory sufficiency of the reflex, and to endorse the Cartesian view that these insects are but machines. For references, see E. Mach, *The Analysis of Sensations*, Eng. trans., pp. 196-7.

[2] Mr. Gardner Murphy, in *An Historical Introduction to Modern Psychology* (p. 2), speaks of Behaviourism as " a refinement of Descartes's automatism and Hobbes's mechanism." This, however, is not to suggest that Watson is a ' Neo-Cartesian.' For, as Bertrand Russell puts it, " the things which Dr. Watson regards as certain are just those which Descartes regarded as doubtful, and the thing which Dr. Watson most vehemently rejects is just what Descartes regarded as absolutely unquestionable. Dr. Watson maintains that there is no such thing as thinking. No doubt he believes in his own existence, but

tended to the explanation of higher orders of human behaviour, intellectual and volitional, would Descartes have parted company with Watson.[1]

But the difficulty that attends Descartes's reduction of matter to space declares itself even more insistently in his attempt to reduce vital activity generally to mechanism. For, here again, however satisfactorily mechanism may ' work ' as a methodological postulate, this is far from establishing the metaphysical conclusion that vital activity in all its forms is nothing but reaction or movement between modes whose intrinsic character wholly consists in being spatially extended and separated. In a world containing literally nothing but three dimensional volumes which are capable of no change except that of internal movement or movement as a whole, what meaning can be found for speaking of *differently organised* ' organs ' and ' glands,' and for supposing differences of a chemical character in the ' fluids ' secreted by those glands ? If qualitative diversity is ultimately excluded from the nature of bodies and quantitative differences alone retained, is it not vain to pretend to explain vital activities that are differentiated in qualitative terms by actions none of whose differences are qualitative ? In a word, what more could purely *geometrical* differences of shape and location of glands and organs explain than difference in mere *direction* of the movements occurrent on their ' stimulation ' ?

Descartes, to be sure, does not commit that absurd blunder of too many physicists of later days—that of maintaining qualitative factors of the existent to *be* really quantitative ones. He does not assert that a colour, for instance, *is* a light wave of certain frequency, but insists on their ultimate disparity. But, on the other hand, neither does he regard it as only a matter of convenience to treat colour as if it were a light wave of certain frequency. That colour is intrinsically qualitative, while whatever is intelligible must be formal and quantitative, is precisely the reason why he denies ultimacy and intelligibility

not because he thinks he can think. The things that strike him as absolutely indubitable are rats in mazes, time-measurements, physiological facts about glands and muscles " (*An Outline of Philosophy*, p. 170). (It must be objected, however, that neither does Descartes believe in his existence "*because* he thinks he can think " !)

[1] How strikingly far Descartes anticipates Watsonian ' conditioning ' and 'unconditioning ' processes, is made plain in the *Passions*, art. 50.

of colour, and assigns it to the order of experiential but inexplicable 'epiphenomena' (*i.e.* "confused ideas"). And in Chapter VI we saw the original and radical difficulty involved here declare itself in its most uncompromising form. There, we observed, his reduction of matter to space and the rational demands it makes on the one hand, and the demands of empirical fact disclosed in perception on the other, lead him inevitably into a vicious circle. That the distinction between mind and body is a "real" and not merely a "modal" or "rational" one is established by resort to sensation. But sensation involves, on his view, the 'substantial' union of mind and body (*i.e.* of substance and mode). Unless this be granted there is no means of accounting for the 'qualitas' characteristic of all sensation. But though the introduction of both mind and body is a condition necessary for explaining that 'qualitas,' it is not a sufficient one. For there is no intelligible connexion between merely determinate spatial forms and motions with definite velocity and acceleration on the one hand, and the non-formal, qualitative character of sense-data on the other. Yet, as M. Gilson has so clearly shown,[1] though Descartes's entire method and metaphysic aim, *inter alia*, at eradicating all dependence on the 'substantial forms,' he is here, at a most crucial juncture, compelled to introduce at least one of them, viz., that of the 'substantial union' of mind and body in man! Thus, in his psycho-physics, is 'writ small' —though made vivid by the relatively concrete character of the terms to which his problem relates—the very same difficulty we first detected 'writ large' in a wider field (p. 254). Some kind of correspondence between qualitative characters and quantitative and formal characters, exhibiting the former as 'appearances' of the latter, there might be, though in particular cases it is difficult to see what could be the formal characters to which the qualitative ones would correspond. But a literal 'reduction'—an identification of qualitative characters with quantitative and formal ones—seems impossible *a priori*, for let the intermediaries interpolated between one of each kind be never so many, any one interpolated term must be either qualitative or formal, hence incapable of facilitating the reduction for which it was introduced, and so, far

[1] *Études*, ch. vi.

from solving the difficulty, would merely emphasise it. Presumably this is why, in Descartes's philosophy, we are left with no genuine explanation of the existence, or the possibility of existence, of 'secondary' qualities generally. For, allowing with Arnauld that there is no reason why a non-physical, cognitive act should not be perceptive of what is qualitatively unlike itself and physical, Descartes would have still to explain how that act should not be perceptive of what is physically given to be perceived (viz., something essentially formal, hence clear and intelligible), but should be perceptive of that which is not physically given at all (viz., something sensory, hence confused and unintelligible). For, after all, the common character of confusedness is something *essential* to sense-data, a positive quality and not mere absence of quality. Therefore the confusedness of sensa requires the assignment of an intelligible cause just as much as the other derivative, but distinct, characters of effects. The issue confronting us here is, indeed, but a special case of a wider one, namely, that which we encountered when trying to give a meaning, within the provisions of Cartesianism, for Descartes's tacit assumption of the " real distinction " (in chemical character) between the fluids secreted by differently located glands, and the tacit assumption of the existence of different natural kinds throughout his particular physical and biological researches. It seems, then, that however permissible and convenient it may be methodologically to reduce as rigorously as possible the number of qualitative terms employed, explaining as much variety as possible by their *formal* determination, there is plainly a grave risk of over-simplification. The principle of qualitative monism—that of reducing all qualitative variety to manifestations of some single, homogeneous quality, susceptible of only formal and quantitative determination—banishes all hope of ever accounting for the qualitative dissimilarity in the variety from which we started.

These difficulties notwithstanding, the historical value of Descartes's attempt remains. He must be considered the founder of that physiological psychology which attained its fullest development towards the end of the last century.[1]

[1] Huxley declared that " Descartes did for the physiology of motion and sensation that which Harvey had done for the circulation of the blood, and opened up a road to the mechanical theory of these processes which has been followed up by all his successors " (*Fortnightly Review*, Nov. 1874). And

SOME MERITS AND DEFECTS OF CARTESIANISM

Cartesian psychology is not an autonomous science. It is dependent on metaphysics no less than on physics and physiology. The idea of a single and separate science of psychology is a ' distinction of reason ' indicating not a radically separate field of data, but only a part (certain modes) of that substance which is Nature. For in the study of affection and conation we are attending to occurrences which, deriving from the primitive connexion of mind with body, would not exist and *be* data for psychological analysis were there no bodies that embodied selves.

IV

Descartes's *Passions of the Soul*, the earliest physiological theory of the emotions, is sometimes regarded as ' over-intellectualised,'[1] but the criticism appears to apply rather to his descriptions and analyses of the phenomena of affection than to his explanations of them. Whatever may be the defects of these phenomenological descriptions and analyses, it is an incontestible merit in Descartes to have emphasised, by his own practice, the necessity of turning to the immediate deliverances of experience to ascertain the proper data of psychology. By so doing he restricted its peculiar field to the operations of the *res cogitans*, so avoiding that confusion of psychology with biology which Aristotle originated and the Scholastics hardened into dogma, with the result that " the science made more progress in two centuries than it had made twenty centuries

---

William James allows that to Descartes " belongs the credit of having first been bold enough to conceive of a completely self-sufficing nervous mechanism which should be able to perform complicated and apparently intelligent acts. By a singularly arbitrary restriction, Descartes stopped short at man, and while contending that in beasts the nervous machinery was all, he held that the higher acts of man were the result of the agency of his rational soul. The opinion that beasts have no consciousness at all was of course too paradoxical to maintain itself long as anything more than a curious item in the history of philosophy " (*The Principles of Psychology*, I, p. 130).—But since James's day, Behaviourism has done its best to re-insist on this " curious item in the history of philosophy," and in fact to apply it further, to all the behaviour of even human beings, so attempting to banish ' consciousness ' from psychology, by explaining " the higher acts of man " as admittedly more complicated but *au fond* equally mechanical actions.

[1] One exception to these objectors is Prof. D. Irons. He says : " Though written in the earliest days of modern science, this work (the *Passions*) will bear comparison with anything that has been produced in recent years. It will be difficult indeed to find any treatment of the emotions much superior to it in originality, thoroughness and suggestiveness " (*Phil. Review*, 1895, p. 291).

before."[1] On the other hand, it is true that Descartes, in his account of the primary emotions, takes as typical states that occur only at mature levels of human development and overlooks their genetically earlier forms. And his classification of the primary emotions is deficient in omitting fear and anger.[2] Yet, despite these blemishes, and despite his hesitant treatment of desire—in which he alternates between the views that the things we desire are desired because of an appraisal made by our intellect, and because of a movement excited in our body— Descartes was certainly the first to have worked out the directive ideas of a psychology in our modern sense of the word.

In conclusion, we pass to forming a critical view of Descartes's conclusions about the self's cognition and its destiny. Our attempt to conceive God's imparting of movement to extension was unsuccessful. No better do we succeed in trying to conceive God's implanting of innate ideas in minds. If, however, it were permissible to strip these postulates of their theological vesture,[3] we may substitute for the latter the assertion that it is simply an ultimate natural fact—one to be accepted without assignable explanation—that minds are not purely ' receptive ' in cognition, but are non-voluntarily formative of at least the *a priori* factors of their knowledge.[4] Similarly, the former

[1] James Ward, *Psychological Principles*, p. 7. The new era Descartes inaugurated in psychology, Prof. G. S. Brett suggests, is less due to his having restated many old views and united in a novel manner the results reached by philosophers and physiologists, and rather to his being gifted with the power of actually experiencing the new freedom of thought. " When others were acquiring traditional formulæ, Descartes was living again through those primitive efforts of the mind by which sciences were first created " (*Hist. of Psychology*, II, p. 197).

[2] Cf. A. Shand, *The Foundations of Character*, pp. 220–1, 518, London, 1920, for objection to including desire among the emotions, as Descartes does.

[3] This, I am inclined to think, Descartes himself would *not* have considered permissible. But so eminent an historian as Professor Gustave Cohen appears to take a contrary view : " Une fois en règle avec la société, dont l'Église est pour lui partie integrante, Descartes se sent libre, absolument libre, et son Dieu métaphysique, garant de la vérité des axiomes et fondement de toute évidence, qui prête son concours ordinaire à la Nature et la laisse agir suivant les lois qu'il a établies, n'a preque rien du Dieu de la religion " (*Écrivains français en Hollande*, p. 427).

[4] Descartes's " innate ideas " are so far preparatory of Kant's " Categories of the Understanding." But whereas Kant's ' Copernican hypothesis ' effectively prevents us ever from knowing whether our cognition represents the structure of ultimate fact (and cannot therefore be taken as being a knowledge of extra-mental reality), it is of the very essence of Cartesian epistemology (viz., of the theory of representative perception, enforced by God's certification of what is ' clear and distinct ') to maintain a correspondence between the *a priori* innate principles and concepts that give form to our knowledge, and

SOME MERITS AND DEFECTS OF CARTESIANISM 265

postulate, relieved of its theological implications, consists in asserting the ultimacy of the factual conjunction of space and movement in Nature. That is to say, so taken, God's imparting of motion would be a seventeenth-century way of expressing that whatever is spatial is in movement, though its movement is not entailed by its spatiality. Interpreted analogously, God's imprinting of innate ideas in minds would mean that our certain knowledge is determined in accordance with a number of general principles and concepts which are native endowments of our minds and are not acquired by abstraction from sense-experience,[1] and that they are not entailed by the very conception of knowledge itself.[2] In this sense of 'innate,' all ideas that are ideas of simple natures are innate, for they can be *apprehended* solely by an operation (intuition) which is innate (*i.e.* not acquired), and all clear and distinct ideas derivable from them are innate in that they can be *produced* only by an operation (deduction) which is innate. But in the end, the simple natures actually constitutive of extra-mental reality. It would seem, therefore, that the charge commonly brought against Descartes of the self being enclosed *within* the circle of its own ideas, hence closed *against* reality and therefore powerless to attain knowledge of it, applies properly not to Descartes but to Kant, who is much more of an idealist where Descartes is a realist. So far it seems erroneous to regard Descartes as a precursor of Kant. Unlike Kant, Descartes is not an 'epistemological idealist'—cf. p. 253, n.1.

[1] That the use of concepts corresponding to the simple natures of, say, geometry (point, line, circle, equality, etc.) is not derivative or acquired but primitive and innate in thinking substances is shown, Descartes considers, by the fact that none of our percepts are exact *instances* of them, but at best only rough approximations to them. Our perceptions are merely suggestive, and their occurrence furnish not the concepts themselves but the occasions on which we tend to think them. Percepts in which points, lines and circles are not in strictness present cannot be materials from which ideas of them could be abstracted. A like view holds of such categorical concepts as those of substance, causality, etc.

[2] Kant held, of course, that those *a priori* concepts and principles he assigned to the understanding are 'necessary' factors of *our actual* knowledge, (*i.e.* knowledge such as we have and attain), and his analysis is restricted to exhibiting the most general principles to which experience must conform in order to be actual knowledge. For Descartes, however, while actual knowledge does conform with, and presupposes for its attainment and expression such *a priori* concepts and principles, their admittedly constitutive function in our actual knowledge is not seen to be necessitated by the very idea of possible knowledge. To put the point in Cartesian language, had God so willed, He could have 'implanted' in our minds *other* concepts and principles than those He did, and our knowledge would have exhibited in consequence a different structure from that which our *de facto* knowledge does exhibit. So, just as 'extension' does not imply (hence, does not 'explain') the origination or existence of the motion present in actual Nature, so 'knowledge' does not imply (hence, does not 'explain') the origination or existence of the concepts and principles present in our *de facto* knowledge.

we saw, Descartes is compelled (by his final view of the constitution of matter and his dogma of ' substantial union ' of self with a mode of matter) to maintain that all ideas whatever are innate[1]—confused no less than clear ones. For the sensory factors present in confused ideas cannot be assigned to bodies[2] (no body really has colour or temperature, but only extension, shape and motion), hence those sensory factors must belong to, be ' in,' the minds conjoined with the bodies in which the correlated physical changes occur. A self thus *requires* the occurrence of certain physical changes in some sense organ of its body as the occasion or stimulus suitable for it to produce, by its own activity, that confused experience that we come to associate with actions of that sense-organ.

Descartes, it cannot be denied, fails to work out fully or clearly enough, his theory of innate ideas. In different contexts different things, we saw (pp. 167 ff.), were said to be innate —mental capacities or dispositions, mental operations, and the ideas present to mind during those operations. He certainly regarded these three as interrelated, but through omitting to investigate their interrelation, he can make no contribution of moment to questions of the very first importance in epistemology and psychology, to the consequent impoverishment of his theory of the self as cognitive. He certainly recognises the dual function of concepts and principles in knowledge, viz., (i) as ' objects ' that can be *thought of* and *combined* so as to yield further concepts, and (ii) as capable of being *applied*, both consciously and unconsciously, to the interpretation of that

[1] Cf. p. 195. His earlier division of ideas put forward tentatively (*Med. III*) —viz., into ' innate ' and non-innate (' adventitious ' and ' factitious ')—turns on the commonly accepted distinction between ideas that are originated by the self through its own proper activity and independently of action by external bodies, and ideas caused by the action of external bodies independently of the self's proper activity. But if, as Descartes thinks he has afterwards shown, a bodily change can cause nothing except *bodily* changes and therefore no ideas, then the distinction between internal and external origination of ideas collapses, as Descartes himself recognised. All ideas must be ' innate,' for ' confused ideas ' require to be originated by the self no less than clear ones, and clear ideas require suitable perceptual situations as the ' occasion' of their being thought no less than confused ones. This, a further consequence of the ' substantial union ' of mind with body, shows again how thoroughly inconsistent is this doctrine of their union with their qualitative disparateness asserted earlier.

[2] In the *Traité de l'Homme* Descartes assigns perceptual, imaginative and affective processes to the body, and regards their occurrence as possible without the body being connected with a self. His later view, indicated above, is stated in the *Principles* and the *Meditations*.

SOME MERITS AND DEFECTS OF CARTESIANISM

which, given in sense-experience, is not itself 'concept.' Thus he assigns to minds as being 'innate' both a tendency to make an interpretative use of concepts and principles, and a capacity to know those concepts and principles in recognising *that* we make such a use of them. And by claiming that their employment is instrumental to the acquirement of knowledge, he assumes that reality does in fact conform to them. So far as his theory of innateness seeks to emphasise that such a procedure on the part of our minds cannot be explained as due solely to 'training' or 'experience,' but is a direct manifestation of its innate constitution or inborn proclivities, the emphasis is no doubt timely and important.

But his theory also ascribes innateness to certain 'ideas' taken in the sense of 'pure thoughts,' 'items conceived' (*e.g.* conceptions of the defining characters of God, infinity, perfection; and of the primitive terms of mathematics and metaphysics),[1] and the legitimacy of this ascription may well be questioned. Its explanatory value, at all events, is negligible, for 'innateness' now means simply 'non-acquired,' and expresses no positive characteristic. The second ascription of innateness therefore enables Descartes to establish nothing, but merely to suggest an analogy—namely, that the mind is able to produce 'from itself' quasi-subsistent universals which are related to it as 'objective' entities present for contemplation, analogously to the way in which seemingly self-subsistent percepts or sensa stand as 'objective' entities to the percipient in his perception.

In the long run, then, 'innateness' of ideas consists in this: in knowing minds do not 'reflect' the character of what is physically available for cognition; minds are so constituted and so connected with bodies that the occurrence of any of a certain range of bodily changes constitutes an occasion on which the self will think one or another idea ('pure thought'), the objective reality of which is not to be found in any sense-datum

[1] Descartes does not appear to distinguish very clearly between 'concepts' and 'principles.' Cf. J. Gibson, *Locke's Theory of Knowledge*, Cambridge, 1917: "There is an almost studied carelessness in the terms used by Descartes to designate the general nature of the contents of intuitions, which are spoken of indifferently as 'simple natures,' 'conceptions' or 'notions,' 'propositions' or 'principles.' This vagueness in their designation may perhaps be regarded as connected with the peculiar Cartesian view which attributed the affirmation or denial which constitutes judgment to the will . . ." (pp. 212-3).

occurrent simultaneously with those bodily changes, nor in the bodily motions themselves. Lastly, we have Descartes's explicit word that he does not mean that there are certain ideas (*e.g.* equality, straightness, circularity, God, etc.) which we are born consciously thinking of or about, and contemplate continuously throughout life, such as Leibniz allows for in his doctrine of unconscious perception. The main merit of Descartes here is in *having raised* an extremely important problem in the theory of knowledge, and in having made a preliminary *esquisse*, the more profound significance of which the criticism and correction of later thinkers has in a measure clarified. In so far, too, as the various attributions of 'innateness' in Descartes can be shown to derive from the notion of innate mental traces and dispositions, he is plainly stressing a mental characteristic the full analysis and explanation of which would be an acquisition of the greatest moment to psychology and philosophy. But it must be admitted that he does little more than indicate the existence of such a power, and show that it is one that cannot be explained by any possible training, and is therefore not acquired. In precisely what terms we are to conceive clearly the existence of dispositions and capacities 'in' the mind, remains with Descartes an unsolved problem, and so, it may be added, it stands in the psychology and philosophy of to-day. How their intrinsic nature and their existence in minds are to be conceived, and how their 'influence' on cognitive activity is properly to be interpreted, is one of the persistent problems of philosophy, the solution of which falls to posterity.[1] The problem, indeed, appears to be a special case of a wider

[1] Cf. C. D. Broad, *The Mind and its Place in Nature*, London, 1925, sect. C, especially chaps. viii and x. " We must remember," writes Dr. Broad, " that before Descartes's time there was a 'faculty-physics,' and that Descartes's greatest achievement was to show that the various causal characteristics of physical things can be connected with each other by correlating them all with characteristic forms of spatio-temporal structure and a few very general and pervasive causal characteristics. No one has succeeded in connecting the various mental 'powers' in any analogous way, and that is why psychology at present hardly deserves the name of a science. It is, I think, quite certain that psychology will remain in this unsatisfactory state unless and until someone succeeds in doing for it what Galileo, Descartes, and Newton did for physics. And the difficulty of doing anything of the kind is obvious when we remember how difficult it is to conceive of purely mental 'structure,' or to imagine what can be the few fundamental causal characteristics which, together with differences of 'mental structure,' will explain and connect the various observable mental powers " (*ibid.* p. 440).

SOME MERITS AND DEFECTS OF CARTESIANISM 269

one (viz., that of the ontological status of 'properties' in the sense of 'powers' or 'potentialities' generally), the impossibility of avoiding which Aristotle showed clearly for all time, but in the analysis of which no hand has yet succeeded. As Dr. Broad puts the matter : " The fact is that we know nothing whatever about the intrinsic nature of traces and dispositions ; they are simply the hypothetical causes of certain observable effects, and the hypothetical effects of certain observable causes."[1]

Passing now to consider critically Descartes's view of the function of understanding and will in knowledge, we noticed (pp. 156-60) that he was fully aware that an acceptable theory of knowledge must show how error can and does arise, and that the solution he proposed to this crucial problem was distinctly valuable. In maintaining that we cannot fall into error until we make an assertion or a denial, so detecting error in the act of judgment (assent or will) passed on what is present in perception or thought, Descartes reaffirms a theory still widely endorsed. There cannot, on this view, be such a thing as misperception or as a false percept, but only a false judgment *about* the perceived.[2] For perception *simpliciter* is no more than a passive awareness of that which is presented. In ' seeing ' but not affirming, we can neither fall into error nor attain to knowledge. But we do desire knowledge, so the risk of error that attends all affirmation must be run. We can *apprehend* the content presented only as it is, but we can *affirm* it to be *as* it is not and *what* it is not. There lies the possibility of error. Being free to pass judgment or to withhold it, our will is unconditionally free. There lies its perfection—the single perfection we possess in common with God. And our ' understanding ' or capacity of apprehension is said also to be perfect in the respect proper to it ; *i.e.* it is capable of forming perfectly clear and distinct ideas. Error, then, is to be traced neither to volition or to apprehension, but to their combination.

It was Descartes's intention originally to show that error is directly due to an improper use of our unlimited freedom in willing, but the conclusion to which he is in point of fact even-

[1] *Op. cit.*, p. 358.
[2] Location of truth and falsity in *assertion* is, of course, not original in Descartes, but a commonplace of Aristotelian epistemology. Cf. *De Anima*, III, 3, 427, b ; 428, a, 11 ; b, 18. Also *De Interpretatione*, c. 4, c. 5.

tually driven is, that the use is 'improper' precisely because of a defect—not in our will, but in our understanding. For, though to yield assent to what is obscure or confused is to abuse our freedom of *will*, the very possibility of such abuse is solely due to a defective *understanding*. For (i) it is solely due to 'understanding' that there is anything obscure or confused *to* apprehend. That which a confused idea is 'of,' is never intrinsically such that, if it is perceived at all, it must be confusedly or obscurely perceived. It is always intrinsically such that, unless the faculty concerned in its apprehension is defective, it must be clearly and distinctly perceived. The confusion or obscurity in the idea is not, therefore, due to the thing of which the idea *is* an idea. But if we had no confused or obscure ideas, there would be no occasions when we ought to withhold assent; *i.e.* it would be *impossible* to fall into error. So, to Descartes's dictum that in willing alone we are responsible for error, we must make the reservation that our defective (confused) apprehension is certainly an accessory before the fact! And (ii) our alleged dependence on a morally perfect and omnipotent God makes it more difficult than ever to explain error. Why the perfectly good and all-powerful God who endowed us with perfect wills should not be held responsible for permitting confusion and obscurity in our understandings when it was possible for him to create us with an understanding uniformly clear in its operations, Descartes does not enlighten us.[1] It seems, then, after all, that God is not free from respon-

[1] To be sure, Descartes does maintain that the limitation of human understanding is inseparable from the finitude of the human self. Cf. *Med. IV*: "It is of the nature of a finite understanding not to comprehend many things, and the nature of a created understanding to be finite" (AT, VII, 60; HR, I, 177). But, it must be objected, whether or no God is responsible for having endowed finite selves with understandings limited in respect to the *extent* of their knowledge, He certainly does seem to be responsible (notwithstanding Descartes's denial) for endowing us with understandings which, even *within* the restricted ranges of their competence, should all too often prove incompetent! Even though we could not have cognitions of everything that is theoretically knowable, why should so many, or any, of the cognitions our constitutions do permit us to have, be *unclear and confused*? For, after all, the elements of confusion in various cognitions are something positive and present, not a mere absence or privation, as Descartes suggests. Why should understanding not 'work' perfectly (clearly and distinctly), even though it is not omniscient in its range? Descartes's remark, "I have no reason to think it was obligatory on God to give to each of his works all the perfections he is able to bestow on some" (*op. cit.*), does not explain, but passes *sous silence* why God should have willed to give the perfection of uniformly clear cognition to *none* of His works. Thus, though Descartes refers only to one restriction, he must in fact confess

SOME MERITS AND DEFECTS OF CARTESIANISM 271

sibility for human error, and that error is *ultimately* to be located in defective understanding and not in will.

Lastly, what shall be said of Descartes's view of the self's immortality ? Mind and Matter must be disparate, so runs his argument, for the latter is divisible into parts and the former is not. The 'thoughts' of a self are not related to it as the members and parts of a body are related to that body (so much follows from the self being a substance and the body being only a mode), therefore we must not suppose what is true of the body is necessarily true of the self. And in particular, it does not follow that because our body is destructible (by separation of its parts), our self must be so too. For our self has no parts to be separated. Hence, from considering the nature of selves or minds, the self's immortality cannot be seen to be impossible. And when we turn to the self's 'substantial union' with its body, no reason is found for denying that the self can exist apart from its body. The most we may infer is that when its body is dead the self can no longer express or communicate its experiences in the accustomed way, *via* actions of its former body. We cannot infer that the self has ceased to exist or that it has no experiences to communicate. Inconclusive, too, are the objections of the type that Kant brought, namely, that the self's not containing extensive parts is no reason for inferring its incorruptibility, since not all that ceases to exist is extensive. As a sound, for instance, does not cease to exist by falling apart into pieces, but by diminishing in intensity, so a self might pass out of existence in the same way, as into a sleep. All this Descartes would deny to be applicable, for a sound is not a substance, and he does not infer the indestructibility of the self from its indivisibility, but precisely from its being a substance and from all substances other than absolute substance requiring only God's concurrence for their persistence. So those reasons commonly alleged against the self's immortality he maintains, rightly on his premises, to be inconclusive, for they one and all make presuppositions that are demonstrably false. He thereby establishes at least the *possibility* of the self's survival of its body's death. But he claims to have

to two, and the second is not, presumably, entailed by the first. And if the former one is not arbitrary, the latter certainly is, and responsibility for the defect it occasions in cognitive beings must, in consistency, be placed wholly in God.

established more than this, namely, the *fact* of the self's immortality, albeit an immortality conditional on God's concurrence. It must be denied, however, that Descartes has proved so much, for his proof presupposes that (i) selves are substances possessing a unique defining attribute, (ii) a God (as defined by him) does exist, and (iii) substances depend for their existence solely on God's concurrence. But even were it allowed that selves are Cartesian substances possessed of a single defining attribute, his proofs of God's existence, we have decided, will not stand. Hence the dependence of selves upon God must be rejected, and so his proof of their immortality with it.

The replacement of Aristotelian by Cartesian science turns on the twofold assumption that specific differences in sensation are causally connected with specific differences in extension, and that sensation, though bodily incited, is mentally apprehended. The existential and qualitative dualism of self and body, the consequent rejection of the Aristotelian thesis that the self is the body's ' form,' and of every suggestion of the self's existential dependence on the body, opened largely the way for the elaboration of a new and fuller psychology of the self. If subsequent psychology has been unable to profit from the emancipation to an extent at all comparable with that to which subsequent physics profited, the failure to have done so cannot be attributed to Descartes. And if the new reasons he proposed for the self's immortality do not convince, they at least retain the advantages for the Christian faith possessed by the older reasons, and have the merit of stressing that the matter is one demanding treatment by reason and is not a mystery to be accepted through faith.

A CARTESIAN BIBLIOGRAPHY

I.—DESCARTES'S WORKS

(a) Collected Editions

Opera Omnia. Amsterdam : 1670–83 ; 1692–1701.
Œuvres complètes, edited by Victor Cousin, 11 vols., Paris, 1824–26.
Œuvres complètes, edited by A. Garnier, 4 vols., Paris, 1835.
Œuvres inédites, par Foucher de Careil, 2 vols., Paris, 1858–60.
Œuvres de Descartes, edited by Adam and Tannery, under the auspices of the Ministère de l'Instruction Publique. (This is the best and most authoritative edition.) 12 vols., Paris, 1896–1910.

(b) Separate Works and English Translations

Discours de la Méthode, Texte et Commentaire par É. Gilson, Paris, 1925 ; 2nd edition, 1930. Annotated by V. Brochard, Paris, 17th edition, 1927.
La Géométrie, English translation by Smith and Latham, Chicago, 1925.
Regulæ ad Directionem Ingenii, Texte et Traduction par G. Le Roy, Paris, 1933.
The Method, Meditations, and Selections from the Principles of Descartes, translation and Introduction by J. Veitch, Edinburgh and London, 15th edition, 1913.
The Philosophical Works of Descartes, rendered into English by E. Haldane and G. R. T. Ross, 2 vols., Cambridge, 1911.

II.—WORKS OF THE CARTESIAN SCHOOL

Arnauld, Antoine, *Œuvres complètes,* 43 vols. (mostly theological), Lausanne, 1780. *Œuvres philosophiques d'Arnauld,* edited by C. Jourdain (containing *Objections contre les Méditations, Logique, Des Vraies et des Fausses Idées*), Paris, 1843. *Œuvres philosophiques d'Arnauld,* edited by Jules Simon (containing *Objections, Des Vraies et des Fausses Idées, Réponse du P. Malebranche, Défense du Dr. Arnauld*), Paris, 1843.
Clauberg, John, *Opera,* Amsterdam, 1691.
Cordemoy, Géraud de, *Les Œuvres du feu M. de Cordemoy,* Paris, 1704.
Forge, Louis de la, *Traité de l'Esprit de l'Homme,* Paris, 1666.
Geulincx, Arnoldi, *Opera philosophica,* edited by J. P. N. Land, 3 vols., La Haye, 1891–93.
Malebranche, Nicholas, *De la Recherche de la Vérité,* edited by Francisque Bouillier, Paris, 1879. *Discourse on Metaphysics,* English translation, M. Ginsberg, London, 1921.

Régis, Sylvain, *Système de Philosophie contenant la Logique, la Métaphysique et la Morale*, Paris, 1690.

III.—WORKS CHIEFLY BIOGRAPHICAL

Adam, C., *Vie et Œuvres de Descartes* (being Tome XII of the Adam and Tannery edition of the *Œuvres*), Paris, 1910.
Baillet, A., *La Vie de M. Descartes*, 2 vols., Paris, 1691. *Abrégé de la Vie de M. Descartes*, Paris, 1692.
Bouillier, F., *Histoire de la Philosophie cartésienne*, 2 vols., Paris, 1854, 3rd edition, 1868.
Cohen, G., *Écrivains français en Hollande dans la première moitié du XVIIe siècle*, Paris, 1920.
De Swarte, V., *Descartes, Directeur spirituel*, Paris, 1904.
Espinas, A., *Descartes et la Morale*, 2 vols., Paris, 1925.
Gouhier, H., *La Pensée religieuse de Descartes*, Paris, 1924.
Leroy, M., *Descartes, le Philosophe au Masque*, Paris, 1929.
Mahaffy, J. P., *Descartes*, London, 1902.
Millet, J., *Histoire de Descartes avant 1637*, Paris, 1867. *Descartes, son Histoire depuis 1637*, Paris, 1870.
Roth, L. (Editor), *Correspondence of Descartes and Constantyn Huygens, 1635-47*, Oxford, 1926.
Sortais, G., *Le Cartésianisme chez les Jésuites*, Archives de Philosophie, Vol. VI, cahier 3, Paris, 1929.

IV.—MONOGRAPHS AND SPECIAL STUDIES

Blanchet, L., *Les Antécédents historiques du ' Je pense donc je suis,'* Paris, 1920.
Bordas-Desmoulins, *Le Cartésianisme*, Paris, 1874.
Boutroux, E., *De Veritatibus æternalibus apud Cartesium*, Paris, 1874. *Des Vérités éternelles chez Descartes* (trans. Canguilhem), Paris, 1927.
Boutroux, P., *L'Imagination et les Mathématiques selon Descartes*, Paris, 1900.
Chevalier, J., *Descartes*, Paris, 2nd edition, 1921.
Cunningham, W., *The Influence of Descartes on Metaphysical Speculation in England*, London, 1887.
Fischer, K., *Descartes and his School* (trans. Gordy), London, 1887.
Fouillée, A., *Descartes*, Paris, 1893.
Gibson, A. Boyce, *The Philosophy of Descartes*, London, 1932.
Gilson, E., *La Liberté chez Descartes et la Théologie*, Paris, 1913. *Index Scolastico-Cartésien*, Paris, 1913. *Etudes sur le rôle de la pensée médiévale dans la formation du système cartésien*, Paris, 1930.
Hamelin, O., *Le Système de Descartes*, Paris, 1911 ; 2nd edition, 1921.
Léon, A., *Les Élements cartésiens de la doctrine spinoziste*, Paris, 1907.
Liard, L., *Descartes*, Paris, 1882.

BIBLIOGRAPHY

Milhaud, G., *Descartes Savant*, Paris, 1921.
Natorp, P., *Descartes Erkenntnisstheorie : Eine Studie zur Vorgeschichte des Kritizismus*, Marburg, 1882.
Sirven, J., *Les Années d'Apprentissage de Descartes*, Paris, 1928.
Smith, N. K., *Studies in the Cartesian Philosophy*, London, 1902.
Wahl, J., *Du Rôle de l'Idée de l'Instant dans la philosophie de Descartes*, Paris, 1920.

V.—SOME IMPORTANT ARTICLES

Adam, C., " Correspondance de Descartes : Nouveau classement," *Revue philosophique*, 1933.
Balz, A., " Dualism in Cartesian Psychology and Epistemology," *Studies in the History of Ideas*, II, 1925. " Clerselier and Rohault," *Philosophical Review*, XXXIX, 5. " Géraud de Cordemoy," *ibid.*, XL, 3. " Louis de la Forge and the Critique of Substantial Forms," *ibid.*, XLI, 6.
Boutroux, P., " Sur la signification historique de la *Géométrie* de Descartes," *Revue de Métaphysique et de Morale*, 1915.
Brochard, V., " Le *Traité des Passions* de Descartes et l'*Ethique* de Spinoza " ; " Descartes Stoïcien " (both in *Études de phil. ancienne et de philosophie moderne*, Paris, 1912).
Brunschvicg, M., " La Révolution cartésienne," *Revue de Métaphysique et de Morale*, 1904.
Caird, " Cartesianism," art. *Encyclopædia Britannica*, 11th edition.
Cantecor, G., " La Vocation de Descartes," *Revue philosophique*, 1923.
Carteron, H., " L'Idée de la Force mécanique dans le système de Descartes," *Revue philosophique*, 1922.
Gibson, B., " The *Regulæ* of Descartes," *Mind*, N.S., VIII., 1898.
Hannequin, A., " La Méthode de Descartes," *Revue de Métaphysique et de Morale*, 1906.
Hubert, R., " La Théorie cartésienne de l'Énumération," *ibid.*, 1916.
Lalande, A., " Sur quelques Textes de Bacon et de Descartes," *ibid.*, 1911.
Laporte, J., " La finalité chez Descartes," *Revue d'Histoire de la Philosophie*, II, 1928.
Levi, A., " Il Problema dell' errore nella filosofia del Descartes," *Logos*, 1928.
Revue de Métaphysique et de Morale, Numéro spécial consacré à Descartes, Paris, 1896.
Vigier, J., " L'Idée de Temps, de Durée et d'Éternité dans Descartes," *Revue philosophique*, 1920.

INDEX

"ABSOLUTE terms," 69, 79, 235
Abstraction, 67–8, 101, 166–7
Académie Française, 6
Action and activity, 134, 173, 204–11, 212, 258–9
   purposive, 147, 258
Adam, C., 7, 20
Adamson, R., 133 n.
Affections, see 'Passions.'
Affirmation, see 'Judgment.'
Agnosticism, 90
Analysis, 69, 92, 235
Anatomy, 42, 144
Animals, 163
"Animal spirits," 146 n., 149 n., 152–153, 173 n., 174, 176 n., 178 n.
Anselm, St., 107
"Anthropological Argument," 104–7, 240–1, 243–4
Appearances, 115, 132, 148, 162, 166, 237–8, 261
Appetites, 174, 175
Archimedes, 37
Aristotle, 30, 31, 37, 52, 61, 63, 145, 146, 187, 231, 233, 263, 269, 272
Arnauld, Antoine, 26, 144 n., 213, 217–21, 245 n., 262
Astronomy, 38–41, 46
Atheist's "knowledge," see 'Knowledge, of the Atheist.'
Atoms, 136, 208
Attributes, 90, 101, 117, 129, 141, 166, 203, 222, 226, 272
Augustine, St., 30, 58
Automata, see 'Body, animate.'

BACON, FRANCIS, 47–50, 128 n.
Bacon, Roger, 37
Balzac, Guez de, 24
Beeckman, I., 9–10, 19
Behaviourism, 147, 259–60, 262 n.
Beliefs—
   common, 81–2, 83–8, 92, 100, 102, 136, 138, 142–3, 251
   "probable," 64, 109
Benevolence, 179
Berkeley, G., 191 n.
Bichat, 259 n.
Blood, circulation of, 43, 146 n.
Body—
   animate, 144–7, 251, 258, see also 'Body, human.'
   human, 94–5, 142–9

Body—continued
   material, 97, 99, 111–6, **243–4**
   and Mind, Ch. VI
Bordas-Desmoulin, 139 **n.**
Boyle, R., 41
Brain, function of, 150
Bréhier, E., 32
Brentano, 154 n.
Brett, G. S., 178 n., 264 n.
Broad, C. D., 50 n., 146 n., 268 n., 269
Bruno, G., 18, 32–3, 34
Butler, S., 147

CABANIS, 259 n.
Campanella, 33, 34
Cantecor, G., 6 n.
Capacities, innate, 168–70, 250, 264–9, see also 'Ideas, innate.'
Caterus, 26
Causality, 101, 102, 106, 114, 127 n., 141, 143, 204, 209–12, 217, 223, 243–4, 250–1
   objective, 104, 108, 115, 243–4
   formal, 105, 107, 117, 243–4, 250
   see also, 'God, causality of,' 'Ideas, causation of,' 'Occasionalism.'
Certainty, 63, 78, 79, 88, 94–6, 100, 109, 112, 132, 232
   criterion of, 79, 89, 109, 160, 209, 247–9
"moral," 81
Chanut, 10 n., 20, 27
Charron, 34
Christina, Queen, 27
Church of Rome, 26, 29–32, 34, 40–1, 45, 229
Church, R. A., 220 n.
Clauberg, J., 204, 206–7, 209
Clearness and distinctness, 63, 75, 78, 97, 109, 159, 160, 172, see also 'Ideas, clear and distinct.'
"Cogito ergo sum," 88, 100 n., 105, 108, 116–7, 209, 246
   its importance, 89–92, 239, 246
   its interpretation, 92–6, 192, 239–40
   transition from, 90, 96, 99–100, 245
   not an inference, 92–3
Cohen, Gustave, 14–5, 46, 264 n.
Compendium Musicæ, 19
Conception and Existence, see 'Existence.'
Concepts, see 'Ideas, conceptual.'
Concupiscence, 179

277

INDEX

Condensation, 135–6, 257
Conduct, moral, 159, 187, 190, 214
Confusedness, 132 n., 142, 172, 175, 262, 270, see also 'Ideas, confused.'
Consciousness, 100, 154
Conviction, 77, 142, 251
Copernicus, 38–41, 46
Cordemoy, G. de, 203, 204, 207, 208, 209, 210
Creation, see 'God, creativity of.'

DA VINCI, L., 32, 37
Death, see 'Immortality.'
Deception, 84, 87, 92, 94, 98, 108, 157, 190, 219–20, 238
Deduction, Descartes's, 61, 65, 70–2, 75, 109, 126–7, 134, 233–6, 265
De Homine et de Fœtu, 16
Delbos, V., 221 n.
Deliberation, see 'Volition.'
Democritus, 208 n.
Demon, malignant, 87–8, 96
De Morgan, A., 234
'De Omnibus Dubitandum,' see 'Doubt, methodical.'
Descartes—
  education of, 6–9, 52–3; travels, 9, 12–16
  attitude to Church of Rome, 17–19, 20–1, 264 n.
  attitude to marriage, 12
  character of, 17 n., 19
  death of, 27
  attitude to philosophy, 5–6
  revolution initiated by, 65, 229–30, 252, 256 n., 268 n.
Desire, 181, 182, 183, 264
Determinism, 186–90, 213 n., 223
Dioptric, 22, 139
Discourse on Method, 6, 21–3, 62, 74–5
Distinctions—
  kinds of, 130
  of reason, 130, 136, 250, 261, 263
  modal, 130, 132, 250, 261
  real, 130, 152, 250, 261, 262
Diversity, 133 n., 252, 254–6, 260
Divine veracity, see 'God, veracity of.'
Doubt—
  experiential, 80
  methodical, 79–81, 83–8, 112, 209, 237–9, 247–9
Dreams, 85–6, 98, 192, 194
Driesch, Hans, 152 n.
Dualism, see 'Universe.'
Duration, 100, 129, 256 n.

ELISABETH, Princess, 143 n., 176 n.
Emotion, see 'Passions.'

Empirical Naturalism, 48–50
Entities, representative, see 'Knowledge, representative.'
'Enumeration,' Descartes's, 70–2, 75
Error, 63, 106, 156–7, 269
Espinas, A., 21
'Eternal truths,' 100, 101, 170, 224
Ethics, Cartesian, 176 n., 209, 213 n., see also 'Geulincx.'
Evaluation, see ' Judgments of value.'
Events—
  physical, 141–2, 149, 211
  mental, 142, 149, 154, 211
Exercise, law of, 152
Existence and 'existential reference,' 90, 94, 97, 99, 102–3, 105–8, 112, 114, 116, 117, 118, 120–1, 123, 125–6, 239–40, 244–5, see also 'Reality.'
" Ex nihilo nihil fit," 102 n., 106 n., 225
Experience, sense-, 84–6, 114, 124–5, 126, 127, 149, 152, 163, 170, 171, 261, 269
  utility of, 128, 132, 140, 148, 163, 175–6
  untrustworthy, 84, 86, 219–20
Experiment and observation, 122, 124–5, 127–8
Explanation, 67–8, 104, 124, 139, 140
Extension, 59 n., 113–4, 132–3, 136, 194–5, 225, 252–8
Eye, 152

FACULTIES, 95, 146 n., see also 'Substantial forms.'
Falsity, see 'Error.'
Feeling, 150, 174, 184
Fontanier, 18, 32
Forge, L. de la, 203, 205, 207
France, Anatole, 19
Freedom, 151–2, 158, 178, 186–90, 224, 269, 270–1

GALEN, 42
Galileo, 7, 17, 18, 21, 38, 40–1, 46, 120 n., 138 n., 145, 255 n.
Gassendi, P., 18, 23, 26, 92–3, 192, 194
Gazali, Al, 83 n.
Géométrie, La, 22
Geometry, Cartesian, 10–11, 22–3, 44, 120, 130, 132, 138
Geulincx, A., 115 n., 176 n., 203, 204, 207, 209–10, 213, 214–6
Gibson, J., 267 n.
Gilbert, W., 41
Gilson, E., 24, 27–8, 51 n., 52 n., 59, 196 n., 248, 261
Ginsberg, M., 220 n.
Gland and glandular activity, 258–60

INDEX 279

Gland, pineal, 153
God, 99, 157, 197, 202, 224–5, 227, 240
  causation and creativity of, 202, 207–8, 210, 211, 213 n., 217 n., 224
  existence of, 107, 108, 114–6, see also 'Anthropological Argument' and 'Ontological Argument.'
  important consequences of, 108, 109, 118, 123, 271–2
  goodness of, 108, 241–2, 270
  idea of, 99, 100 n., 102, 104–6, 154, 166, 240
  imparts motion, 137, 206, 225, 254, 255 n., 264, 265
  nature of, 106 n., 108, 134, 166, 211, 244–5
  veracity of, 108, 109 n., 110, 112, 116, 245–51

Habit, 187, 188 n.
Hagues de St. Victor, 51
Hamelin, O., 59, 248 n.
Hardness, 131 n.
Harvey, W., 42–3, 146 n., 262 n.
Hatred, 178–9, 182, 185
Hegel, 5, 63, 221 n., 232 n., 243
Herriot, T., 43
Hicks, G. Dawes, 220 n., 228 n.
Hobbes, T., 6, 7, 50, 51–2, 95, 187, 191 n., 232 n, 259 n.
Holbach, Baron, 205
Homme, Traité de l', 140
Humanism, 32
Hume, D., 8, 217 n.
Huxley, T., 262 n.
Hypnosis, 192–3, 194

Idea, 96, 97, 117, 154–5, 217
  senses of, 103, 218, 242–3
  "to have," 93, 103, 161, 166
  clear and distinct, 97, 159–60, 171, 181, 189–90, 245, 247, 266
  unclear (confused), 97, 114, 148, 163, 171, 181, 249, 261, 266, 270, see also 'Confusedness,' 'Sensa,' 'Sensation'
  conceptual, 162, 164–5, 171, 265 n., 266–7
  innate, 161, 164, 165–72, 190, 236 n., 264–9
  causation of, 98, 103–7
  adventitious and fictitious, 168, 171, 266 n.
  positive and negative, 167 n., 241–2
  representative, see 'Knowledge, representative.'
  of God, see 'God, idea of.'
  of non-existents, 86, 98, 105–6, 164, 166

Idea—*continued*
  of material bodies, 97, 99, 112, 113, 116, 171, 249–51
  of simple natures, 165, 168, 169, 170, 171, 236 n., see also 'Simple Natures,' and 'Ideas, innate.'
  of reality, see 'Reality, formal,' 'Reality, objective.'
  Impulse to assert, natural, 63, 97, 98, 134, 151, 250–1
Illusions—
  of memory, 109 n.
  of perception, see 'Deception.'
Images, 106, 115, 150, 154, 162, 166, 250
Imagination, 86, 113, 169
Immortality, 196–7, 271–2
Infinite, see 'Perfection.'
  and Indefinite, 158 n.
Innateness, see 'Ideas, innate,' 'Capacity, innate.'
Instinct, 146
"Intellectus," see 'Understanding'
Interaction, 147–53, 165–6, 204, 213, 217, see also 'Action.'
Intuition, 70–2, 75, 79, 95, 100, 109, 110–2, 143, 235–6, 247–8, 265, 267 n., see also 'Memory, fallibility of.'
"Intuitive Induction," 89, 93–4, 101, 113, 126 n., 240
Irons, D., 263 n.
"Irrationals," 139 n., 145, 147, 187, 191, 255 n., 256 n.

James, William, 46, 262 n.
Johnson, W. E., 89 n., 155, 161 n.
Joy, 177, 180, 184–5
Judgment, 63, 97, 99, 103, 125–6, 154–5, 156–8, 161, 189, 267 n., 269
Judgments of value, 178, 180, 181, 183, 187

Kant, 92 n., 134, 165, 217 n., 264 n., 265 n., 271
Kepler, 39–40, 41, 46, 255 n.
Keynes, J. M., 237 n.
Kinematics, 114, 130, 137, 249
Knowledge—
  certain, 63, 78–9, 110
  and conjecture, 64, 65
  and disagreement, 65
  D.'s sense of, 73–6, 120, 122, 161–2, 169, 170, 267
  of the atheist, 76–7, 111, 121, 240
  of nature, 121–8
  objectivity of, 111, 265 n., see also 'Existence and Existential reference.'

INDEX

Knowledge—*continued*
 possibility of radical incapacity for, 96
 privacy of, 110–1
 representative character of, 161, 217–21, 236 *n.*, 262, 264 *n.*
 structure of, 11, 67–70, 164–5, 170–171, 231–6, 264–5, 265 *n.*

LA FLÈCHE, 6, 7 *n.*, 8, 40, 52
Laird, J., 220 *n.*, 239
Lalande, A., 50 *n.*
Language, misleading, 92–3, 95, 179 *n.*
Laws, scientific, 123–4, 126, see also 'Motion, laws of.'
 deducibility of, 124
Leibniz, 4, 45, 138, 145, 156 *n.*, 191 *n.*, 203, 211, 221, 225–8, 232 *n.*, 234, 243, 255, 268
Leroy, M., 20, 21, 46
Le Roy, see 'Regius.'
Liard, L., 59, 81
Light, 140
Lipstorp, 8
Liquids, 139
Locke, J., 13, 170, 191 *n.*
Logistic, 45, 233–4
Love, 178–9, 180–3, 215
Lovejoy, A. O., 220 *n.*

MACHINES, 140, 144–5, 146, 163
Malebranche, N., 187, 203, 204, 207, 210, 211, 213, 217–21
Mariotte, 41
Mass, 138, 254–5
Materialism, 52, 94, 205
Material world, see 'Nature, constitution of.'
Mathematics, 43–5, 64, 67, 86–8, 108, 114, 235, 238, 249, 253 *n.*
Matter—
 definition and properties of, 113, 116, 153, 223, see also 'Nature,' 'Extension,' 'Body.'
 identified with space, 135, 252–8, 260
"Maxims," 100
McTaggart, J. McT. E., 182 *n.*, 183 *n.*, 191 *n.*
Mechanics and mechanism, 37, 140, 146, 149, 152 *n.*, 164, 207, 208, 258–9, 260
Meditations, The, 25, 74
Memory, 152, 163, 169, 184, 247
 fallibility of, 71–2, 78, 109 *n.*, 247–9
Mersenne, M., 6, 16, 51, 120, 122 *n.*, 145, 168 *n.*
Metaphysics, D.'s, 57–8, 73, 100 *n.*, 117–8, 119, 121–4, 134, 201, 233, 236, 252–3
 to support the Method, 73–8

Meteors, The, 22
Method, D.'s, 11, 15, 21–3, 50–1, 78, Ch. III, 230–7, 246
 order in, 67
 of Mathematics, 65–6
 relation to Metaphysics and Physics, 60–1, 73
Mettrie, De la, 205
Meyerson, E., 139 *n.*, 256 *n.*
Milhaud, G., 9 *n.*, 50 *n.*
Mill, J. S., 234
Miracle, 203, 208
Modes, 91, 129, 155, 162, 165, 168, 174, 197, 202, 208 *n.*, 213 *n.*, 223, 254, 256
Monde, the, 16–17, 18, 21, 58, 59, 139–140
Montaigne, M. de, 15, 34–6
Moore, G. E., 132 *n.*
Morin, J., 13
Motion—
 and Extension, 134, 136–7
 and laws of, 133, 134, 137–9, 151, 163, 166, 175, 225, 254–5
 communication of, 137, 150, 257
 direction of, 203, 260
 quantity of, 137, 141, 207
 ultimate, 134–5

"NATURAL light," 161
Natural philosophy, D.'s, see 'Philosophy, D.'s.'
Nature—
 constitution of, 128–40, 141, 236, 249, 252
 knowledge of, see 'Knowledge, of nature.'
 "taught by," 160–1, 250–1
Natures—
 absolute, see 'Absolute terms.'
 complex, 68, 103
 relative, see 'Relative terms.'
 simple, see "Simple Natures."
Necessity, 79, 93, 101–2, 108, 131, 134, 143 *n.*, 148, 170, 203, 211, 212, 213 *n.*, 224, 231, 244–5
Nerves, 149, 151–3, 174, 259
Newton, I., 22, 50, 138, 257
Nicholas of Amiens, 51
Nicholas of Cusa, 31
Noël, Père, 52
Notions—
 common, 91, 100
 primitive, 143, 144, 190
November 10th, 10–11
Number, 143 *n.*

OBSERVATION, see 'Experiment.'
Occam, William of, 31

INDEX

"Occasion," 144, 147, 163, 208–9, 210, 212
Occasionalism, 201, 207, 209–11, 212, 213 *n.*, 217, 220, *see* also 'Causality'
"Occult qualities," *see* 'Substantial forms.'
Omnipotence, *see* 'God, nature of.'
"Omnis peccans est ignorans," 159, 183, *see* also 'Conduct, moral.'
"Ontological Argument," 94 *n.*, 107–8, 241, 244
Operations, cognitive, *see* 'Intuition,' 'Deduction,' 'Enumeration.'
Optics, 41, 139 *n.*
Oresme, N., 23 *n.*, 51
Oughtred, W., 43

PAIN, 159, 181, 185
Parallelism, 147
Pascal, B., 41, 173 *n.*
"Passions," 150–2, 154, 173, 174–7, 178–9, 180, 182–5, 263–4, 266 *n.*
Passions of the Soul, The, 19, 27, 176 *n.*, 263
Patterson, R. Leet, 83 *n.*
Perception, *see* 'Experience, sense-,' 'Idea.'
representative, *see* 'Knowledge, representative.'
Perfection, and idea of, 90, 106 *n.*, 107–8, 115, 129, 137, 157–8, 166, 167 *n.*, 185, 211, 241–2, 244, 269, 270 *n.*
Phenomenalism, 121
Philosophy, D.'s view of, 73, 119–21, 126, 128–40, 141, 225, 236, 253 *n.*, 255
Physics, 41–2, 272
D.'s, 58–60, 119–21, 122, 126, 231–2
Physiology, 42–3
D.'s, 144, 147, 163, 252
Place, 134–5
Plato, 30, 31, 220, 243
Plemp, 124
Pollock, F., 221 *n.*
Pomponazzi, P., 30, 32
Principles, 91, 100–1, 170, 171, 265 *n.*, 266–7
Principles of Philosophy, The, 27, 40
Probability, D.'s view of, 64, 231–2
Propositions, 157, 161, 226
existential, *see* 'Existence and existential reference.'
Pseudo-sciences, 46
Psychology, 119, 235, 262–4, 272
Ptolemy, 38

"QUAESTIONES," 66–7, 78, 96, 232

RAMUS, P., 33–4
Rarefaction, 135–6, 257
Rationalism, 118
Realism, 118
Reality—
formal, 103–7, 115–6, 117, 164–5, 227, 243
objective, 103–7, 114–5, 164–5, 243
degrees of, 106–7, 243–4, *see* also 'Perfection.'
Régis, P. S., 201, 203, 204, 206, 207
Regius, H., 20, 26, 144, 167 *n.*, 168 *n.*, 204–5
Regulæ ad directionem ingenii, 13, 15, 16, 60, 62, 63, 77, 79, 80, 83, 144 *n.*
Reid, T., 92 *n.*, 220
"Relative terms," 69, 140, *see* also "Absolute terms."
Renaissance, 32
Reneri, 20
Representative perception, *see* 'Knowledge, representative.'
Revelation, 57, 208, 211
Ribot, T., 177 *n.*
Rosicrucians, 21, 46
Russell, B., 45, 232 *n.*, 259 *n.*

SADNESS, 177, 180, 184–5
Scepticism, 35, 36, 81
Scholasticism, 7, 42, 45, 51, 53, 112, 117, 146 *n.*, 196 *n.*, 263
Self, 91, 95, 100–1, 105, 107, 116, 141, 142–3, 149, 153, 156, 162–3, 171, 173, 180–1, 185, 191, 193, 197, 205, 209, 214, 217, 239–40, 258, 264–72
persistence of, 109–10, 191–2, 194–7
Sensa, 147–8, 162, 261
as 'signs,' 148, 150
Sensation, 84–5
kinæsthetic and organic, 150, 181
Shand, A., 264 *n.*
"Simple Natures"—
of Bacon, 49
of Descartes, 67–70, 90–1, 93, 94, 100–1, 103, 129, 143, 148, 164, 235, 236–7, 265 *n.*, 267 *n.*
Snell, 41
Socrates, 159
Soul, *see* 'Self.'
Space—
empty, 135, 136, 257
relational view of, 135, *see* also 'Extension.'
Spinoza, B. de, 5, 93 *n.*, 201, 203, 215, 221, 222–6, 228, 243, 254 *n.*

INDEX

States, mental, 91, 94, 96, 173, 181, 192, 193, 191–6; *see also* 'Consciousness.'
Stebbing, L. S., 237 *n*.
Stoicism, 45
Substance, 95–6, 100, 101, 116, 128, 133 *n*., 134, 173, 191 *n*., 192, 194–7, 201–3, 222–3, 226, 239, 254, 271
"absolute" and "secondary," 128–9, 202, 204–5, 207, 211, 213 *n*., 222
"Substantial forms," 9, 145, 146, 196 *n*., 253, 261
Substantial unity, *see* 'Union, of body and mind.'
Surprise, *see* 'Wonder.'
Syllogism, 92–3, 101 *n*., 233–5, 236
Synthesis, 69, 98, 235

TANNERY, P., 11 *n*., 146 *n*.
Taylor, A. E., 3, 50, 149 *n*., 256 *n*.
Telesio, 31
Thales, 146 *n*.
Theology, its exclusion from Metaphysics, 57–8, 116, 202, 208
Thinking, *see* 'Consciousness.'
Thomas Aquinas, St., 30, 31, 52, 166
Thought, pure, *see* 'Understanding.'
Thouverez, E., 214 *n*.
Time, 129, 256 *n*.
Torricelli, 41
Truth, 156, 163
Tycho Brahé, 39

UNCONSCIOUSNESS, 192–3

"Understanding," 94, 100, 157, 158, 162, 223, 269–71
"Union" of body and mind, 142–4, 146, 152–3, 191, 206–7, 225, 261, 266, 271, *see also* 'Body, human.'
our knowledge of, 143
Universe, D.'s view of, 117, 201, 203, 222, 225
University of Utrecht, 26–7

VACUUM, *see* 'Space, empty.'
Vanini, 18, 32
Variety, concrete, 133 *n*.
Velocity, 138
"Vérités de foi," 116
Véron, Père, 52
Vesalius, 42
Viète, 43, 44
"Vincula" of knowledge, 101, 102, *see also* 'Principles.'
Vitellion, 123
Volition, 98, 115, 135, 151, 154–8, 174, 178, 185–90, 192, 205, 207–8, 210, 212, 214–5, 223, 250–1, 259, 269–271, *see also* 'Necessity.'

WARD, J., 138 *n*., 264 *n*.
Watch, simile of, 145
Watson, J., *see* 'Behaviourism.'
Wax, example of, 113, 131
Whitehead, A. N., 4, 29, 43, 45, 256 *n*.
Will, *see* 'Volition.'
"Wisdom," 73
Wonder, 177–8, 184

DATE DUE